Exploring Cultural ANTHROPOLOGY

Keri A. Canada

revised printing

Kendall Hunt
publishing company

Kendall Hunt
p u b l i s h i n g   c o m p a n y

www.kendallhunt.com
Send all inquiries to:
4050 Westmark Drive
Dubuque, IA 52004-1840

Copyright © 2014 by Kendall Hunt Publishing Company

ISBN 978-1-5249-3320-3

Published in the United States of America

TABLE OF CONTENTS

Chapter 1

Body Ritual among the Nacirema

Horace Miner
University of Michigan

How does our own cultural worldview influence how we see people from other cultures? In this article, Horace Miner describes in detail a culture seemingly very different from our own. In examining those cultural attributes we find strange, we become aware that we tend to focus on cultural differences, rather than similarities, when we come into contact with groups of people we may not be familiar with. Is there value in concentrating on differences, or should we make more of an effort to find common ground in diversity? How much difference really exists?

The anthropologist has become so familiar with the diversity of ways in which different peoples behave in similar situations that he is not apt to be surprised by even the most exotic customs. In fact, if all of the logically possible combinations of behavior have not been found somewhere in the world, he is apt to suspect that they must be present in some yet undescribed tribe. This point has, in fact, been expressed with respect to clan organization by Murdock (1949: 71). In this light, the magical beliefs and practices of the Nacirema present such unusual aspects that it seems desirable to describe them as an example of the extremes to which human behavior can go.

Professor Linton first brought the ritual of the Nacirema to the attention of anthropologists twenty years ago (1936:326), but the culture of this people is still very poorly understood. They are a North American group living in the territory between the Canadian Cree, the Yaqui and Tarahumare of Mexico, and the Carib and Arawak of the Antilles. Little is known of their origin, although tradition states that they came from the east. According to Nacirema mythology, their nation was originated by a culture hero, Notgnihsaw, who is otherwise known for two great feats of strength—the throwing of a piece of wampum across the river Pa-To-Mac and the chopping down of a cherry tree in which the Spirit of Truth resided.

Nacirema culture is characterized by a highly developed market economy which has evolved in a rich natural habitat. While much of the people's time is devoted to economic pursuits, a large part of the fruits of these labors and a considerable portion of the day are spent in ritual activity. The focus of this activity is the human body, the appearance and health of which loom as a dominant concern in the ethos of the people. While such a concern is certainly not unusual, its ceremonial aspects and associated philosophy are unique.

The fundamental belief underlying the whole system appears to be that the human body is ugly and that its natural tendency is to debility and disease. Incarcerated in such a body, man's only hope is to avert these characteristics through the use of the powerful influences of ritual and ceremony. Every house-hold has one or more shrines devoted to this purpose. The more powerful individuals in the society have several shrines in their houses and, in fact, the opulence of a house is often referred to in terms of the number of such ritual centers it possesses. Most houses are of wattle and daub construction, but the shrine rooms of the more wealthy are walled with stone. Poorer families imitate the rich by applying pottery plaques to their shrine walls.

While each family has at least one such shrine, the rituals associated with it are not family ceremonies but are private and secret. The rites are normally only discussed with children, and then only during the

From "Body Ritual Among the Nacirema" by Horace Miner as published in *American Anthropologist*, 58(3), June 1956. American Anthropological Association.

period when they are being initiated into these mysteries. I was able, however, to establish sufficient rapport with the natives to examine these shrines and to have the rituals described to me.

The focal point of the shrine is a box or chest which is built into the wall. In this chest are kept the many charms and magical potions without which no native believes he could live. These preparations are secured from a variety of specialized practitioners. The most powerful of these are the medicine men, whose assistance must be rewarded with substantial gifts. However, the medicine men do not provide the curative potions for their clients, but decide what the ingredients should be and then write them down in an ancient and secret language. This writing is understood only by the medicine men and by the herbalists who, for another gift, provide the required charm.

The charm is not disposed of after it has served its purpose, but is placed in the charm-box of the household shrine. As these magical materials are specific for certain ills, and the real or imagined maladies of the people are many, the charm-box is usually full to overflowing. The magical packets are so numerous that people forget what their purposes were and fear to use them again. While the natives are very vague on this point, we can only assume that the idea in retaining all the old magical materials is that their presence in the charm-box, before which the body rituals are conducted, will in some way protect the worshipper.

Beneath the charm-box is a small font. Each day every member of the family, in succession, enters the shrine room, bows his head before the charm-box, mingles different sorts of holy water in the font, and proceeds with a brief rite of ablution. The holy waters are secured from the Water Temple of the community, where the priests conduct elaborate ceremonies to make the liquid ritually pure.

In the hierarchy of magical practitioners, and below the medicine men in prestige, are specialists whose designation is best translated "holy-mouth-men." The Nacirema have an almost pathological horror of and fascination with the mouth, the condition of which is believed to have a supernatural influence on all social relationships. Were it not for the rituals of the mouth, they believe that their teeth would fall out, their gums bleed, their jaws shrink, their friends desert them, and their lovers reject them. They also believe that a strong relationship exists between oral and moral characteristics. For example, there is a ritual ablution of the mouth for children which is supposed to improve their moral fiber.

The daily body ritual performed by everyone includes a mouth-rite. Despite the fact that these people are so punctilious about care of the mouth, this rite involves a practice which strikes the uninitiated stranger as revolting. It was reported to me that the ritual consists of inserting a small bundle of hog hairs into the mouth, along with certain magical powders, and then moving the bundle in a highly formalized series of gestures.

In addition to the private mouth-rite, the people seek out a holy-mouth-man once or twice a year. These practitioners have an impressive set of paraphernalia, consisting of a variety of augers, awls, probes, and prods. The use of these objects in the exorcism of the evils of the mouth involves almost unbelievable ritual torture of the client. The holy-mouth-man opens the client's mouth and, using the above mentioned tools, enlarges any holes which decay may have created in the teeth. Magical materials are put into these holes. If there are no naturally occurring holes in the teeth, large sections of one or more teeth are gouged out so that the supernatural substance can be applied. In the client's view, the purpose of these ministrations is to arrest decay and to draw friends. The extremely sacred and traditional character of the rite is evident in the fact that the natives return to the holy-mouth-men year after year, despite the fact that their teeth continue to decay.

It is to be hoped that, when a thorough study of the Nacirema is made, there will be careful inquiry into the personality structure of these people. One has but to watch the gleam in the eye of a holy-mouth-man, as he jabs an awl into an exposed nerve, to suspect that a certain amount of sadism is involved. If this can be established, a very interesting pattern emerges, for most of the population shows definite masochistic tendencies. It was to these that Professor Linton referred in discussing a distinctive part of the daily body ritual which is performed only by men. This part of the rite involves scraping and lacerating the surface of the face with a sharp instrument. Special women's rites are performed only four times during each lunar month, but what they lack in frequency is made up in barbarity. As part of this ceremony, women bake their heads in small ovens for about an hour. The theoretically interesting point is that what seems to be a preponderantly masochistic people have developed sadistic specialists.

The medicine men have an imposing temple, or *latipso*, in every community of any size. The more elaborate ceremonies required to treat very sick patients can only be performed at this temple. These ceremonies involve not only the thaumaturge but a permanent group of vestal maidens who move sedately about the temple chambers in distinctive costume and headdress.

The *latipso* ceremonies are so harsh that it is phenomenal that a fair proportion of the really sick natives who enter the temple ever recover. Small children whose indoctrination is still incomplete have been known to resist attempts to take them to the temple because "that is where you go to die." Despite this fact, sick adults are not only willing but eager to undergo the protracted ritual purification, if they can afford to do so. No matter how ill the supplicant or how grave the emergency, the guardians of many temples will not admit a client if he cannot give a rich gift to the custodian. Even after one has gained admission and survived the ceremonies, the guardians will not permit the neophyte to leave until he makes still another gift.

The supplicant entering the temple is first stripped of all his or her clothes. In every-day life the Nacirema avoids exposure of his body and its natural functions. Bathing and excretory acts are performed only in the secrecy of the household shrine, where they are ritualized as part of the body-rites. Psychological shock results from the fact that body secrecy is suddenly lost upon entry into the *latipso*. A man, whose own wife has never seen him in an excretory act, suddenly finds himself naked and assisted by a vestal maiden while he performs his natural functions into a sacred vessel. This sort of ceremonial treatment is necessitated by the fact that the excreta are used by a diviner to ascertain the course and nature of the client's sickness. Female clients, on the other hand, find their naked bodies are subjected to the scrutiny, manipulation and prodding of the medicine men.

Few supplicants in the temple are well enough to do anything but lie on their hard beds. The daily ceremonies, like the rites of the holy-mouth-men, involve discomfort and torture. With ritual precision, the vestals awaken their miserable charges each dawn and roll them about on their beds of pain while performing ablutions, in the formal movements of which the maidens are highly trained. At other times they insert magic wands in the supplicant's mouth or force him to eat substances which are supposed to be healing. From time to time the medicine men come to their clients and jab magically treated needles into their flesh. The fact that these temple ceremonies may not cure, and may even kill the neophyte. in no way decreases the people's faith in the medicine men.

There remains one other kind of practitioner, known as a "listener." This witch-doctor has the power to exorcise the devils that lodge in the heads of people who have been bewitched. The Nacirema believe that parents bewitch their own children. Mothers are particularly suspected of putting a curse on children while teaching them the secret body rituals. The counter-magic of the witch-doctor is unusual in its lack of ritual. The patient simply tells the "listener" all his troubles and fears, beginning with the earliest difficulties he can remember. The memory displayed by the Nacirema in these exorcism sessions is truly remarkable. It is not uncommon for the patient to bemoan the rejection he felt upon being weaned as a babe, and a few individuals even see their troubles going back to the traumatic effects of their own birth.

In conclusion, mention must be made of certain practices which have their base in native esthetics but which depend upon the pervasive aversion to the natural body and its functions. There are ritual fasts to make fat people thin and ceremonial feasts to make thin people fat. Still other rites are used to make women's breasts larger if they are small, and smaller if they are large. General dissatisfaction with breast shape is symbolized in the fact that the ideal form is virtually outside the range of human variation. A few women afflicted with almost inhuman hypermammary development are so idolized that they make a handsome living by simply going from village to village and permitting the natives to stare at them for a fee.

Reference has already been made to the fact that excretory functions are ritualized, routinized, and relegated to secrecy. Natural reproductive functions are similarly distorted. Intercourse is taboo as a topic and scheduled as an act. Efforts are made to avoid pregnancy by the use of magical materials or by limiting intercourse to certain phases of the moon. Conception is actually very infrequent. When pregnant, women dress so as to hide their condition. Parturition takes place in secret, without friends or relatives to assist, and the majority of women do not nurse their infants.

Our review of the ritual life of the Nacirema has certainly shown them to be a magic-ridden people. It is hard to understand how they have managed to exist so long under the burdens which they have imposed upon themselves. But even such exotic customs as these take on real meaning when they are viewed with the insight provided by Malinowski when he wrote (1948:70):

Looking from far and above, from our high places of safety in the developed civilization, it is easy to see all the crudity and irrelevance of magic. But without its power and guidance early man could not have mastered his practical difficulties as he has done, nor could man have advanced to the higher stages of civilization.

References Cited

Linton, Ralph
    1936 The Study of Man. New York, D. Appleton-Century Co.

Malinowski, Bronislaw
    1948 Magic, Science, and Religion. Glencoe, The Free Press.

Murdock, George P.
    1949 Social Structure. New York, The Macmillan Co.

Discussion Questions

1. Who are the Nacirema? What clues exist in the article that helped you to determine the group's true identity? Was it easy or hard to figure this out?
2. Think of what you do every day before you leave your house. What body rituals do you practice? Why might someone from another culture find these rituals strange?
3. Is there a way to write about the Nacirema to make the group sound less strange? How could this be accomplished? Provide specific examples.
4. What can this article teach us about cultural relativism? Why is cultural relativism an important concept to understand in anthropological research?
5. What does this article teach us about the importance of attempting to *understand* a culture, rather than just reporting it?

Chapter 2

Undergraduates Deserve Methods Too: Using a Research Laboratory Model to Engage Students in Cognitive Anthropological Research

H. J. François Dengah II and Erica Hawvermale
Utah State University
Essa Temple
Western Washington University
Mckayla Montierth
U.S. Navy
Talon Dutson, Tyler Young, Elizabeth Thomas, Kirsti Patterson, Abigail Bentley, and David Tauber
Utah State University

An anthropological education is invaluable – though we've seen the value of an anthropology degree questioned publicly in the past few years. What those unfamiliar with the discipline fail to realize, however, is that anthropology is incredibly relevant, and not just to those with PhDs. This article details the importance of undergraduate students having the opportunity to develop applied anthropological skills (those often sought by employers), and shows the reader concrete examples from the Collaborative Anthropological Research Laboratory (CARL) at Utah State University.

Introduction

In 2011, Rick Scott, then Governor of Florida, made a statement that unfortunately characterizes the challenges faced by our discipline:

> We don't need a lot more anthropologists in the state ... I want to spend our dollars giving people science, technology, engineering, and math (STEM) degrees. That's what our kids need to focus all their time and attention on, those types of degrees, so when they get out of school they can get a job.

The flagship organization of the discipline, the American Anthropological Association, quickly replied, affirming that anthropologists are often scientists as well, who use STEM knowledge to make "groundbreaking discoveries" in areas such as health and medicine, genetics, evolution, and more. Yet the media coverage of this story was mixed, with some organizations such as National Public Radio (NPR) defending the discipline, explaining that the Bureau of Labor Statistics (BLS) Report predicts a 28 percent job growth for anthropologists between 2011 and 2018 (O'Conner 2011). Others, such as the *Business Insider*, supported Gov. Scott's sentiment and argued that even if BLS statistics are accurate, these jobs are open to all social scientists—and very few *cultural* anthropologists, particularly with undergraduate degrees, have the training in math and science to meet the requirements for these positions (Harper 2011).

We disagree with the belief that an anthropology degree is less valuable than those in STEM fields. Nevertheless, it is undeniable that the hard sciences receive the bulk of the resources from most public universities and funding agencies, indicating that the governor's sentiments are not isolated. This unbalanced investment leaves anthropology departments, and other humanities and social science disciplines, to make do with less. Importantly, such disciplinary distinctions are unfortunate, as many anthropologists see themselves as part of STEM fields, regularly and seamlessly infusing science, technology, engineering, and math with their holistic approach. Moreover, methodological and/or scientifically oriented anthropology is particularly relevant within the applied sector, where practicing anthropologists are using a variety of methods to bring ethnographic insights to a variety of social problems and issues.

What is at issue is the devalued perception of cultural anthropology among various stakeholders and financial gatekeepers (e.g., students, parents, universities, politicians, employers). If we want to challenge and change the view that an anthropology degree is somehow less valuable than a STEM degree, we need to ensure that there is a trained workforce of anthropology graduates to fill the growing demand for social science professionals in the public and private sectors. Many within academia recognize this, if the rise in the number of applied anthropology programs and applied graduate degrees are any indication. Importantly, however, there is reason to think that we need to do a better job training this next generation of applied anthropologists. A recent Center for Innovation and Research in Graduate Education (CIGRE) report finds that new anthropology PhD graduates receive only "adequate" or "poor" training for grant and technical writing, presentations, and publications; it can be surmised that such training is similarly lacking for Masters students and all but nonexistent for most undergraduates (Rudd et al. 2008). It is this latter group of students, who James Peacock calls the "bread and butter" of our discipline and who Gov. Scott references, that are arguably the most underserved and ill-prepared (Peregrine et al. 2012:596).

It should come as no surprise that anthropology undergraduates are often left out of practical skills training and engaged learning. In the university "publish or perish" climate, many academics are expected to spend at least half of their productive energy on research. As a result, in-depth methods training (e.g., mixed methods, participating in an actual anthropological study that leads to a peer-reviewed publication) is traditionally reserved for graduate students (Upham et al. 1988). Even then, it is not uncommon for graduate students to learn specific methods only *after* they are in the field, doing their own thesis or dissertation fieldwork (see Stein et al. 2016).We contend that there are practical ways to improve the undergraduate educational experience within anthropology (e.g., see Copeland 2016; Glass-Coffin 2016; Snodgrass 2016, Stein et al. 2016 in this issue). Fundamentally, this requires aligning the research interests of academic anthropologists with the applied career goals of our students. This mental shift on the part of academics rests on the realization that the divide between academic and professional anthropology is arbitrary. As Baba (2009:380) reminds us, "disciplines and professions appear to be interdependent in that professions are the means to livelihoods, and disciplines often hold amonopoly on granting credentials that are the gateway to the professions." The credentials that we impart to our students must be more than a title or a degree on the wall; they need to be connected to concrete marketable skills that clearly signify capability in a diverse range of careers. While the job opportunities for social scientists are expected to increase, we need to position our students and more broadly our discipline to benefit from these opportunities and to show the Scott Walkers of the world the value of anthropology.

This paper argues that *undergraduate* students, as the lifeblood of our departments, must not be left out of applied training. In an era of budgetary cutbacks and politically driven oversight, anthropology must provide students with a valuable bachelor's level education that includes specific skills for entry into the marketplace. The standard line given to undergraduates regarding the value of their degree is largely the same as when I (the first author) was in their shoes, "we make well-rounded, well-educated citizens, capable of critical thought and cultural inclusion and sensitivity" (see Loker 2016). This is simply not something most employers are looking for in potential employees, leaving graduates confused about how to apply their degree in the marketplace (see Harper 2011). Instead, we need to provide students of all levels with tangible skills that they can then apply in concrete ways in future careers. This paper provides one example of how to accomplish this with a group of undergraduate students at Utah State University (USU). We suggest that small lab settings provide undergraduate students with the hands-on training and personal mentorship to teach the skills necessary for applied and practicing anthropological work.

In particular, we highlight the role cognitive anthropological methods serve in this education and training. These methods are relatively easy to teach and employ, but they are backed by rigorous and robust analytical strength that translate well in practicing settings (see Briody et al. 2014). We present a specific example of a cognitive anthropological research project carried out by the undergraduate students in this laboratory. Their work demonstrates the possibilities for the "research-teaching nexus" of student-involved research. Finally, we conclude with a renewed call for engaged-learning opportunities for students, and provide recommendations for accomplishing this worthy feat.

The collaborative anthropological research laboratory

Here, I (the first author) expand on the inspiration and motivation to create an undergraduate research group. The Collaborative Anthropological Research Laboratory (CARL) was founded in Fall 2014 at USU by the first author with the help of a few intrepid undergraduate students, who are co-authors on this paper. The model for this group is based on my prior experiences with collaborative research groups while a student at Colorado State University and the University of Alabama. In both of these contexts, faculty members worked alongside graduate and advanced undergraduate students in joint research-teaching activities. By doing so, students learned to *do* anthropology through involvement in actual projects. As a Masters student, I worked in Snodgrass's (2016) Ethnographic Research and Teaching Laboratory (ERTL), investigating the experiences of online gamers in massively multiuser online games such as World of Warcraft and League of Legends. Often ERTL exists as an instructional course, providing students with the opportunity to learn ethnographic methods within a research context that results in tangible products (e.g., publications and presentations) for the students (see Snodgrass et al. 2012, 2014, 2016). Later, as a PhD student, I had the opportunity to take these experiences and apply them in Lynn's (see Stein et al. 2016 this volume) Human Behavioral Ecology Research Group (HBERG). This group similarly engaged graduate and undergraduate students in joint study. Uniquely, HBERG is not offered as a course, but as an extracurricular "club" that gives students the opportunity to apply theory and methods obtained in the classroom to research projects in field-like settings. Since HBERG is not limited by course requirements or the semester schedule, the group evolves organically, and oscillates its focus between shared group projects and more individually oriented studies derived from the students' own theses and dissertations. This flexibility also allows attention to mentorship and development activities, including grant writing, conference presentations, and post undergraduate placement.

The experiences offered by both ERTL and HBERG provide students with opportunities to *learn* anthropological skills by *doing* anthropology. These small, focused groups provide students with a place to learn and practice a variety of anthropological methods, while also giving them the experience of designing and carrying out research projects and, importantly, adjusting to the inevitable challenges and roadblocks of fieldwork. As mentioned above, few students—even at the graduate level—are given opportunities to engage in collaborative projects with a senior anthropologist where they can shadow experienced ethnographers before carrying out research by themselves. When I accepted a position at USU, one of my first goals was to establish a setting that would combine the research-teaching nexus for my new students. Unlike my previous labs, CARL focuses solely on undergraduate students by engaging them in experiential and skill-based learning. This population of students, often occluded from fieldwork opportunities, would have their own research lab.

I knew that for this collaboration to flourish, CARL would require a clear outline of expectations and goals. The success and longevity of this program rest solely on the potential of undergraduates to learn methods outside of a formalized classroom setting and to produce research of publishable quality. A major part of this group's success derives from allowing students to develop a sense of ownership in the lab and our research (see Stein et al. 2016). Thus, it was essential to involve students in all aspects of the research process, from devising the research question, developing the research proposal, and the analysis and presentation of results. In doing so, the students become invested in the process, feeling that their insights and interest guide the direction of the research endeavor. Here, mentoring plays a critical role. Students need to be given the confidence to take on the role of "junior" researchers and colleagues. At the same time, they must be guided and taught—something particularly true for undergraduates who often have no prior research experience. As such, before each research phase, I provide students opportunities to shadow me in data collection techniques before they try them. Senior members of the lab are now conducting this mentoring role as they demonstrate and teach these methods to the newer students. Finally, this collaborative lab emphasizes professional development through the acquisition of skills and professional knowledge. To ensure they obtain the skills for entry into the marketplace, I emphasize that CARL members need to become experienced in more than "just" data collection and analytical techniques. They need to become well versed in other essential aspects of professional anthropology as well, including grant and proposal writing, and the presentation of their results in reports, conference presentations, and academic articles.

In sum, CARL is derived from my own work in similar groups that utilize the research-teaching nexus to shape the educational experience of students. As a spiritual successor to these collaborative research groups, CARL is focused on providing students with the skills necessary to succeed in both the academic and professional setting after graduation. This can be facilitated through a unified theoretical and methodological approach that provides a common narrative strand through the distinct phases of research. The next section outlines my own reasoning for incorporating an explicitly cognitive anthropological approach to the research conducted by members of CARL.

A cognitive anthropological approach for practicing careers

One of the goals of CARL is to provide methodological training and experience to undergraduates, so that they have the practical skills necessary for applied work upon graduation. There is of course a wide variety of methods available to any ethnographer, and this is arguably one strength of anthropology. The holistic orientation of the anthropological approach provides space for qualitative, experience-driven insights, as well as more rigid, standardized measurements, and data collection. Good ethnographic and anthropological research can make use of either of these methodological traditions. The combination of these so-called mixed-method or integrated approaches is often used in applied and practicing work (see Miller et al. 2004). Not to diminish the role of critical, interpretive, or deconstructionist anthropology, but anthropology outside the ivory tower often requires that the research design and methods be framed in ways that communicate findings across disciplines and to various stakeholders or clients. In such settings, anthropologists are often part of collaborative teams, where interdisciplinary, methodological pluralism is the norm, rather than the exception (Weisner 2012). One approach that combines both qualitative and quantitative traditions, and has enjoyed success within the applied and practicing world, is that of cognitive anthropology. This is also the primary methodological approach utilized within CARL.

Cognitive anthropology is concerned with how cultural knowledge is structured and shared among members of a community. Here, culture is specifically understood as the systems of knowledge necessary to function within a social and/or ecological setting. Units of such cultural knowledge, variously conceptualized as prototypes, models, and schemas, provide common frameworks for people to individually understand and jointly communicate their experiences of reality. Of course, variation between individuals and subgroups are expected, and in fact, necessary for social learning, innovation, and distinction. The qualitative and quantitative methods that lie at the heart of cognitive anthropological research are as varied as the topics studied. For instance, schema analysis—the evaluation of common and salient ideas—can be applied to unstructured and semistructured interviews. Cultural domain analysis—the analysis of cognitive "lists"— relies on more structured methods such as free listing and pile sorting. The point here is not to provide an exhaustive description of cognitive anthropology— there are many great sources that serve that role (e.g., Bernard 2011; Bernard and Gravlee 2014; d'Andrade 1995; Kempton et al. 1996; Medin et al. 2006)—but rather to provide a brief background of a specific cultural anthropological approach that has found a central place within many applied anthropologists' tool kit.

The methods utilized by any researcher should be apropos to the question and hypothesis being considered. In many anthropological research projects, there are two general questions: How does community *A* view/understand phenomena *B*; and how does *B* affect community *A*? In answering both of these questions, a cognitive anthropological approach proves particularly useful. In an early study, Harding and Wulf (1979) described how cognitive anthropological methods were beneficial in architectural planning. In particular, they used this approach to identify the uses and meanings ascribed to different structural layouts and spaces. Utilizing the simple, but analytically powerful free-listing method, they elicited meanings and emotions associated with particularly architectural styles and designs. Based on commonalities of terms, Harding and Wulf assisted architects in building a more effective and culturally appropriate school for a Navajo community. Similar approaches have also been applied toward health studies. Poehlman (2008) for instance, utilized free lists to identify ideal masculine behaviors among African-American men, and the connection of these cultural behaviors with HIV/AIDS risk. After collecting the free lists, Poehlman had his informants sort the most salient items by importance and commonality, which was then subjected to a statistical analysis of similarity, known as cultural consensus analysis (see Romney et al. 1986). This cognitive approach allows researchers to empirically identify shared cultural knowledge and determine its distribution among a sample of informants. After finding evidence of a shared model for masculine behaviors, Poehlman evaluated how enactment of this cultural ideal was associated with HIV/AIDS exposure, in a process called "cultural consonance" (Dressler 1996). In this way, Poehlman utilizes the cognitive anthropological approach to answer the general questions faced by applied anthropologists: how does a population, in this case African-American men, view a cultural phenomenon, such as masculine expectations?; and how does the action or adherence to this model affect an outcome, like HIV/ AIDS risk?

To date, much of the published applied work that utilizes an explicitly cognitive methodology focuses on projects that address human-environment questions. These cognitive methods, which provide an empirical approach toward documenting "culture," can be useful for conveying research findings with stakeholders and collaborators who may be more policy or "scientifically" driven. For example, in response to a fish-die off associated with an algae bloom, Paolisso and Maloney (2001) utilized cognitive anthropological methods to identify cultural models and schemas which people used to understand environmental hazards and pollution risks. They found that the way by which they did their work contributed to the acceptance and validation of the role and value of anthropological perspectives to clients and stakeholders:

> [I]n addition to producing insightful substantive findings, the construct "cultural model" has also served us well in helping to establish rapport with scientists and environmental professionals. The construct of a "model" is central to the research paradigm of our colleagues. Our colleagues did understand that we were attempting to construct models, and although our models are not nearly as specified or predictive as say economic or ecosystem models, they do share underlying similarities in terms of their utility in capturing key relationships among cultural as well as biological variables. In the end, we appear to other scientists and environmental professionals as very scientific, which we suspect contrasts with any existing cultural understanding they have of anthropologists and anthropology.... Our use of a cultural model approach, supported by well-respected and prestigious scientific funding sources, helped to legitimize us among scientists and policymakers as one of many research projects on *Pfiesteria* and now other environmental issues for the Bay. (Paolisso and Maloney 2001:44, 46)

Shirley Fiske (2008) echoes this point in her own work with the federal government by arguing that often clients and bureaucracies value empirically driven, quantitatively analyzed research over other types of methodologies. A cognitive approach, she contends, provides methodological similarities to convey information across disciplinary divides. Further, the replicability of these methods allows for the perception of objectivity, thereby making them attractive for use by various stakeholders, particularly on issues of environmental and health-related social problems (Miller et al. 2004). Importantly, however, cultural models and cognitive methods are not a panacea, and like in any project, the researcher has to use the methods most appropriate to the research questions, setting, and goals. As Vivelo (1980) reminds us, in the adoption of "new," rigorous methodologies that may provide "legitimacy" of anthropology in the eyes of others, we must not lose sight of what makes anthropology unique within the social sciences. Applied anthropologists, must "remain the most adept at what is, unquestionably, the most difficult social science research technique to master: participant-observation. No other methodology demands so much personally from the researcher in terms of time, labor intensity, creativity, adaptability, hardship, and commitment" (Vivelo 1980:346). That is, for anthropologists, the emic and holistic viewpoints are particularly valuable contributions, and while we need to speak a common language with stakeholders and collaborators (often involving scientific methods and quantitative data), we should not forgo what makes anthropology so unique among the social sciences.

A brief example of an undergraduate cognitive anthropological project

These cognitive anthropological methods are accessible to undergraduate students. In fact, the first project performed by the undergraduates in CARL focuses on identifying cultural models of secular and religious gender roles held by students on their college campus. Student researchers are very interested in the negotiation and distribution of these expectations among their peers and themselves. The reasons for this attention vary, from a personal interest to a sense of concern about the well-being of their community. As fellow USU anthropologist, Bonnie Glass-Coffin (2016) explores in this special issue, there is a substantial amount of discord lying just beneath the surface of the USU-Logan community. This distress, particularly among students, comes from the religious (Mormon) pressures to adhere to certain cultural norms and expectations; and from their more secularly oriented professors and peers, many of whom "push back" against the traditional and conservative values of the Mormon (or LDS, Latter-day Saints) Church. Gender role negotiation—something the students view as a salient pressure within this period in emerging adults' lives—was to be the domain of interest.

Utilizing a cognitive anthropological approach, the undergraduate students set out to identify religious and secular models of gender. The students and research both benefit from the method's rigorous empirical evaluation and ease of execution. Students administered 22 semistructured interviews combined with a free-listing exercise to fellow students, asking them to describe the traits valued in men and women from both a Mormon and secular American perspective. This sample (20.2 ± 3.7 years old; 36 percent male, 86 percent LDS) roughly approximated the gender, age, and religious demographics of students at the university. Students administered these interviews until we felt the domain was saturated and respondents were not generating new terms.

The researchers of CARL analyzed the free lists through Visual Anthropac (Borgatti 2003), a computer program that assists in determining the saliency and frequency of elicited terms. Concurrent with these interviews, the researchers also engaged in participant-observation of the USU and LDS communities. This was facilitated by a number of the student researchers who operate as "halfie" anthropologists—anthropologists who at least partially identify with the communities of study. In this case, all of the researchers are USU students and half are active members of the LDS Church. In conjunction with the more empirical results from the free lists, and the more subjective insights from participant-observation and semistructured interviews, the researchers constructed models of what USU students view as the religious and secular expectations for men and women. This process resulted in four "cultural models" that were tested for cultural consensus—significant interinformant agreement of the structure and composition of how the community views these gendered expectations (see Romney et al. 1986). Undergraduate researchers then administered a pile-sorting task to test the proposed models for consensus. Thirty-three items were chosen that were indicative of the necessary and forbidden characteristics of religious and secular gender roles across all four models. A separate sample of 33 undergraduate students (20.4 ± 2.4 years old; 42 percent male, 82 percent active LDS) conducted a constrained pile sort of these terms, identifying traits that "were" and "were not" valued among each of the four gender role models. We reasoned that by having the informants construct models from a common pool of terms, we would be able to compare the composition of each model, and determine areas of both overlap and distinction. These pile sort data were evaluated using formal cultural consensus analysis via the computer program UCINET.

We found strong consensus for three of the four models we tested. By convention, indications of significant sharing via cultural consensus includes: an eigenvalue ratio greater than 3:1, which signifies that a single dimension explains over three times the variance than the next; an average competency score above 0.5, suggesting that an informant knows the culturally appropriate response to at least half of the queried items; and few to no negative competency scores, indicating that no informant was completely dissonant or contrary to the responses provided by the aggregate. Both LDS gender roles show a high level of cultural consensus. The gender model for Mormon women shows the greatest agreement among informants, with an eigenvalue ratio of 9.5, an average competency of 0.8, and no negative competency scores. The model for LDS men also shows high consensus, with an eigenvalue ratio of 8.2 and an average competency of 0.64 with no negative scores. There was similarly high consensus for the ideal characteristics of American men (eigenvalue ratio of 5.9; average competency of 0.65 with no negative scores). The gender model for American women, however, shows less consensus with an eigenvalue ratio of 2.3 and average competency of 0.48 with one negative score. Further analysis suggests that the American female model may represent a "contested domain" with the majority of informants identifying a liberal "feminist" leaning model; whereas some informants alternatively identified more traditional characteristics (e.g., nurturer, wife, homemaker) as indicative of the expectations for an American woman (see Caulkins and Hyatt 1999). Because each model is composed of the same possible terms, the relationship of each can be displayed as a Venn diagram of similarities and differences (Figure 1).

A brief discussion of the data

Areas of cultural knowledge, understood here as cultural models, exist in synergistic relationships with one another. Rather than being isolated domains, their content and boundaries are formed in relation to what it *is*, and what it *is not*. Such is the case for gender roles within American and Western societies, where male and femaleness are often constructed in opposition to one another (West and Zimmerman 1987). Similarly, religion within American society is often constructed at odds with, in opposition to, or distinct from "everyday" secular society (see Mauss 1994). Both of these distinctions—between genders and between the secular and the sacred—are evident with Utah. Uniquely, however, Mormonism as the majority religion also shapes the dominant culture within Utah, and specifically that on the USU campus.

Church members and nonmembers alike easily identify the ideal model for LDS men and women. In general, these gender roles follow traditional and conservative roles once endorsed by larger American society during the early and mid-20th century (Mauss 1994). LDS men are expected to be the head of the household, responsible for the economic and physical health of the family. LDS women, on the other hand, are expected to be the primary nurturers of the family, taking care of the children and domestic duties of the household. This distinction is what church goers call "different but equal"; men and women are "endowed" with different traits that are suitable for specific spheres of life. This distinction is further codified within Mormon theology as Church members view themselves as being gendered not only in earthly life, but also in the pre-existence and afterlife. The church decree, "The Family: A Proclamation to the World," provides the organization's doctrine for these roles. In this supposed divinely ordained statement, earthly genders and

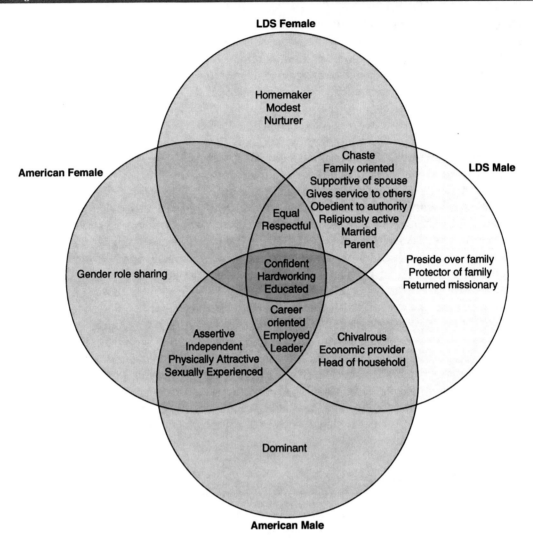

FIGURE 1.   Venn diagram of cultural models for secular and mormon gender roles. Items that correspond to particular gender roles are located within the (overlapping) circles.

families are seen as replicating heavenly order: "Gender is an essential characteristic of individual premortal, mortal, and eternal identity and purpose"; and men and women are viewed as occupying different roles and endowed with unique traits: "By divine design, fathers are to preside over their families in love and righteousness and are responsible to provide the necessities of life and protection for their families.... Mothers are primarily responsible for the nurture of their children." Yet, there is substantial overlap between the LDS male and female modeling, coinciding with the genders' shared focus on the family and the faith. Our cultural consensus results show that at least among our sample, the message of the church is clearly heard and understood by members and nonmembers alike.

The American gender models show a slightly different pattern. The American male model is more salient in the minds of our informants, and appears to share many similarities with LDS men. The similarity with the LDS male model likely stems from the patriarchal position of both male roles. American men, like their religious counterparts, are viewed to be leaders within the public and private sphere— career driven, economic providers who are confident and hardworking. However, they are also seen as domineering, taking pleasure in their position over others. As mentioned prior, there is less agreement on the American female model, with informants seemingly at odds between a more modern and liberal role, versus one that is more conservative and traditional. Most respondents do view American society as promoting the former, characterized as career-oriented leaders, sexually experienced, and independent. These are also characteristics the female model shares with the secular male model. Uniquely, our informants saw the secular female role as endorsing more "gender role sharing"—the idea that a woman could and should do anything a man can do.

Taken together, these gender models show what one should *and* should not be—and demonstrates the contradictions and negotiations USU undergraduates must contend with in their own displays of gender. In the next phase of this study, the students are performing a cultural consonance analysis to determine how adherence with these gendered cultural models shapes psychological well-being. For the students, they are hoping to use these findings to address the culturally derived pressures that are distressful for parts of the population. While the research is ongoing, the students are hypothesizing that the greater disconnect between the religious female model endorsed by their faith and the American female model endorsed by society (e.g., importance of being career oriented, leader, employed) presents unique challenges to Mormon women. This disjuncture, combined with the differences between the LDS female and male roles, may explain some of the disproportionate psychological distress that Utah women experience (see Kaiser Family Foundation 2014; Norton et al. 2006). The student researchers are hoping that these insights will foster dialogue across campus for ways of mitigating divergent cultural expectations and to create opportunities for "third ways" of being.

Teaching applied methods and preparing students for careers

Perhaps we should not be surprised by the sentiment of Governor Scott. Anthropology has been losing the battle for relevance in the public eye for some time. Over 25 years ago, Upham et al. (1988) lamented that an anthropology degree was losing relevancy in a changing marketplace that increasingly valued STEM and business degrees for securing job placement after graduation. This perception of which majors translate into better economic security is not lost on students, parents, or university administrators. These various educational stakeholders are doing a cost-benefit analysis, determining which disciplines and majors offer the most value for the ever-increasing costs of higher education. Gradually, these clients and sponsors are cutting support and funding for liberal arts, humanities, and social science departments (Cohen 2016). The model for how we train our students, however, has changed little in the intervening time. A recent column from the AAA executive director Ed Liebow (2016) once again addresses this issue by calling for the discipline to convey the value of our majors by showing that a bachelor's degree within anthropology does yield a "significant payoff." But without professional utility of an anthropology B.A., the "payoff" will be disconnected from economic value, which is becoming more difficult to justify to our students and ourselves. Clearly, our discipline requires a fundamental shift in how we approach teaching anthropology to our biggest patrons—our undergraduate students.

It is not for a lack of great ideas that our discipline finds itself in this position. Returning to Upham et al. (1988), they suggest restructuring the curricula to better reflect the training and expertise required to succeed in the job market. For example, while French social theory is certainly important for understanding the conceptual foundations of anthropology today, it holds little practical worth for an undergraduate who wants to get a job after graduation. Indeed, compared to other social sciences, anthropology arguably offers more in the realm of practical and marketable skills—which further begs the question why "methods" is not already central to an undergraduate curriculum. As the authors point out, "too often teaching of these skills is saved for the end of graduate training and is not made available to undergraduate students at all" (Upham et al. 1988:212, see also Hart Research Associates 2015; Rudd et al. 2008). In particular, Upham et al. suggest that an anthropological undergraduate education include training in "applied anthropological research, such as research design, statistical analysis, program evaluation, and communication through writing and speaking" (Upham et al. 1988:211). The suite of skills and tools that the anthropologist utilizes can and should be taught to all of our students. This includes both mixed-method approaches (e.g., participant-observation, ethnographic interviewing skills, cultural domain analysis; formal and informal survey and sampling methods, video ethnography, etc.) as well as the dissemination of findings (e.g., technical reports, journal articles, blogs, research proposals, etc.). Crucially, students must be given the background and confidence to effectively communicate their ability to perform jobs that may not be explicitly marketed toward "anthropologists." In short, "these skills are salable and marketable and could give anthropology undergraduates access to careers" where they are often overlooked (Upham et al. 1988:213; see Goldmacher 2016).

This shift in focus away from classroom learning toward experiential, skill-development learning is not an easy transition (Kuh 2008). For the many academic anthropologists who are charged with instructing the next generation, teaching is often a secondary obligation in the role statement. As Copeland (2016) expresses in her article, many academic anthropologists are discouraged from making such engaged training a focal point of their careers, lest it threaten their "research" output. Yet, there is good reason to encourage academic anthropologists to make research a teaching enterprise, where this so-called "research-teaching nexus" provides students with opportunities for collaborative research participation, and provides a strategy for professors to combine the conflicting demands of time dedicated to research and time dedicated to teaching (Elsen et al. 2009; Griffiths 2004). Indeed, by having courses that provide "research-oriented" (curriculum focused on learning by practicing research activities) and "research-based" (curriculum focused on students conducting actual research) experience, core anthropological *concepts* connect with the *process* of knowledge construction, and the potential *outcomes* for such inquiries. Further, a collaborative research-teaching environment helps students learn by more fully integrating them within a community of their peers, allowing them to share their knowledge and skills with each other, and develop positive attitudes toward learning and knowledge. For the academics, the research-teaching nexus provides a "stimulating and rejuvenating milieu" where research and teaching are no longer distinct expectations, and both inform one another (Elsen et al. 2009). Within such a system, courses would explicitly have a research-based focus that gradually move undergraduates from the audience (consuming the knowledge of their discipline) to active participants (creating knowledge for their discipline; Elsen et al. 2009). The ability, however, to institute this system within an undergraduate curriculum would require the collaboration of entire departments, as well as university administration. Part of the challenge, therefore, will be to change existing beliefs within academia. This will require supporting professors who are designing and implementing courses with a research-based focus, by providing resources and flexibility to experiment within the research-teaching nexus.

Here, the model provided by CARL (and the other groups highlighted in this issue) offers entry points for implementing collaborative research models. These groups focus on teaching hands-on anthropology within actual research projects among local populations. In this way, the costs, in terms of time and resources are kept at a minimum for professors and students. By having the research take the form of extracurricular clubs or senior seminars, research can overlap with teaching and service requirements for professors, and the regular availability of these groups will encourage student participation. Further, by focusing on local communities, resource costs for "field schools" are kept at a minimum, ensuring more students access to this experience. Indeed, local field schools arguably offer a better alternative to the foreign locale. Collaborative projects that take place in the students' own communities allow students to focus more on the methodological training and the applied potentials of the research (rather than the "foreign" conditions). This has the potential to take on what Kozaitis (2013) calls the "engaged university" model, in which the mission of the institution and its departments is to serve the larger local community (see Copeland et al. 2016; Funkhouser et al. 2016). This allows students to see the practical value of the anthropological approach that they are acquiring. Ideally, the community likewise sees the value of anthropology within its society, cementing a place for the discipline and our students within the local marketplace.

The student view

Ultimately, however, students need to be the driving force behind the group. Without their interest, involvement, and investment, initiatives such as CARL are ineffective and unsustainable. Students need the freedom to take on an ownership role, identifying areas of importance within their community, or even themselves, for anthropological study (see Brownell and Swaner 2009; Upham et al. 1988). For example, in CARL, students chose the topic—how Mormon culture shape behaviors and identities— as the focus of research. Allowing students to study something that they are personally connected to encourages them to go beyond developing methodological skills, and develop as individuals and citizens. In fact, more than one lab member identified their own religious identity, and even struggles with being LDS, as a motivator to engage in this particular line or research.

> I joined the group during a flux of personal transition between being an active member of the LDS church and leaving the LDS church. This process put me in a state of limbo that caused me to feel a sense of rejection from many groups at school. Being a member of CARL has opened up a new avenue to interact with other students with different religious perspectives and spiritual practices. CARL brought me in with a welcoming environment that encouraged open expression of opinions and thoughts with zero prejudice and discrimination in the group.

Here, Talon found the research, but more importantly the group, as helping him to reflect on his own religious identity, and his place within the community. Similarly, Tyler remarked,

> Since coming back from my (LDS) mission, I felt like I was thrown back into a community that had never seen any other way to life that wasn't focused around the Church. Then I joined CARL, where we talked about the Church in a way that wasn't how we would talk about it within the (Mormon) culture. I was able to look at my own culture from an outsider's perspective. We have a variety of religions and statuses within the group, allowing for wider insight into our research. I myself began to see the Church as a system, with strengths and flaws like any other group. It has been a great mind-opening experience.

Still active in his faith, Tyler started reflecting on some of the more "status quo" ideals and behaviors embodied in his community. His research within CARL, particular the collaboration with his peers, has allowed him to explore some of these views, facilitating him to develop a more mature understanding and appreciation of his community and his faith.

Indeed, the cooperative relationships built between the "halfie" and the "outsider" members demonstrate the value of collaborative partnerships with community of focus. However, this synergy of ideas and backgrounds can be difficult at times. Elizabeth occasionally found the interaction challenging, but ultimately rewarding:

> Participating as an active Mormon studying Mormons is an incredible experience. Have I learned about my own religion? Yes. Have I learned about how other people see my beliefs? Yes. Have I been offended from time to time? Yes. Have I offended others? I'm sure I have. For me, I appreciate the opportunity to explain my religion in an academic light and to study it from an academic perspective.

Elizabeth found the exchange of conflicting ideas to be part of the academic experience. Within a context of mutual respect, students feel free to share their ideas, opinions, and insights with one another. While at times those ideas challenged and offended, these exchanges provide valuable perspectives to the research question at hand. Similarly, Kirsti made the connection that such collaborations fulfill the anthropological edict of capturing both an emic and etic perspective:

> I believe that the participation of members of the groups being studied, as well as those not members, allow for a greater understanding by providing multiple perspectives on an extremely complex topic. Only by having someone

inside a box taking pictures, and outside the box taking pictures, can a full understanding of the box be obtained. I have learned so much about what I see as a real meaning of collaboration: filling in where others cannot.

And this insight, of learning about anthropological methods, by doing anthropological methods, is viewed by Erica as essential, but lacking in traditional classroom courses:

> CARL has taught me things that you really can't learn in a classroom. You can't listen to a lecture on interviewing someone and then do it like a professional. Watching a professor talk about data analysis isn't the same as working through a question you thought of yourself. No amount of English essays truly prepare you to have to go through the IRB. It's a kind of hands on learning that makes up the nuts and bolts of what it means to practice anthropology. And that really puts me a step above my non-research peers. Students who only go to class may graduate with an anthropology degree, but they aren't anthropologists.

Students also appreciate the opportunity to focus their future academic and professional goals, by having the opportunity to practice what they study. For example, some CARL students, such as Essa, decided to commit to graduate studies in the discipline.

> CARL showed me what it really means to be an anthropologist. It wasn't just theoretical anymore: we were doing actual research. The IRB process, the interviews, the transcriptions, the analyzing, the writing, the editing— CARL taught me valuable skills that I will use throughout my career, and instilled in me the value of group research. I formed connections with other anthropologists, both in and out of CARL, that are very dear to me. I would definitely not feel as confident about starting grad school if not for my time in CARL ... I definitely feel like I have a head start! I know the methods. I have the tools.

Indeed, navigating graduate school and professional careers can be a complex and stressful experience, particularly for undergraduates. However, the professional development labs such as CARL provide students the opportunity to network with other academic and professionals, and give them the confidence that they have the professional skills to succeed at the next level (Kuh 2008). Not all students, however, will go on to earn graduate degrees in anthropology. Nevertheless, undergraduate research opportunities can still instill personal and professional skills that will help them succeed in other fields.

> How does CARL help me install anchor baskets on an F/A-18 or fixing composite material? The first thing that comes to mind is how CARL and programs like it benefit the student in ways nothing else could. Everybody knows how the workplace is a very competitive one. What sets you apart from anyone else applying for the same position? In the Navy, the ones who get promoted are those who are showing that they are trying to better themselves constantly and don't just do their job for the day and go home. And CARL offers those same opportunities for students. So they can learn and expand all the skills (beyond the classroom) needed in their careers.

Here, Airman McKayla Montierth comments that while "anthropology" has little to do with her current job repairing U.S.Navy fighter jets, the work ethic instilled by the research group showed her the importance of being self-directed in one's professional career. That is, for both Erica and McKayla, the things that separate them from their peers (for either graduate schools or Navy promotion) are the skills, experiences, and confidence that are part of personal and professional development.

Conclusion

The CARL is providing students at USU the opportunity for meaningful and practical skill development during the undergraduate years. These students are more than capable of learning and engaging in anthropological projects, as their research on campus gender roles indicates. Collaborative spaces such as CARL provide opportunities for students to model the methods and behaviors of senior anthropologists, which the students can then utilize in their own academic and professional careers. It is essential, if we as a discipline are to provide students with a valuable and practical degree, that the major confer skills that include the abilities to design, conduct, analyze, and present research. This training should not wait until graduate school, but start early and be included as part of the basic education for all our students.

Providing opportunities for faculty-student collaboration is not difficult, but it does require a conscientious effort on the part of faculty, students, and departments in order to maximize both the research and educational outcomes. To summarize, we learned six key things through our experience working in the research-teaching nexus of CARL:

1. Undergraduates are capable of meaningful contribution to research if given the opportunity. This is facilitated by a unifying research project that the students have an invested interest in pursuing.
2. Most undergraduates will not have prior methodological experience, so it is important to provide this training and to suggest courses that will provide further developmental opportunities. Having an integrated and iterative research plan helps students see how the various approaches in the ethnographer's toolkit fit together.
3. Similarly, having a clear methodological and theoretical orientation helps students understand how theory, method, and analysis are interconnected. In the first-author's experience, a cognitive anthropological approach encompasses a suite of mixed methods that link to a specific theoretical and analytical school of thought. This approach is also widely and successfully employed within the applied realm, making it a (somewhat) known quantity among (some) employers, agencies, and stakeholders. The point here is not to advocate for any particular method or theory, but to recommend that the methods taught to students have professional value that students can clearly articulate to potential employers.
4. These groups provide valuable mentorship opportunities that allow students to model "professional" behavior. This includes developing positive habits and work ethics, as well as social networking and collaboration skills. Students will also have the opportunity to become mentors for each other, allowing the development of leadership skills and furthering their investment in the group.
5. Faculty-student collaborations can also provide opportunities for personal development beyond and above "professional" skills. Fostering an open, respectful collaborative work environment can facilitate the experience of community citizenship, and the growth and maturity of personal identities.
6. Finally, it is essential that students are taught how to clearly articulate their skills and experience for future projects and employment opportunities. It is a mistake to think the connections between theory and practice are self-evident, and students will need to be shown how to connect their anthropology degree with what employers are seeking.

To conclude, we should not lose sight of what makes the anthropology degree unique—creating well-rounded, well-educated citizens, capable of critical thought, cultural inclusion, and sensitivity. Rather, we need to *add* the skills and knowledge that are valued in STEM into the basic curriculum. This should not be a difficult task, as many of these approaches are fundamentally anthropological as well. This paper, along with the contributing authors in this special issue, provides strategies, experiences, and tips for providing such integrated and holistic anthropological training. Part of the challenge will be confronting existing trends and beliefs within academia. This will require supporting academics who are designing and implementing courses with a collaborative-study focus by allowing them resources and flexibility to experiment with the research-teaching nexus. The unfortunate truth is that in the present university environment, many public institutions have taken on a neoliberal economic slant, focusing on the most "productive" and "profitable" majors and cutting back funding on others. This is threatening the socially responsible education that universities have excelled at, and instead placed more emphasis on a piecework education that values certifications and the like. If we are successful, we will be helping more than just our students, we will be reshaping the role of the discipline within academic, civic, and public life.

References cited

Baba, Marietta
2009 Disciplinary-Professional Relations in an Era of Anthropological Engagement. Human Organization 68(4):380–391.

Bernard, H. Russell
2011 Research Methods in Anthropology: Qualitative and Quantitative Approaches. Lanham, MD: Rowman Altamira.

Bernard, H. Russell, and Clarence C. Gravlee
2014 Handbook of Methods in Cultural Anthropology. Lanham, MD: Rowman & Littlefield.

Borgatti, Steve
2003 ANTHROPAC4.98.Natick, MA: Analytic Technologies.

Briody, Elizabeth Kathleen, Robert T. Trotter, and Tracy L. Meerwarth
2014 Transforming Culture: Creating and Sustaining Effective Organizations. Palgrave Macmillan.

Brownell, Jayne E., and Lynn E. Swaner
2009 High-Impact Practices: Applying the Learning Outcomes Literature to the Development of Successful Campus Programs. Peer Review 11(2):26–30.

Caulkins, Douglas, and Susan B. Hyatt
1999 Using Consensus Analysis to Measure Cultural Diversity in Organizations and Social Movements. Field Methods 11(1):5–26.

Cohen, Patricia
2016 A Rising Call to Promote STEM Education and Cut Liberal Arts Funding. The New York Times, February 21. http://www.nytimes.com/2016/02/22/business/arising-call-to-promote-stem-educationand-cut-liberal-arts-funding.html?_r=0, accessed October 14, 2016.

Copeland, Toni
2016 Teaching the Research Process through Student Engagement: Cultural Consensus Analysis of HIV/AIDS. Annals of Anthropological Practice 40(2):137–152.

Copeland, Toni, Donna Ploessl, Avery McNeece, Curtis Kennett, Victoria Lee, and Dylan Karges
2016 Creating a Better Tomorrow: Teaching Applied Cultural Anthropological Research by Reimagining Service Learning and Community Engagement. Annals of Anthropological Practice 40(2):218–232.

d'Andrade, Roy G.
1995 The Development of Cognitive Anthropology. Cambridge: Cambridge University Press.

Dressler, William W.
1996 Culture and Blood Pressure: Using Consensus Analysis to Create a Measurement. Field Methods 8(3):6–8.

Elsen, Mariken G.M. F., Gerda J. Visser-Wijnveen, Roeland M. Van der Rijst, and Jan H. Van Driel
2009 How to Strengthen the Connection between Research and Teaching in Undergraduate University Education. Higher Education Quarterly 63(1):64–85.

Fiske, Shirley J.
2008 Working for the Federal Government: Anthropology Careers. NAPA Bulletin 29(1):110–130.

Funkhouser, J. Lynn, Juliann Friel, Melinda Carr, and Christopher D. Lynn
2016 Anthropology is Elemental: Anthropological Perspective through Multi-Level Teaching. Annals of Anthropological Practice 40(2):233–244.

Glass-Coffin, Bonnie
2016 Building Capacity and Transforming Lives: Anthropology Undergraduates and Religious Campus-Climate Research on a Public-University Campus. Annals of Anthropological Practice 40(2):245–256.

Goldmacher, Amy
2016 Helping Faculty Prepare Students for the Job Market. Anthropology News 57(4):e22–e23. doi:10.1111/j.1556- 3502.2016.570512.x.

Griffiths, Ron
2004 Knowledge Production and the Research–Teaching Nexus: The Case of the Built Environment Disciplines. Studies in Higher Education 29(6):709–726.

Harding, Joe, and Robert Wulff
    1979 Special Section: Anthropology and Architectural Planning. Practicing Anthropology 1(5–6):3–25.
Harper, Janice
    2011 Why Florida Gov. Rick Scott Was Right to Slam Studying Anthropology. Business Insider, October 21. http://www.businessinsider.com/rick-scott-thinks-liberal-arts-degrees-are-not-neededunless-you-want-to-work-for-him-2011-10, accessed October 14, 2016.
Hart Research Associates
    2015 Falling Short? College Learning and Career Success: Selected Findings from Online Surveys of Employers and College Students. Association of American Colleges & Universities. http://www.aacu.org/sites/default/files/files/LEAP/2015employerstudentsurvey.pdf, accessed October 14, 2016.
Kaiser Family Foundation
    2014 Kaiser Family Foundation Analysis of the Centers for Disease Control and Prevention (CDC)'s Behavioral Risk Factor Surveillance System (BRFSS) 2014 Survey Results. http://kff.org/other/stateindicator/poor-mental-health-by-gender, accessed October 14, 2016.
Kempton, Willett, James S. Boster, and Jennifer A. Hartley
    1996 Environmental Values in American Culture. Cambridge: MIT Press.
Kozaitis, Kathryn A.
    2013 Anthropological Praxis in Higher Education. Annals of Anthropological Practice 37(1):133–55.
Kuh, George D.
    2008 High-Impact Education Practices: What They Are, Who Has Access to Them, and Why They Matter. Washington, DC: Association of American Colleges and Universities.
Liebow, Ed
    2016 Look Outside the Classroom to Draw Students in. Anthropology News, April. http://www.anthropology-news.org/index.php/2016/03/02/look-outside-the-class room-to-draw-students-in/, accessed October 14, 2016.
Loker, William
    2016 WhatDoWeWantOur Students to Learn?: Learning Outcomes for Anthropology. Anthropology News 57(9–10):8.
Mauss, Armand L.
    1994 The Angel and the Beehive: The Mormon Struggle with Assimilation. Champaign, IL: University of Illinois Press.
Medin, Douglas L., Norbert O. Ross, and Douglas G. Cox
    2006 Culture and Resource Conflict: Why Meanings Matter: Why Meanings Matter. New York: Russell Sage Foundation.
Miller, Marc L., John Kaneko, Paul Bartram, Joe Marks, and Devon D. Brewer
    2004 Cultural Consensus Analysis and Environmental Anthropology: Yellowfin Tuna Fishery Management in Hawaii. Cross-Cultural Research 38(3):289–314.
Norton, Maria C., Ingmar Skoog, Lynn M. Franklin, Christopher Corcoran, JoAnn T. Tschanz, Peter P. Zandi, John C.S. Breitner, Kathleen A. Welsh–Bohmer, and David C. Steffens
    2006 Gender Differences in the Association between Religious Involvement and Depression: The Cache County (Utah) Study. The Journals of Gerontology Series B: Psychological Sciences and Social Sciences 61(3):P129–P136.
O'Conner, John
    2011 Explaining Florida Gov. Rick Scott's War On Anthropology (and Why Anthropologists MayWin). State Impact, NPR, October 20. https://stateimpact.npr.org/florida/2011/10/20/explaining-florida-gov-scottwar-on-anthropology-why-anthropologists-win/, accessed October 14, 2016.
Paolisso, Michael, and R. Maloney
    2001 Building a Constituency for Applied Environmental Anthropology through Research. Practicing Anthropology 23(3):42– 46.
Peregrine, Peter, Yolanda T. Moses, Alan Goodman, Louise Lamphere, and James Lowe Peacock
    2012 What Is Science in Anthropology? American Anthropologist 114(4):593–597.

Poehlman, Jon
  2008 Masculine Identity and HIV/AIDS Risk Behavior among African-American Men. Practicing Anthropology 30(1):12–17.

Romney, A. Kimball, Susan C.Weller, andWilliam H. Batchelder
  1986 Culture as Consensus: A Theory of Culture and Informant Accuracy. American Anthropologist 88(2):313–338.

Rudd, Elizabeth, EmoryMorrison, Joseph Picciano, and Maresi Nerad
  2008 Social Science PhDs Five+ Years Out: Anthropology Report. Center for Innovation and Research in Graduate Education. Seattle, WA: University of Washington. February 14.

Snodgrass, Jeffrey
  2016 Online Virtual Worlds as Anthropological Field Sites: Ethnographic Methods Training via Collaborative Research of Internet Gaming Cultures. Annals of Anthropological Practice 40(2):123–136.

Snodgrass, Jeffrey, Greg Batchelder, Scarlett Eisenhauer, Lahoma Howard, H.J. François Dengah II, Rory Sascha Thompson, Josh Bassarear, Robert Cookson, Peter Defouw, Melanie Matteliano, and Colton Powell
  2016 (In Online First) A Guild Culture of "Casual Raiding" Enhances Is Members' Online Gaming Experiences: A Cognitive Anthropological and Ethnographic Approach to World of Warcraft. New Media and Society.

Snodgrass, Jeffrey G., H. J. Francois Dengah II, Michael G. Lacy, Jesse Fagan, David Most, Michael Blank, Lahoma Howard, Chad R. Kershner, Gregory Krambeer, and Alissa Leavitt-Reynolds
  2012 Restorative Magical Adventure or Warcrack? Motivated MMO Play and the Pleasures and Perils of Online Experience. Games and Culture 7(1):3–28.

Snodgrass, Jeffrey G., Michael G. Lacy, H. J. Francois Dengah II, Scarlett Eisenhauer, Greg Batchelder, and Rory Sascha Thompson
  2014 A Vacation from Your Mind: Problematic Online Gaming Is a Stress Response. Computers in Human Behavior 38:248–260.

Stein, Max J., Ashley Daugherty, Isabella Rivera, Jessica Muzzo, and Christopher D. Lynn
  2016 Thinking Outside Anthropology's Box: Socializing Undergraduates through Collaborative, Interdisciplinary Research. Annals of Anthropological Practice 40(2):153–166.

Upham, Steadman, Wenda R. Trevathan, and Richard R. Wilk
  1988 Teaching Anthropology: Research, Students, and the Marketplace. Anthropology & Education Quarterly 19(3):203–217.

Vivelo, Frank
  1980 Anthropology, Applied Research, and Non-academic Careers: Observations and Recommendations, with a Personal Case History. Human Organization 39(4):345–357.

Weisner, Thomas
  2012 Mixed Methods Should Be a Valued Practice in Anthropology. Anthropology News 53(5):3–4.

West, Candace, and Don H. Zimmerman
  1987 Doing Gender. Gender & Society 1(2):125–151.

Discussion Questions

1. Why is a degree in anthropology often seen as "less valuable" than one in the STEM fields? Is there data available to support this? Please explain.
2. Why is it important for undergraduates in anthropology to obtain training in anthropological methods? Please explain and support your answer with examples.
3. Briefly describe the project on gender roles described in the article. How could learning these types of methods be useful in a field outside of anthropology?
4. How can participating in the type of research outlined in this article change an undergraduates' view of her or his own education and work? Please provide examples.
5. How can undergraduate training in anthropological methods provide opportunities for collaboration with faculty members? What ideas can you come up with for anthropological research at an undergraduate level?

Chapter 3

What Words Bring to the Table: The Linguistic Anthropological Toolkit as Applied to the Study of Food

Jillian R. Cavanaugh et al.

B oth food and language are integral parts of our everyday lives, but how are they connected – and to what extent? This article examines linguistic anthropological methods and questions whether the methods generally used to study cultural material from an anthropological point of view are the same as the methods developed by the authors to study foodways. The authors note the importance of using not only language and food, but a range of other expressive media, to promote cross-cultural research. Food *is* culture, and the authors here have provided us with the toolkit needed to study such culture.

This article offers an introduction to the methods being developed by scholars interested in studying food and language as interrelated phenomena. First, we explore a few of the intriguing parallels that have inspired a number of researchers to study food and language simultaneously. Then, we look at how the study of language led each of us to the study of food and consider if and how the methods we have used for this new enterprise differ from linguistic anthropological methods used to study other cultural material. Finally, we expand upon the specific methods we have developed for studying how foodways and language use are intertwined. In passing, we note some of the new research terrains and theoretical questions that may be explored by interweaving food-and-language methodologies in these ways. This multiauthored article, which emerged from a roundtable at the 2013 American Anthropological Association Annual meeting on the same topic, has a dialogic structure that reflects the ongoing conversation in which we are engaged while also manifesting the unfinished nature of the project. [methods, food, language, research]

Food and language have frequently been served up together on the same plate at the anthropological research table. Ethnographers have described how yams are grown with magic spells (Malinowski 1935), how ordering drinks orders people (Frake 1964), how children learn not to whine for their sago (Schieffelin 1990), how Reese's Peanut Butter Cups can help elicit landscape narratives (Basso 1996), and how mock Spanish is used to structure social relations at a Tex-Mex restaurant (Barrett 2006). Recently, however, and parallel to a rapid expansion in the study of food in cultural anthropology and other disciplines, there has been a more deliberate turn within linguistic anthropology toward the purposeful study of language use and foodways (how food is produced, prepared, distributed, and consumed) as meaningfully intertwined modalities (e.g., Manning 2012). And this analytic turn requires some explicit methodological attention, which this jointly authored article begins to provide.

In this article, we look first at some of the intriguing parallels linking food and language in ways that have inspired us to study them simultaneously. We next consider how the study of language led us to the study of food, and if and how the methods we have used differ from linguistic anthropological methods used to study other cultural material. Third, we focus on the specific methods we have expanded upon in order to study food and language as interrelated phenomena. By way of conclusion, we briefly note some of the new research terrains and theoretical questions that may be explored by interweaving food-and-language methodologies in these ways.

But first a note to clarify the textual structure before we begin. This piece grew out of a roundtable at the 2013 American Anthropological Association Annual Meetings in Chicago entitled, "Food Talk as Semiotic Substance: Steps toward an Integrated Anthropology of Foodways and Discourse." The roundtable participants included Jillian Cavanaugh, Alexandra Jaffe, Christine Jourdan, Martha Karrebæk, Anne Meneley, Amy Paugh, and Kathleen Riley. For this article, we solicited the contributions of participants (not all of whom were able to contribute) and worked to integrate their singly authored texts into a dialogic structure that reflects the ongoing conversation in which we are engaged while also manifesting the unfinished nature of the project to bring these methodologies together. As you read, you will find unmarked contextualizing paragraphs, authored by Riley and Cavanaugh (see also our two jointly authored articles on food-and-language methodology: Cavanaugh and Riley forthcoming and Riley and Cavanaugh forthcoming). These will be punctuated by the specific contributions in italics of our coauthors and ourselves as we reflect on our research and methods.

Food and Language Parallels: How We Were Hooked

While the need to eat and the need to communicate can both be seen as basic human essentials, they may also both be approached as semiotic systems, engaging sensually embodied forms in the expression of socio-culturally situated meanings. Indeed, the initial impetus for many of us to engage in the joint study of food and language arose out of a range of fundamental alignments between these two forms of social practice. However, as this article demonstrates, such connections can be multiplex and approached from a number of angles as both food and words are produced and processed, stored and exchanged, consumed and digested in diverse social contexts within specific communities with distinctive meanings and towards particular ends as these food-and-language ways are variously socialized, enacted, and transmitted across generations.

Jourdan: *Work on language often takes advantage of the sociability of food production and the commensality of the meal to start and continue inquiries on other topics. Oftentimes, food serves as a conduit through which research on other topics can take place. I surmise, this is the case because food lies at the center of social production and reproduction. Thus, methods used for the study of language socialization or language transmission are eminently suited to the study of the more symbolic dimensions of food practices and ideologies within families.*

Karrebæk: *Food and language are among the many signs (money, clothes, pictures, music ...) that people use in their everyday life to create meaning, individual and group identity, and sociality, and all of this is very basic to human life. But it is through language that we are able to make clear our (metapragmatic) understandings of other types of signs, such as food, and we only get a very loose grip on the role of food in the social life of human beings if we do not attend closely to the way food is treated linguistically. For instance, food items involved in food events are typified and sorted into linguistic categories such as healthy, halal, gross, delicious, etc. On the other hand, food has a specific meaning (and communicative) potential, which differs from that of language because it is necessary for survival. Both food and language are also part of consumer culture and globalization in late modernity; as a commodity as well as a semiotic resource, food travels along with global discourses about food, thus influencing local ways of producing, promoting, and understanding it.*

Riley: *Whether participating in mealtime conversations or plans to go fishing, the researcher learns how to eat and procure food and how to talk about these activities, how to interact while doing them and how to do them while interacting, how such forms of food talk may contribute to the functioning of food practices and how food practices may contribute to the meaning of the food talk. Frequently, we are led to do and study both food and talk simultaneously because both are essential for our efficacy as anthropologists.*

Cavanaugh: *For researchers not looking at contexts of food consumption, connections between food and language may be less obvious. For many years, my research on food (Cavanaugh 2005, 2007) and my research on language (Cavanaugh 2009) proceeded in parallel, as separate projects with little overlap. Clearly, the food producers with whom I was working used language, and the poets and other speakers I was recording ate and talked about food (I work in Italy, after all!). But it wasn't until I realized how essential various linguistic activities had become to the successful production of food—talking to customers and government officials, producing documents in pursuit of source protection designations (such as the European Union's PDO or Protected Designation of Origin schemes), selecting among linguistic varieties to construct appealing product labels—that the two came together as necessarily and interestingly intertwined. A twin focus on food and language from the vantage point of production can enable one to consider both the role of language and the place of food within contemporary political economic structures and processes.*

From Language to Food: How We Were Plated

All of the contributors to this article started out their careers as linguistic anthropologists interested in issues of language in use (e.g., language shift, language ideologies, language socialization, multilingual repertoires and strategies, and language in education). A subsequent focus on food emerged for all of us out of the ethnographic practices of earlier projects as we came to see food as either complexly intertwined with language issues or as a new topic of interest wound round with some of the analytical challenges that had drawn us to the study of language in the first place. Thus, we all arrived at our food-oriented projects with linguistic anthropological toolkits in hand, ready to see how language in use contextualized or otherwise interacted with the foodways we found so compelling. Here we ponder if and how the methods we use differ from those used in nonlinguistic studies of food as well as in linguistic anthropological studies of cultural material other than food. We also intimate how unexpected research directions are developing out of the application of linguistic anthropological methods to the study of food.

Jourdan: *As with any other type of research in anthropology, the study of food frequently starts with language: what people say about food, how they speak about it, what they do not say about it, and what they say that hides or stands for something else. Thus, the methods I have used to research food are really methods I have also employed to research other dimensions of social life. Yet, minute attention to discourse reveals that language and food are symbolic systems that have great complementary salience because they have the same type of immediacy when defining oneself or the other.*

Cavanaugh: *In many ways, the ethnographic methods that I use in my research on language and food are not so different than those which I used when investigating language shift and language ideologies: conducting participant observation and diverse types of interviews, recording and selectively transcribing language in use (often with native-speaker transcription assistants), attending to various media forms, and collecting documents of various sorts. What is different are the contexts in which I employ them and thus the activities which I participate in and document: sites of food production (slaughterhouses, farms, food production facilities) and circulation (open-air and farmers markets, specialty stores, supermarkets), as well as food activism events (tastings, food fairs, food exhibitions). In these contexts, gathering linguistic anthropological evidence while studying practices involved in food production and circulation allows me to capture a vital interactional layer of what people are doing to, around, and because of food. There are differences, however, in how I conduct research around food. The issue of what it means to participate, as well as observe, across ethnographic contexts takes different forms (I am asked to taste salamis rather than recite phrases in dialect, for instance). There are also technical challenges built into the study of food via linguistic methods: where to put one's recording device in a slaughterhouse, for instance, or how to ensure IRB compliance when recording market exchanges. Overall, however, the challenges have been outweighed by the richness of the data I have been able to gather.*

Paugh: *My research on food and language emerged from two projects—neither of which began with a focus on food interactions. My first project explored language shift and children's cultures on the Caribbean island-nation of Dominica, where I have conducted ethnographic and linguistic fieldwork since 1995 (Paugh 2012a). While my analysis privileged code-switching practices and language ideologies, the social interactions that I recorded in homes were full of talk about food, a primary concern for parents and young children. For example, a regular socializing activity concerned teaching children to overcome greediness and share food with others in their social networks. My second project examined dinnertime narratives about work among dual-earner American families in the UCLA Sloan Center on Everyday Lives of Families (CELF) study, where I was a postdoctoral fellow (Paugh 2012b). Here my interests in food talk emerged in conversation with a medical anthropologist on the project, Carolina Izquierdo. We explored how to combine approaches from linguistic and medical anthropology to study families' construction of health and well-being (rather than illness, the focus of much research) through everyday social interaction (Paugh and Izquierdo 2009).*

Karrebæk: *I started as a student of language, more particularly language-in-use, specifically within the theoretical/methodological framework of Linguistic Ethnography (Rampton 2007). My point of entry into food research was through a study of language socialization at an ethnically diverse primary classroom in Copenhagen, Denmark. My methods included ethnographic fieldwork (participant observation) and audio- and video-recordings in class, during breaks, and in the afterschool centers; I conducted interviews with parents, teachers and the principal. I then selected recordings for transcription, transcribed these in great detail, subjected these transcriptions to thorough microanalysis, and compared my classroom data with larger scale societal discourses. Most of my preconceived ideas had to do with more traditional sociolinguistic questions (e.g., "what linguistic resources do the children make use of?", "do we find hybrid linguistic practices?", "when do they then emerge?", and "what is the relation between the linguistic repertories we observe and those that we are told that the children know of?"; see, e.g., Karrebæk 2013b). None had to do with food. It was only during fieldwork that the enormous role of food and health in this classroom became clear to me; as we all know, ethnography may (and maybe even should) lead us into unforeseen and unexplored areas. But of course, it was my basic linguistic ethnographic approach that enabled to me to reach my conclusions about food and language (e.g., Karrebæk 2012, 2013a, 2013c, 2014).*

Riley: *My first research project was on language socialization, language shift, and cultural identity in French Polynesia (Riley 2007), and though I was already recording talk around food, I did not discover that this was a hidden focus until I went to study language socialization in France (this I did in order to better understand what was French and what was Polynesian about how French Polynesians socialize their children into language and culture). The ease of gathering a French family together at mealtime to record their talk made me realize how "unnatural" had been my attempts to do so in French Polynesia. Mealtime there is not an ingrained time-and-space in the day as it is in France, and no one is expected to talk at the table if they do come together. Based on this realization that sociality is not necessarily attached to consuming food as I had assumed, I returned to the study of food-and-language socialization in French Polynesia with a new perspective (although children weren't necessarily learning how to talk around the dinner table, they were definitely learning to negotiate the procuring, distribution, and preparation of food in other contexts). Then, in turn, I have been reexamining as a cultural particularity of European cultures (especially of the bourgeoisie) the assumption that one has not really learned to eat properly until one learns to speak while dining.*

(E)merging Food-and-Language Methodologies

In this section, we explore how newly food-focused methods have emerged for all of us out of the specific methods we were trained to use for the study of language in use. We examine how these methods become particularly fruitful when merged with the goal of simultaneously studying the two modalities of food and language. And we consider how, in the process, our methods are being enriched for the study of new food-and-language research problems in unfamiliar food-and-language contexts.

Participant Observation

The anthropologist's signature tool is participant observation. All the contributors to this article have engaged in participant observation across diverse cultural contexts. For some of us, this has included working in culturally familiar research settings, showing us firsthand how research conducted in an "other" community demands a different analytic lens than research conducted in our "own" communities. When working in a foreign community, we may be presented with the challenge of learning enough of the language to examine how it is used meaningfully and appropriately; we may also need to acquire a taste for unfamiliar foods (or at least some understanding of our participants' taste for them). By contrast, when working within our own backyards, we must work to pierce the veil of the normal and not assume too much about how other individuals are using what seem to be familiar words or negotiating the value of what seem to be typical foods.

Karrebæk: *My studies took place in an urban Copenhagen classroom. This is very much "my home turf." I was born and raised in Copenhagen, I went to a school rather similar to the school I did fieldwork in, and today I have children of the same age as the children I studied and who attend a school within the same time-space. My office is even situated next to the fieldwork site. More generally I am well-integrated in the Danish cultural context, have a family background without much migrational history, and the food discourse, semiotic meanings and indexicalities that I focused on are imprinted in me through a lifelong socialization into dominant food hegemonies; they form part of my own everyday understandings. What I discovered during my fieldwork were the potential negative effects of these hegemonic understandings on individuals who had different backgrounds and understandings. In fact, this study became a personal eye-opener in gaining new insights into my own cultural biases and myself as a representative of majority society.*

Riley: *I have now conducted food-and-language participant observation in three settings, one alien, one familiar and one in between. In French Polynesia, I engaged in participant observation in two languages I do not master (French and Marquesan); I also acquired a taste for foods that I would not otherwise have eaten (e.g., fermented breadfruit and fish) while learning to do without foods that I otherwise crave (e.g., vegetables). By contrast, my fieldwork in New York City was carried out in my mother tongue at the school I attended as a child, watching the students grow, cook, eat, and evaluate foods that are excruciatingly familiar (e.g., pizza and M&Ms). In my third research site, France, I had only one foreign language to deal with and most of the food bore a family resemblance to what I grew up eating, but the details of difference can be all the more striking when one is lulled by a sense of the familiar. In all three settings, food-and-language situations abound; yet even in the most familiar contexts, it was not always easy to identify the food-and-language events worth observing and participating in, much less the significant details worthy of analysis. As a result, I have been formulating a new food-and-language research tool modeled on Hymes's well-known SPEAKING mnemonic for the study of speech events (Hymes 1964). To conduct ethnographies of SPEAKING-and-EATING events, one attends not only to the Setting, Participants, Ends, Acts, Keys, Instrumentalities, Norms, and Genres, but also to a number of other facets of the event encoded in the EATING mnemonic: Etiquette, Actions, Tools, Ingredients, Notions, and Gender (this last being a reminder to look not only at gender but also at age, class, ethnicity, and any other relevant identity categories). So far this protocol has been utilized by my students to analyze meals they have observed and participated in preparing and consuming. However, this method could clearly be expanded to the study of any situation in which food is being processed, sold, or composted. The advantage here is that food and language are treated as functional and significant elements of a common cultural system.*

Jaffe: *My focus on tasting events in Corsican markets is both ethnographically familiar and new. It is familiar because eating and discussing the merits of traditional products is one of the currencies of everyday relations and ethnographic practice. These discussions presuppose and activate notions of authenticity and the criteria used to assess it. Those shared assessments constitute a shared esthetic and epistemic social ground in which different participants (including ethnographers) can take up various novice and expert positions and their attendant social relationships. Due to my long-standing ethnographic experience on the island, however, I tended not to engage much in tasting/purchasing events at markets and festivals because I had been socialized to seek and "trust" traditional products obtained through informal and personal networks, where the producer was known and endorsed by someone known to me. Thus the positionality of assessing origin, authenticity and value in the markets as an ethnographer was a new one, and involved thinking about how the ubiquitous practice of tasting foods as part of a discursive sales process compared and contrasted to the other social/noncommercial tasting contexts I had experienced.*

Ethnolinguistic Analysis

Linguistic anthropologists have a long history of investigating language and other nonverbal modes of communication as implicated in the expression of particular sociocultural realities, and food is no exception. Indeed, the analysis of words, phrases, idioms, metaphors, and gestures related to food continues to be a key way to investigate a group's relationship to food.

Jourdan: *My research into rice localization in Honiara in the Solomon Islands started when I noticed that people had been developing phrases about rice, an imported food, in the local pidgin language. They would say: mi kaekae raes nating (I eat only rice); drae raes nomoa (only dry rice); kaekae blong iumi (our food); kaekae blon saenaman (the food of the Chinese), etc. Over 30 years of research, I saw that these comments were becoming stock phrases to refer to how people lived. So raes nating, which meant "eating rice only," also progressively came to mean being poor, even destitute; drae raes nomoa, which also meant "eating only rice," came to mean being stern or severe (e.g., man ia hemi drae raes nomoa means "this man is really stern"); while kaekae blong iumi speaks about the cultural localization of rice in Solomon Islands as a true island food, and kaekae blong saenaman expresses bitterness about the power of Chinese merchants in the control of the economy of the Solomon Islands. Rice, then, has become a metaphor for life and social relations. Tracking and collecting these stock phrases referring to rice enabled me to do a study of the enculturation of rice, and I used them for the architecture of a paper I presented at a AAA panel on Food and Language that Kate Riley and I co-organized in 2009, and subsequently transformed into a paper on food, with a bit of language in it (Jourdan 2010). Although the linguistic dimension took second stage to the social dimension in this version, it was language that alerted me to the cultural significance of rice in the Solomon Islands.*

Jaffe: *The market contexts I have observed are ideologically aligned with the "slow food" movement: the promotion of regional/local products and cuisine, a focus on "sustainability," and an opposition to big agribusiness. Valuing local, fresh, organic produce was also understood as a dominant discourse; as "what consumers want" and thus as a product itself. This has led to both the development and linguistic rebranding of local farmer's markets: a Marché des Producteurs [Producers' Market] held every Saturday morning in a small pull-off from one of the main road arteries of the region, a Marché des Producteurs du Pays [Local Producers' Market] during the summer in one of the coastal tourist offices, the Mercati Muntagnoli (Mountain Markets) in villages that were located away from typical tourist and nontourist itineraries, and a Bio Mercatu—organic market—organized in Bastia as a supplement to the long-standing, traditional produce, cheese, and fish market that has been held on one of the main squares of the city as long as people can remember. We can note here the way that language is at work in the labeling of these markets in order to produce certain kinds of culturally inflected localness. First, there is the use of the Corsican word mercatu for "market" in the latter two initiatives above. Given Corsican's status as a regional, minority language, this choice carries indexical associations with intimacy, smallness of scale, and traditional circuits of agricultural distribution. In the case of the mercatu muntagnolu, the word "mountain" is also in Corsican; given the geography of the island, this signifies remoteness and rurality—valued elements of authenticity for the products in question. The mention of "producers" in the event types also marks producers—and not just products—as salient.*

Food-Oriented Interviews

Food-focused and food-situated interviewing may produce data that can be analyzed not only for the information collected about the subject's foodways (e.g., in Counihan's (2004) food-centered life histories) but also for the speech acts and genres prompted by the presence of food (e.g., the kitchen chat (Abarca 2006)). In other words, food may become both topic and context for the interview. As many of us can attest, when surrounded by food and engaged in food activities (butchering animals, canning, marketing produce, or setting the table), an interviewee may not only supply information about his/her foodways, but also display rich metapragmatic entanglements with it (e.g., "Oh, God, look what my mom put in my lunch box today!"). While conducting food-focused interviews, the question arises: Is talk about food within ongoing food contexts more metapragmatically oriented than talk about other topics and contexts (e.g., knitting or video games)? If we have an intuition that they are, we must ask ourselves questions such as: What are the features of communication directly involved in the event as a sensory activity?

Riley: *In my work in New York City (2012b), I interviewed parents about their foodways and requested that we carry out the interviews at their homes in plain sight of their refrigerators, kitchen counters, and dining tables. Many of my participants were clearly moved (both upset and excited) by the experience of reexamining their own past foodways and comparing these to how they presently procure and prepare the food that they and their children eat. Many expressed embarrassment as they explored how differently their children were learning to eat—in this case, money and urbanism appeared to be the factors driving the changes: many of these well-to-do parents had grown up "in the country" with gardens and mothers who cooked a family meal daily; by contrast, their own children eat apart from the adults food prepared by the nanny, much of it high-end but processed. Talking about food triggered memories that contrasted heavily with their present way of life, indexed by the food props surrounding them as they spoke. Not only the affect displayed, but also the features of their late-acquired class habitus provided data worthy of analysis.*

Jourdan: *I used the linguistic life history approach in the Solomon Islands to study how family members across generations handle changes in the language repertoires of their kin over the years and in the language ideologies that govern these shifts. I use life histories because in this way subjects have opportunities to tell me what matters linguistically to them, and how the ideological and practical dimensions of urban living inform their linguistic self (Jourdan 2008). I then decided along with my co-researcher and coauthor Sylvain Poirier to apply this particular method to the study of the transformations of food ideologies and practices in the food-crazy city Montreal has become by asking people to reflect on these changes (Jourdan and Poirier 2012). We worked with three generations in six middle-class families. The narratives they built focused on relationships, morals, emotions, memories, all being conveyed mainly through words and sentences they attributed to their mothers. At times, they appropriated these words and expressions just as they appropriated the underlying ideologies and food practices. At other times, they expressly rejected both their mothers' words as well as the underlying ideologies. We asked them to explain what these expressions and words meant in their current understanding of food-based relationships, and were then able to peel away at the meaning of food in these families by paying attention to how they spoke about it amongst themselves (many interviews were carried out with two people in the same family). The food life histories proved to be important research tools for a few reasons: they allowed us to put into perspective what other members of the families had said about the family foodscape; they served as a canvas where food changes within families through time were painted; they showed the importance of food events and food related consciousness for the production of self and the reproduction of the families; finally, they gave flesh to the concept of food lineage that we are exploring elsewhere.*

Paugh: *The CELF study was designed to investigate the everyday lives of 32 middle-class families with children in Los Angeles, California (see Ochs and Kremer-Sadlik 2013). This team-based project employed diverse methods. Two videographers filmed family members over a period of one week including two weekdays and a weekend. During filming, families prepared and ate meals and snacks, dined at restaurants, got takeout, and shopped for food. Researchers also interviewed parents about their families' health practices, and couples provided narrated tours of their refrigerators and kitchens. In examining interview data, Carolina Izquierdo and I found that parents prized eating as being central to good health. They took responsibility for their children's food choices and eating practices, but often felt they fell short in practice, largely due to children "not wanting" the healthy foods they claimed to prepare. When we examined the dinnertime interactions, however, we were struck by the extensive negotiations that took place. For example, 8-year-old Anna and her mother battled daily about how many pieces of each kind of food she needed to consume. This included protein foods and vegetables, but also pizza in the presence of a visiting friend. In other interactions, parents asked children what they "wanted" to eat only to tell them what they "needed" to eat instead. Still others evinced caregivers using conditional promises (eat this and you will get that), threats if certain foods were not consumed, nutrition lessons, directives, bargaining for replacement foods (string cheese instead of milk), and rule statements (you have to eat your vegetables). Through analyzing the turn-by-turn construction of food interactions from the videos, we demonstrated how conflicts over food build sequentially as family members co-construct and evaluate one another's eating choices and preferences (Paugh and Izquierdo 2009), in contrast to the more straightforward notions of parent-child interactions around food offered in interviews.*

Jaffe: *I interviewed several apiculteurs [honey producers] and observed their interactions with clients in the summer of 2013. One of these interactions took place at the Mercatu Muntagnolu [Mountain Market] that was held in the village I live in during the summer. At the beginning of the day, I chatted with the young apiculteur setting up his wares at the first of these stands. I asked him where he was from, and he told me that he'd "married" and now lived in Ponte Novu, a town in a neighboring valley about 25 minutes away. But as we talked about his honey, he located his business in a much larger geographical space than the one town. He had four kinds of honey, and he told me that he moved his hives from one locale to another in different seasons to benefit from the differences in vegetation in those different habitats. As we spoke, he gestured both "up" (toward the mountains behind and further inland from our location at 700 meters in the foothills) as he spoke about his "spring honey" and waved his arm northeastward in the direction of the next mountain range over, a microregion famous for its chestnut trees, to indicate where his chestnut honey was collected. Thus his use of linguistic and gestural deixis to orient me to the various "there"s where he located his bees circumscribed the contours of the local and described the trajectories of movement (production, processing, packaging, marketing). That is, it was discourse and semiosis that produced the "territory" in which he, his bees and his product were anchored and in which the act of purchase would be too.*

Language Socialization

The methods used for the study of language socialization, first developed in the 1970s and '80s by Elinor Ochs and Bambi Schieffelin (see Ochs and Schieffelin 2012 for an overview of the paradigm), have been expanded and used for the ethnographic study of food-and-language socialization by contributors to this article as well as other scholars (e.g., Blum-Kulka 1997; Ochs et al. 1996). Although language socialization methods can be applied to socializing interactions across the lifespan, most language socialization approaches to the study of food socialization have so far focused on children in family settings or at schools. Here, the recording, transcribing, and analysis of interactions among children and their caregivers while preparing and eating food becomes the groundwork for understanding not only how children learn to use language in the presence of food (talking about it and around it, politely or not), but also how they learn to *do* food through language—i.e., to negotiate the use and value of food in their community (from quality and quantity to culinary know-how and sexual innuendo). While a language socialization approach can be (and frequently is) applied to many other cultural forms, practices, and values that are acquired by novices in new settings, the special significance of studying food-and-language socialization may arise from early developmental ties between food and communication (e.g., the early engagement of children in the emotional negotiation of food shares or our embodied associations of certain tastes with certain early social settings and interactions).

Paugh: *For both of my projects I employed the language socialization paradigm as my primary theoretical and methodological framework. Language socialization research explores how children and other novices acquire cultural and linguistic knowledge and practices as interrelated processes through everyday social interaction with those around them. In order to document and analyze language socialization, a primary method in both studies was the use of video recording and transcription of naturalistic daily social interactions involving children, their caregivers, and others in their verbal environments. As discussed above in the section on interviews, the study of language socialization proves to be a key method for getting at the disjunctures between ideologies concerning food and health, and how they play out in practice. Novices in both of my studies were learning both how to engage in eating practices and how to talk, negotiate, and bargain about those practices. Talk about food emerged as a key site for socializing children, constructing and contesting social identities, and negotiating a frequently fraught moral and social terrain.*

Jaffe: *Language socialization is of course a lifelong process, and takes place among many different kinds of experts and novices. In tourist contexts, consumers/ tourists can be drawn into language socialization routines that "teach" them how to understand the connection between local linguistic forms and the cultural features of the local context that constitute the meaning and value of the tourist experience. One feature of such food discourse I have been attentive to is the extent to which talk between locals and tourists represents local foodways, labels, and forms of discursive evaluation of food on a continuum between the exotic and the known/accessible to those tourists. In one mountain hike that included a lunch in a remote shepherd's cabin I observed and participated in, the guide used Corsican terms for food items (cheese fritters, different kinds of cheeses and smoked meats) that were being served and sold, but did not engage the (continental) French-speaking customers in "repeat-after-me" labeling activities. That is, he explained without using an overtly instructional discourse. Later in the walk, one particularly attentive client used several of these words and also told him that she had "recognized" other Corsican terms he'd used with an assistant guide because of her knowledge of Italian but also because she was a repeat client of his. Corsican ways of talking about food (in the form of terminology) and, by extension, Corsican foodways, were thus figured as fundamentally accessible, shareable, commensurate. Here we can make the connection between "commensurable" language to "commensality" as a core feature of eating that asserts a common humanity.*

Collaborative Transcription

Language socialization methodology, as Ochs and Schieffelin originally formulated it, ideally involves participant-assisted transcription of the language socialization routines (Garrett 2007). But this collaborative method may be applied to any discourse—including talk generated and recorded around the production, distribution, and consumption of food—and is a fruitful extension to the primary methodology of participant observation. By engaging discourse participants in the transcription process, researchers may reach a more accurate and nuanced representation of what, why, and how interlocutors communicated during some food-related recorded event. Additionally, community members who were not actually present for the recording may also be employed to collaborate on the transcription as they too may shed light on both the language used and the values expressed during what are to them socioculturally familiar interactions. Of note here are two potentially important methodological moments: one in which food discourse is collected when and where food is present and consequential, followed by a second reflexive moment in which food becomes the object of metadiscursive linguistic activity but is no longer necessarily present. Again, this method could be applied by linguistic anthropologists interested in any cultural topic of interest to participants; however, the particularity of the food-and-talk link is how people from so many cultures are willing to stop and reflect upon not only food (its form and value) but also how their linguistic practices relate to their food practices.

Riley: *Following conventional language socialization methodology, I have recorded natural discourse among children and their caregivers in all three of my field sites (always audio, but sometimes video as well) and have employed one or more participating adults (usually the mother, but I have also been aided by a father, two aunts, and a grandmother) to assist me in transcribing these interactions in both the Marquesas (Riley 2009) and France (Riley 2012a). Data collected in this way have proven to be as interesting as the transcribed discourse itself as my assistants provided background information about not only why the participants spoke as they did but also why they related to the food as they did (e.g., why a 3-year-old Marquesan girl had a tantrum when there were no more crackers for breakfast or why a 6-year-old French girl was critiquing her mother for having oversalted the soup).*

Cavanaugh: *I have used native-speaker transcription consultants in both my projects. Although not participants in the events being transcribed, my transcription consultants are members of the broader community. What is lost in terms of specific insider knowledge about the unfolding of a particular event is balanced out by more generalized metalinguistic and metapragmatic reflections, as well as outsider views that may illuminate broader language and/or food ideologies. For instance, in my first project on language shift in northern Italy (Cavanaugh 2009), the comments of my transcription assistants were invaluable for giving voice to usually unspoken facets of language ideology, but also for pointing to the exact parts of speech that were most laden with ideological valences (such as accent markers). In my current project, my transcription assistants' comments have helped me recognize the social entailments involved in market exchange interactions, as well as the complicated stance-taking patterns involved in food production events such as inspections of food-making facilities.*

Semiotic Analysis of Documents and Media

Another array of methods developed within linguistic anthropology and now applied within food-and-language studies are those that support the semiotic analysis of intertextual relationships between everyday interaction and written texts, including mass-mediated public discourses. In this case, connections among and across written texts and spoken utterances about and around food can be examined to reveal the moral and political valence of food and language. In addition to the growth of food-related issues as fodder for public mediated discourse, the modern food system itself is characterized by a proliferation of documents—certificates of authenticity, ingredients lists, inspection reports, and food policy white papers—all produced according to rigid norms, situated within particular ethnographic contexts, circulated in specifically constrained manners, and thus carrying a wealth of analytic potential. Linguistic anthropologists are in a prime position to analyze these documents not only for their referential content in terms of how they describe and delimit the world around them, but also to explore how such documents are connected to various types of interactional contexts (policy-making sessions, inspections of production facilities, meetings in which origin designations are pursued, etc.) in consequential ways.

Jourdan: *In a research project conducted with one of my PhD students Stephanie Hobbis, we used language to track how people expressed their reactions to a food scare that erupted in Europe in 2011. The food scare appeared when cucumbers imported by Germany from Spain were identified as the source of a deadly enterohemorrhagic bacterium, resulting in a crisis of confidence in food and food systems across Europe. To understand the crisis of confidence, we focused on how readers of three major European newspapers (Germany's Die Welt, Spain's El Mundo, and France's Le Monde) reacted. We collected all comments that appeared after every article on the crisis published in these newspapers and did a comparative discourse analysis. Our findings reveal that pronouns such as "they" and we," along with expletives and affective particles did much to signal aggressive posturing, negative othering, and distrust, as commentators positioned themselves in the debates via a careful selection of linguistic weapons. But it was clear also that food was a sensitive topic that lay at the center of people's emotions. How food was produced, how it circulated, how it was eaten, how it related to national character … each was used as a weapon to attack various types of "others" (Jourdan and Hobbis 2013).*

Cavanaugh: *My recent research has involved collecting the myriad types of documents foundational to modern food production, such as certificates, checklists, authorizations, even bills of lading, as well as audio recording whenever possible in production and circulation contexts, like tasting events or farmers markets. In analyzing these data, I have sought to track how documents and talk are made to work together, or at times are at odds with one another, to produce cultural and economic value for particular foods. In a recent piece I coauthored with Shalini Shankar (Cavanaugh and Shankar 2014), we demonstrated how authentication processes are built from linguistic and material practices that work together to construct chronotopes—images of time and place that emerge from discourse that links different communicative contexts to one another (Bakhtin 1981). Brochures that described foods as genuine and talk at food tastings that depicted the exact location in which they had been produced, combined with time-honored—i.e., recurring across multiple generations, usually of the same family—material production processes helped to render certain foods as authentic, while leaving others out of the picture. In another project, I looked at a case of what has been called "gastronomic racism," by analyzing texts on social media sites that formed part of the public and highly politicized debate over the opening of a kebab stand in the historic city center of Bergamo (Cavanaugh 2013). I demonstrated how participants used various linguistic and semiotic resources to participate in, or protest against, the framing of this stand as problematic by analyzing how posters to a Facebook group against the stand's opening used various linguistic elements (such as code and pronoun choice, use of markers of heightened affect such as all caps and exclamation points) to depict themselves, various types of foods, and other people in positive or negative terms.*

Karrebæk: *In conjunction with my work on food socialization and education I have looked at societal discourses. Milk, rye (bread) and pork all figure in (re)interpretations (and reimaginations) of Danish food, such as the so-called New Nordic Cuisine. These newer trends added weight to teachers' health-oriented work in the school as they could find support for their interpretations of what were the healthiest foods in the public media on a daily basis. One of the main responsible persons behind the rise of interest in Danish gastronomy and the New Nordic Cuisine, Claus Meyer, joined forces with a health researcher Arne Astrup and together they received 100 mio D.kr. (17 mio Euros) to fund a center, OPUS, situated at the University of Copenhagen, which aims at demonstrating how the New Nordic diet is healthier than other diets. This work is ongoing, and we have frequent news releases broadcast by the national media about their work. Still, the ideological basis of OPUS is very obvious, and it has even been argued, by a former PhD student and with much media attention, that results that do not validate the hypotheses and intentions are suppressed. In addition to this I am currently working on a project on how food and food products are used by a peripheral place in Denmark to create value (and thereby attract capital, work places and tourists) in their market oriented discourse, how the EU and other nonlocal actors finance this, and how local food producers and food entrepreneurs, in exchange, use their affiliation to this specific site (and terroir) to create value for their products. We also look at the way that this added-value is communicated through linguistic and nonlinguistic signs.*

Paugh: *My research in Dominica was designed to investigate language shift toward English from an Afro-French creole called Patwa, but as I followed national discourses about the loss of Patwa and other aspects of Dominican culture, what also came to the fore were discussions of a shift from creole foodways to more processed imported food types considered to be more modern. These changes in Dominican diets have been noted in development, tourism, health, and cultural preservation discourses, where creole foods and cooking methods are joining a litany of "traditional" cultural heritage forms considered on the decline and in need of rescue. This was exemplified during a research visit to Dominica in 2008, when I attended a "Panel Discussion on Village Feasts and Cultural Renewal" held in one village and broadcast throughout the nation. During the panel, creole food emerged as a salient marker of change, but also as a potential site of cultural renewal, health improvement (since they tend to contain local produce and fresh fish or other lean meats), and economic possibility. In light of the expansion of this type of public discourse, I returned to my language socialization data to investigate this issue and found that while public discourses promoted the consumption of local foods, in the home I saw the daily socialization of children to prefer imported processed foods versus locally obtained ones. Adults used packaged snacks and foreign foods as rewards for good behavior, or threats to withhold them as punishment for bad behavior, linking such foods to both "goodness" and positive affect, and denigrating local foods in the presence of and to children. Thus the data produced through a language socialization project allowed me to link and contrast daily food practices with public food discourse, although multilingual language use and ideologies were my initial concerns.*

Surveying these food-and-language methods demonstrates how standard anthropological and linguistic anthropological methodologies from participant observation and interviewing to discourse transcription and document analysis can be reworked to focus on a particular set of cultural practices and ideologies, in this case foodways.

Food-and-Language: New Methods, New Terrain, New Topics ...

In composing this article, we have sought to contribute to ongoing discussions about the nature and conditions of doing linguistic anthropological research (e.g., Philips 2013). First, broadly speaking, we hope to promote the value of looking across cultural modalities, not only language and food, but also language and a range of other expressive media. Second, and more specifically, we are seeking to encourage the application of linguistic anthropological and linguistic ethnographic methods and analytical tools to the study of food in order to open up new and productive terrains and topics.

As for exploring new contexts, it is instructive to realize how many language-rich settings involve food in ways we rarely think about—not only kitchens and dining tables, but also primary school classrooms and conference broadcasts. Similarly, obvious food-focused locations (e.g., butcher shops and farmers markets) turn out to offer excellent opportunities for studying the use of language and other communicative media. Thus, not only the inherent connections between foodways and language practices, but also the many overlapping contexts for their joint study may evoke new perspectives on new topics.

Some of the subjects broached by the researchers contributing to this article include the ideological (re) evaluation of food(s) and language(s) as "good" or "authentic," the production and reproduction of moral order via food-and-language socialization, and the loss or transformation of food-and-language regimes over time. Such recurrences indicate the rich theoretical possibilities afforded by studying food and language together. Of course, research on food OR language within any of these theoretical domains is not hard to find. But what offers the potential for new and fascinating findings is a simultaneous focus on both foodways AND discourse.

In short, we hope that this brief article on the integration of food-and-language methodologies will spur researchers to locate new and interesting field sites while also taking steps toward conceptualizing how local everyday forms of semiosis and large-scale, long-term forces of change involving food and language intersect.

References

Abarca, Meredith E.
> 2006 Voices in the Kitchen: Views of Food and the World from Working-Class Mexican and Mexican-American Women. College Station: Texas A&M University Press.

Bakhtin, Mikhail
> 1981 The Dialogic Imagination: Four Essays. M. Holquist, ed. Austin: University of Texas Press.

Barrett, Rusty
> 2006 Language Ideology and Racial Inequality: Competing Functions of Spanish in an AngloOwned Mexican Restaurant. Language in Society 35:163–204.

Basso, Keith H.
> 1996 Wisdom Sits in Places: Landscape and Language among the Western Apache. Albuquerque: University of New Mexico Press.

Blum-Kulka, Shoshana
> 1997 Dinner Talk: Cultural Patterns of Sociability and Socialization in Family Discourse. Mahwah NJ: Lawrence Erlbaum.

Cavanaugh, Jillian R.
> 2005 Lard. *In* Fat. Don Kulick & Anne Meneley, eds. Pp. 139–151. New York: Tarcher/Penguin USA.
> 2007 Making Salami, Producing Bergamo: The Transformation of Value. Ethnos 72(2):149–172.
> 2009 Living Memory: The Social Aesthetics of Language in a Northern Italian Town. Malden MA: Wiley-Blackwell.
> 2013 Il y a Kébab et Kébab: Conflit Local et Alimentation Globale en Italie du Nord. Anthropologie et Sociétés 37(2):193–212.

Cavanaugh, Jillian R., and Kathleen C. Riley
> Forthcoming Foodways and Discourse: Language-Oriented Approaches to the Study of Food. *In* Research Methods for Anthropological Studies of Food and Nutrition. John Brett and Janet Chrzan, eds. New York: Berghahn.

Cavanaugh, Jillian R., and Shalini Shankar
> 2014 Producing Authenticity in Global Capitalism: Language, Materiality, and Value. American Anthropologist 166(1):1–14.

Counihan, Carole
> 2004 Around the Tuscan Table: Food Family, and Gender in Twentieth Century Florence. New York: Routledge.

Frake, Charles O.
> 1964 How to Ask for a Drink in Subanun. American Anthropologist 66(6, pt. 2):127–132.

Garrett, Paul
> 2007 Researching Language Socialization. *In* Encyclopedia of Language and Education (2nd ed.), Volume 10. Nancy H. Hornberger, ed. Pp. 189–201. Heidelberg: Springer.

Hymes, Dell
> 1964 Introduction: Toward Ethnographies of Communication. American Anthropologist 66(6):1–34.

Jourdan, Christine
> 2008 Language Repertoires and the Middle Class in the Solomon Islands. Social Lives in Language: Sociolinguistics and Multilingual Speech Communities. M. Meyerhoff and Naomie Nagy, eds. Pp. 43–67. Amsterdam: John Benjamins.
> 2010 The Cultural Localization of Rice in Solomon Islands. Ethnology 49(4):263–282.

Jourdan, Christine, and Stephanie Hobbis
> 2013 Tensions Internationales autour d'un Concombre Tueur: Confiance et Glocalisation Alimentaire. Anthropologie et Sociétés 37(2):173–192.

Jourdan, Christine, and Sylvain Poirier
> 2012 Le Goût en Héritage: Exploration des Transformations Alimentaires dans quelques Familles Montréalaises. Anthropologica 54(2):281–292.

Karrebæk, Martha Sif
> 2012 "What's in Your Lunch-Box Today?": Health, Ethnicity and Respectability in the Primary Classroom. Journal of Linguistic Anthropology 22(1):1–22.

2013a Lasagna for Breakfast: The Respectable Child and Cultural Norms of Eating Practices in a Danish Kindergarten Classroom. Food, Culture and Society 16(1):85–106.

2013b "Don't Speak Like That to Her!": Linguistic Minority Children's Socialization into an Ideology of Monolingualism. Journal of Sociolinguistics 17(3):355–375.

2013c Rye Bread and Halal: Enregisterment of Food Practices in the Primary Classroom. Language & Communication 34:17–34.

2014 Healthy Beverages?: The Interactional Use of Milk, Juice and Water in an Ethnically Diverse Kindergarten Class in Denmark. *In* Language and Food: Verbal and NonVerbal Experiences. Polly E. Szatrowski, ed. Pp. 279–299. Amsterdam: John Benjamins.

Malinowski, Bronislaw

1935 Coral Gardens and Their Magic: A Study of the Methods of Tilling the Soil and of Agricultural Rites in the Trobriand Islands. New York: American Book Co.

Manning, Paul

2012 Semiotics of Drink and Drinking. London: Continuum.

Ochs, Elinor, and Tamar Kremer-Sadlik, eds.

2013 Fast Forward Family: Home, Work and Relationships in Middle Class America. Berkeley: University of California Press.

Ochs, Elinor, Clotilde Pontecorvo, and Alessandra Fasulo

1996 Socializing Taste. Ethnos 61(1–2):7–46.

Ochs, Elinor, and Bambi B. Schieffelin

2012 The Theory of Language Socialization. *In* The Handbook of Language Socialization. Alessandro Duranti, Elinor Ochs, and Bambi B. Schieffelin, eds. Pp. 1–21. Malden: Wiley-Blackwell.

Paugh, Amy

2012a Playing with Languages: Children and Change in a Caribbean Village. New York: Berghahn.

2012b Speculating about Work: Dinnertime Narratives among Dual-Earner American Families. Text & Talk 32(5):615–636.

Paugh, Amy, and Carolina Izquierdo

2009 Why Is This a Battle Every Night?: Negotiating Food and Eating in American Dinnertime Interaction. Journal of Linguistic Anthropology 19(2):185–204.

Philips, Susan

2013 Method in Anthropological Discourse Analysis: The Comparison of Units of Interaction. Journal of Linguistic Anthropology 23(1):82–95.

Rampton, Ben, ed.

2007 Linguistic Ethnography: Links, Problems and Possibilities. Special issue of the Journal of Sociolinguistics 11(5).

Riley, Kathleen C.

2007 To Tangle or Not to Tangle: Shifting Language Ideologies and the Socialization of Charabia in the Marquesas, F.P. *In* Consequences of Contact: Language Ideologies and Sociocultural Transformations in Pacific Societies. Miki Makihara and Bambi B. Schieffelin, eds. Pp. 70–95. New York: Oxford University Press.

2009 Who Made the Soup? Socializing the Researcher and Cooking Her Data. Language and Communication 29(3):254–270. 2012a Learning to Exchange Words for Food in the Marquesas. *In* Food: Ethnographic Encounters, Leo Coleman, ed. Pp. 111–126. Oxford: Berg.

2012b "Don't Yuck My Yum": Negotiating Physical Health and Moral Goodness via Food. Nanterre: European Association of Social Anthropology.

Riley, Kathleen C., and Jillian R. Cavanaugh

Forthcoming Food Talk: Studying Food and Language in Use Together. *In* Research Methods for Anthropological Studies of Food and Nutrition. John Brett and Janet Chrzan, eds. New York: Berghahn.

Schieffelin, Bambi B.

1990 The Give and Take of Everyday Language. Cambridge: Cambridge University Press.

Discussion Questions

1. Why might researchers want to study food and language simultaneously? How are these topics connected in your own life?
2. How did the authors of this article use participant observation to conduct research? What did they learn?
3. The authors wondered if and how the methods they use differ from those used in nonlinguistic studies of food as well as in linguistic anthropological studies of cultural material other than food. What conclusions did they reach?
4. The article states "Linguistic anthropologists have a long history of investigating language and other nonverbal modes of communication as implicated in the expression of particular sociocultural realities, and food is no exception" – can you think of examples other than food that could be studied this way? Please discuss.
5. How can using food (directly, by having it present or indirectly, by discussing it) help the interview process? Can you think of examples?

Chapter 4

Making Immigrants Illegal in Small-Town USA

Hilary Parsons Dick
Department of Historical & Political Studies Arcadia University
hilarypdick@gmail.com

I n a discussion on immigration, is talking about race an important clarifying factor, or is it an obstacle to discussion? What are the consequences of seeing people as groups or stereotypes rather than individuals? U.S. immigration policy has long created a significant contradiction, particularly for Mexican immigrants – this country has a demand for their labor, but does not issue enough visas for their legal entry.

Using two discourse-analytical lenses, one genealogical and the other textual, this article traces the interdiscursive history through which the social categories "Mexican immigrant" and "illegal alien" have become conflated in the United States, effectively criminalizing Mexican immigrants as dangerous Others. Today, this conflation is a prime source for the racialization of not only Mexican immigrants, but other Latin American immigrants as well, where racialization is understood as a form of social differentiation that marks people as inherently threatening and foreign. This article focuses on the ways this conflation has been established and circulated in U.S. immigration policy. After offering a genealogy of the relevant federal policy, I provide a textual analysis of an anti-immigrant ordinance penned in Hazleton, Pennsylvania. I trace the interdiscursive strategies used by municipal officials in constructing the ordinance, showing that they extend the "legal racialization" in federal code by expanding the categories of behavior associated with immigrant illegality.

[Legal discourse; racialization; interdiscursivity; performative nomination; Latin American immigration; Hazleton]

Introduction

> What I'm doing here is protecting the legal taxpayer of any race. And I will get rid of the illegal people. It's that simple: they must leave.
>
> —*Hazleton Mayor Louis J. Barletta (in Powell and Garcia 2006)*

On July 13, 2006, Hazleton, Pennsylvania passed the "Illegal Immigration Relief Act" in response to a sudden increase in immigration into the town, especially by Mexicans and Dominicans—an immigration that municipal officials assume is "illegal." The act would punish town employers and landlords for hiring or renting property to undocumented immigrants. This ordinance immediately garnered national media attention, making the law's principle champion, then-mayor Louis J. Barletta, a hero to anti-immigrant[1] groups and inspiring municipalities across the country to propose similar ordinances. In a ruling on a suit filed by the American Civil Liberties Union and several other organizations, the ordinance was declared unconstitutional by a federal judge in 2007; it is currently in a process of appeal that Barletta, now a newly seated member of the U.S. House of Representatives, promises to take to the U.S. Supreme Court. As the legal challenges unfold, the ordinance has altered the social landscape of the town as many Latin American immigrants have departed for friendlier climes, and as those who remain, along with Latino U.S. citizens, negotiate heightened suspicions that they are "illegal."

Hazleton's ordinance speaks to pressing questions about who is authorized to inhabit sovereign nation-state territory and which governing bodies get to make such decisions. These questions point to a politics of national belonging that delineates who is allowed to become a legitimate member of the "we of the nation" and who is not. Throughout U.S. history, such debates have always differentiated among immigrant groups; some are constructed as desirable, as enhancing "who we are," and others are constructed as undesirable, as a threat to U.S. sovereignty and national identity. Although groups thus classified have changed over time, this process of differentiation has consistently relied on the racialization of the "undesirable," as national belonging aligns with racial hierarchies that construct whiteness as neutral and prototypically "American" and nonwhiteness as fundamentally Other and unassimilable. Thus, the construction of immigrant illegality is about more than the delineation of "foreignness"; it is also a racial code. Though this process is expressed through discourses of exclusion that designate categories of outsiders, it is, in fact, an incorporation regime that positions some immigrants as worthy of "above-table" belonging, while relegating others to "under-the-table" exchanges that render them suspect and, thus, make them exploitable and dispensable—a pattern found in many nation-state-building projects (Hall 2004; Ngai 2004; Soysal 1994).

At present in the United States, immigrants from Mexico are especially vulnerable to this incorporation regime, as the country's economy depends on their labor while much of its public discourse and policy construct them as dangerous Others (De Genova 2002, 2005; Massey 2007); consider, for example, Samuel Huntington's (2004) polemic, which argues that Mexican immigration is one of the greatest present threats to U.S. national unity and security. The targeting of Mexican immigration is no coincidence. Since the early 20th century, U.S. immigration policy has created a core contradiction: the country aggressively recruits Mexican laborers—indeed, its economic development has depended on this labor since the late 19th century—but at the same time, the U.S. government consistently provides an insufficient number of visas for their legal entry. This contradiction legitimates the integration of people of Mexican descent through their positioning as "illegal people," to use Barletta's phrase from the opening quotation. This positioning relies on a conflation between the category "illegal alien" and a cultural image of the Mexican immigrant as a criminal Other, so that when one speaks of illegal immigration, one pictures not the white British nanny who has overstayed her visa, but a menacing movement of dark-skinned people from south of the border (Chavez 2001; Santa Ana 2002).

It is this history of "south-of-the-border illegality" that creates the conditions of possibility for the Hazleton ordinance; without this history, the draconian legal response to the influx of Latin American immigrants would be socially and politically incongruous. This article examines the relationship between the Hazleton ordinance and federal immigration policy, considering how the former works to extend the racializing effects of the latter. There is a robust literature on the ways in which federal immigration policy has criminalized and racialized Mexican and other Latin American immigrants (Coutin 2005; Coutin and Pease Chock 1995; De Genova 2005; Hagan 1994; Stephen 2004). But there has been little work on the impact of state and municipal policies on these processes (but see Varsanyi 2010), despite the fact that, in the past decade, local governments have increasingly produced immigration policy. These policies are important to track not only because they shape local incorporation processes; they also influence federal legal trends, as happened with California's Proposition 187: although it was declared unconstitutional, its restrictions on immigrant access to social services became a feature of the 1996 Illegal Immigration Reform and Financial Responsibility Act (Durand and Massey 2003).

Crucially, the conflation of immigrant illegality with "south-of-the-border immigration" affects not only immigrants from Mexico, but immigrants from all over Latin America. As other scholars have shown (e.g., DeGenova and Ramos Zayas 2003; Hill 2008; Mendoza-Denton 2008; Zentella 1995), the diversity of Latin American communities and nationalities present in the United States is seldom recognized by people who are not of Latin American descent. Rather, people from countries as distinct as the Dominican Republic,

Guatemala, and Colombia become incorporated into a system of stereotypes developed to characterize Mexican immigrants and Mexican Americans—e.g., that Mexicans are lazy, stupid, vulgar, criminal, and corrupting (Hill 2008:121): a process of erasure that Zentella (1995) has called "chiquita-fication." Chiquita-fication represents a common racializing process through which people from an entire region become associated with members of a single nation-state marked as suspect; consider, for example, the common practice of calling people from all over Asia "Chinese." Because of chiquita-fication, the racializing conflation of illegality and Mexican immigrants becomes available as an interpretive lens when communities confront influxes of immigrants from Latin America.

This conflation is racializing because it affects only some immigrants—Mexicans or those presumed to be Mexican—constructing this group as inherently foreign and unauthorized, regardless of actual legal status (Flores and Benmayor 1997; Flores 2003). This racialization depends on a process of iconization in which the conflation between "illegal alien" and "Mexican" is symbolically loaded with phenotypic stereotypes: the idea that "Mexicans" look a certain way—they are dark-skinned, small in stature, possess "indigenous" features such as broad noses, and so on—and so can be visually identified. These stereotypes align with others that mark Mexicans as outsiders, including linguistic ones, evidenced by the popular (and inaccurate) assumption that Mexicans do not learn English, but "irrationally" hold onto a language seen as suspect (cf. Huntington 2004); speaking Spanish, then, becomes iconic of illegality and public illegitimacy (Hill 2001; Woolard 1990). Not coincidentally, the Hazleton ordinance originally included a provision to make English the official language of the town, which was later implemented as a separate ordinance. These iconic alignments can also affect the incorporation of other Latin American immigrants, as they met up with "chiquita-fication."

The central claim of this article is that the Hazleton ordinance's ability to extend the racializing effects of federal policy depends fundamentally on the construction of *interdiscursivity* at and across two discursive scales: genealogical and textual. Interdiscursivity describes the forms of relationship between discourse produced in "phenomenologically distinct spatiotemporal" frameworks (Silverstein 2005:6). Genealogically, I examine the broad ideological links between the ordinance and a history of federal law that has created the conflation between the "illegal alien" and "the Mexican immigrant" as a criminal outsider. This approach is Foucauldian, addressing the socio-politically interested regime of preconditions, or warrants, for making claims about national belonging, which have overwhelmingly constructed Mexican and other Latin American immigrants as inherently "too foreign." Textually, I examine the actual forms of resemblance between the Hazleton ordinance and federal policy, explained below. The approach is linguistic-anthropological, examining the "actual material presence ... of language-in-use" and the forms of interaction between actors involved in such use (Hill 2008:32). The distinction between Foucauldian and linguistic-anthropological discourse does not describe an absolute difference in types; rather, it is an analytical distinction used to show how the micro-interactions of textual construction draw on broader sociocultural formations.

Immigration policies function as racializing discourses primarily through the inherently interdiscursive activity of performative nomination (Silverstein 2005:11): the baptizing of categories of person that, in this case, take broadly circulating, informal us/them dichotomies and transform them into highly entextualized, codified lexical labels that carry the backing of the state, such as "illegal alien" and "immigrant harborer" (Mehan 1996:253; 1997). As argued above, these categories become racializing when they are disproportionately applied to some kinds of people, producing, for instance, the construction of Mexicans as illegal. This process is not born *ex nihilo* out of the minds of lawmakers, but relies on genealogical and textual interdiscursivities between everyday social distinctions and immigration policy. Therefore, the genealogy that has conflated the category "illegal alien" with an image of the Mexican immigrant as a criminalized Other is necessary to demonstrate how the ordinance is a racializing discourse, and not just an "innocent" effort to defend sovereign borders, as is often claimed by Barletta and his supporters.

The Hazleton ordinance participates most incisively in national processes of immigrant racialization through two tactics of textual interdiscursivity: citation of federal code and iconic replication of that code. Bauman and Briggs (1990; see also Briggs and Bauman 1992) characterize the intertextual relationship between instances of like discourse "as being inherently variable—resulting in an intertextual gap—and this variability can be minimized or maximized as a discursive strategy" (Matoesian 2000:882–883). If citation involves deferring to the original version of a prior text, "iconic replication" concerns the faithful copying of discourse produced in a prior instance: endeavoring to generate an exact replica, thus minimizing the intertextual gap as much as possible. Through citation and iconic replication, the ordinance makes the federally sanctioned categories that racialize Latin American immigrants applicable to life in Hazleton. Therefore, the second part of this article offers a textual analysis of two drafts of the ordinance and the areas of federal code that they replicate and transform. As officials in Hazleton rewrote the ordinance between July and September of 2006, its interdiscursivity with federal law changed such that the textual similarity between the ordinance and federal law becomes increasingly explicit: the September 2006 version not only adopts the terminology of federal law; its denotational content contains ever more iconic replication of that law. At the same time, the ordinance's position with respect to federal law changes. If initially it worked to substitute the categories of federal law with categories of its own, now it works within the categories available in existing law, seeking to expand federal categories so that they speak to locally relevant types of interaction. Of particular interest in this regard is what I call the "landlord sanction:" the effort to include those who rent property to undocumented immigrants within the category of "immigrant harborer."

Historical and Demographic Background

Hazleton is an economically depressed and diminishing mining town located in Luzerne County, part of Pennsylvania's once-booming anthracite coal region. U.S. census data show that between 2000 and 2006, the municipal population contracted by 6%. As in many depressed parts of the United States, population loss in Hazleton has been offset by immigration, largely by Mexicans and Dominicans, many of whom moved into Pennsylvania from New York after September 11, 2001 (Tilove 2007). These immigrants have opened restaurants, clothing stores, and other businesses, stimulating economic growth in a town whose main street had been all but boarded up prior to this immigration. This movement coincided with another important landmark in an ongoing change in Hazleton's economy: the establishment of a meat-packaging plant by Cargill Meat Solutions, a major national corporation that owns dozens of brands (such as Shady Brook Farms) and has an established history of hiring immigrant labor (De Jesús 2006). Cargill set up shop in Hazleton in 2001 after being courted by the town's Community Area New Development Organization (CAN DO); CAN DO was able to attract Cargill and other major manufacturers, such as Office Max, when Hazleton became designated as a Keystone Opportunity Zone by the state of Pennsylvania, a status that allows the town to waive taxes on outside corporations in order to attract jobs (Fleury-Steiner and Longazel 2010).

The growth of the Latin American population in Hazleton has thus been recent and rapid. In 2000, "Latinos" (the U.S. Census designation that includes Latin American immigrants) represented less than 5% of the population. The Census Bureau estimates that they now represent close to 30%—this in a town that was, in 2000, over 90% white (Fleury-Steiner and Longazel 2010:161). Indeed, during the 2000s, the Latino population in Hazleton increased at the fourth-fastest rate of all large U.S. counties (El Nasser and Heath 2007). The abrupt emergence of Latin American immigrant communities in mostly white receiving areas is a trend found across the country (Massey et al. 2002; Wortham et al. 2002). The swiftness with which these communities emerge understandably sparks public debate, as demographic shifts create economic and social strains in municipalities lacking the public services to facilitate the integration of immigrants. Demographics, however, do not determine the character of emergent immigration politics. As Fleury-Steiner and Longazel (2010) argue about the Hazleton ordinance, these politics are, instead, part of a political-economic order in which the municipality aggressively courts industries with known histories of hiring immigrant labor, such as Cargill, thereby effectively encouraging that labor to come to Hazleton, while at the same time criminalizing immigrants. As I describe in the next section, such "politics of contradiction" (Durand and Massey 2003) have long characterized federal immigration policy toward Mexico and have helped generate an incorporation regime in which immigrants from "south of the border" are integrated into the United States through a criminalization that makes the exploitation of their labor politically irrelevant and therefore invisible.

Moreover, as Wortham et al. (this issue) explain, places like Hazleton that have not experienced immigration for decades do not necessarily have locally generated "models of identity" that allow native-born residents to make sense of new arrivals; as they seek to comprehend the changes to their town, they search for such models. One ready source of these models are the categories of person established in immigration law and circulated by national debates of immigration and their coverage in the media. To be sure, the Hazleton ordinance was inspired by the December 2005 passage of House of Representatives Bill 4437: The Border Protection, Antiterrorism, and Illegal Immigration Control Act. HR 4437 included a provision that would make undocumented immigration a felony (Chavez 2008:9). Because of this provision, the bill sparked massive protests led by immigrants and immigrant advocates in the spring of 2006. Among the largest in U.S. history, these protests inspired some to claim that they heralded the next great civil rights movement, while others argued that they were proof of "invading illegal alien armies" (Chavez 2008:70–102). The protests stirred resistance to HR 4437 in the Senate, which blocked its passage. In 2006 and 2007, Congress failed to pass any immigration bill and, with the 2008 elections pending, federal lawmakers tabled the fraught issue.

After Congress's failures to pass reform, many local governments took formal actions to deal with immigration. Some towns decided to welcome immigrants, developing infrastructure that would facilitate their integration and, in some cases, formally declaring themselves "sanctuary cities" where officials are not allowed to inquire about immigration status (Degnen 2007). But other places, like Hazleton, promoted a staunchly nativist politics, passing ordinances that empower the municipality as an immigration law enforcer. This was, partly at least, in response to the interdiscursive web spun that spring between proposed federal law, protests of HR 4437, and the nationally broadcast mainstream and conservative media coverage of both, which helped motivate action among local lawmakers by providing frameworks through which local officials could interpret demographic and economic changes and think through how to address the impact of these changes on their towns. A study of municipal anti-immigrant proposals shows that they spiked after the spring of 2006; between 2000 and 2005, roughly ten to twenty municipalities drafted anti-immigration proposals each year; but in the summer of 2006 alone, 52 municipalities drafted such proposals (Hopkins 2008:2, 8, 24; Hopkins 2010). These spikes are found at the state level as well: in 2005, state legislators considered some 300 immigration-related bills, passing approximately 50; in 2006, they considered 500, passing 84; and in 2007, they considered 1,562, passing 240 (Varsanyi 2010:3). The spread of these policies has been so rapid that it has prompted their review by the United Nations' Special Rapporteur on the Human Rights of Migrants.[2] They vary in scope—some concentrate on the elimination of day-laboring, while others, such as Hazleton's, are more comprehensive—but all of them impose conditions that are meant to drive away presumably undocumented, and evidently nonwhite, immigrants.

Racialiation and Immigration Law

Race is a primary category of social differentiation in the United States, and it profoundly shapes the distribution of material and ideological resources, including legitimate belonging in the polity (De Genova 2005; Flores 2003; Ngai 2004). Scholars generally use the term "race" to describe types of social difference constructed to appear fixed, involuntary, hierarchically organized, and anchored in inherited phenotype. "Race," thus conceived, is often contrasted with "ethnicity," used to describe types of social difference constructed to appear relatively more flexible, less hierarchical, and anchored in inherited cultural beliefs and practices (Brubaker 2009). Of course, in everyday interactions, such contrasts are often blurred. Therefore, racializing and ethnicizing practices, including those of discourse, are usefully conceptualized as manifestations of a single domain of social difference that relies on the symbolic loading of inherited features, physical or cultural. What unites them is that both race and ethnicity construct actors as deviant from a putatively normative type, such as Anglo-Protestant whiteness in the United States. In this respect, racializing and ethnicizing practices do not produce fixed statuses, but shifting ones, as groups become more or less racialized or ethnicized across time and space. For instance, in the United States, Italians, Eastern Europeans, Jews, and other former "white races" became redesignated as "ethnic groups" when Black/White racial distinctions emerged as the organizing principle for racializing practices in the post-World War II era (Roediger 1991; Sacks 1994).

Where "race" and "ethnicity" are understood to describe distinct, if related, types of social difference, the kinds of nonnormative marking achieved by ethnicizing and racializing practices are divergent. Ethnicizing practices mark actors by casting cultural difference as "colorful"—Other and perhaps inferior, but non-threatening (Urciuoli 1996:17). By contrast, racializing practices mark actors as nonnormative by dehumanizing them, representing them as undifferentiated, immoral, dangerous—inherently and irredeemably Other. These concepts are used as analytics to describe differences in the consequences of social marking: the consequences of ethnicized social positioning are less severe than those that result from racializing. Ethnic groups, for example, may be barred access to membership in the local country club and its associated networks of upward mobility, but their mere physical presence will not inspire police surveillance and detention, as does that of a racialized group. To be sure, racialization often goes hand-in-hand with criminalization. Consider the U.S. "war on drugs." Studies by the National Institute on Drug Abuse and the National Household Survey on Drug Abuse have shown not only that White youth are seven to eight times more likely than African American youth to use heroin, powder cocaine, and crack cocaine, but also that White youth are one-third more likely than African American youth to have sold illegal drugs (Thompson 2010:708). However, "[i]n the 1980s alone ... African Americans' 'share' of drug crimes jumped from 26.9% to 46% ... If convicted, African Americans of every age 'were more likely than whites to be committed to prison ..., and they were more likely to receive longer sentences' " (Thompson 2010:709). Such patterns of disparity in law enforcement construct some populations (African American youth, Mexican immigrants) as suspect classes who are "inherently" criminal.

Immigration Law As Racializing Discourse: Performative Nomination and Interdiscursivity

As explained in the introduction, immigration policies function as racializing discourses principally through the performative nomination of categories of illegality that are disproportionately applied to groups constructed as dangerous and unassimilable. This process is related to what Hill (2008:21) describes as the broader racializing project to categorize people according to taxonomies, such as those of the U.S. census. Here I deal with taxonomies of immigrant criminality, in which the illegality of Latin American immigrants is considered to be of the greatest social concern. The nomination of legal categories powerfully transforms existing social distinctions, making them consequential in novel ways (Lee 1997; Urban 2001:93–142). Everyday accusations of illegality are ambiguous and open to contestation; legal designations, though often quite ambiguous when applied in the courts (cf. Philips 1998), confer a guise of absoluteness: either you are an "illegal alien" or you are not. This absoluteness allows legal labels to be divorced from the interactional complexities of immigration and to move freely across time and space, which creates the illusion that they are essential and timeless. Moreover, recruitment into legal categories (being designated an "illegal alien") introduces one into a network of consequences that further naturalizes these categories by requiring immigrants to participate in activities that enact them as law-breaking, such as deportation proceedings.

But contemporary immigration policy, whether penned in Washington or Hazleton, does not overtly name particular immigrant groups as illegal and undesirable; rather, it works surreptitiously to exclude them, as I show in the next section. Consequently, immigration law is a *covert* racializing discourse in which talk about "illegal aliens" becomes code for racial difference (Hill 2001:84). Covert discourse operates at two levels of social indexicality: indirect and direct (Ochs 1990). On one hand, immigration policy overtly points to and creates realms of legal practice that ostensibly pertain to any noncitizen. On the other hand, U.S. policy history has created a "fully naturalized set of understandings" (Hill 2005:114) that allow the category "illegal alien" to function as a synonym for "Mexican immigrant." This synonymous relationship sometimes also meets with other racializing processes, such as chiquita-fication, creating a logic in which anyone who "looks Mexican" can be assumed to be "illegal." Immigration categories, not explicit markers of race, thereby become indirect racial indexicals. This indirectness allows anti-immigrant activists to create policies that overwhelmingly affect Mexicans and other Latin Americans while claiming that such actions have nothing to do with race—as Barletta has done in defending his ordinance, saying, "[t]his isn't racial, because 'illegal' and 'legal' don't have a race" (Powell and Garcia 2006). As this suggests, the racializing effects of legal categories come not from explicit propositional content, but from interdiscursivity with the policy history that has restricted Mexicans from the "we of the United States."

The term *interdiscursivity*, coined by Silverstein (2005), emerges from work in linguistic anthropology on entextualization processes (Agha 2005, 2007; Bauman and Briggs 1990; Briggs and Bauman 1992; Silverstein and Urban 1996b). Entextualization refers to the ways in which discursive practice forms discrete "texts" that can be lifted out of moments of production and recontextualized in new interactional settings, where a "text" is a unifying poetic structure of discourse produced in real time—one that, though ordered, emerges out of the contingencies of ongoing social action. Scholars have looked to the analysis of intertextuality—the likeness between texts produced on different occasions—as a way to understand relationships between the micro-interactions of particular discursive events and large-scale discursive formations such as "genre" (Briggs and Bauman 1992) or "culture" (Silverstein and Urban 1996a)—or Foucauldian discursive regimes. This work has always been concerned with how intertextual relationships index, (re)create, and thus illuminate forms of social power, such as racializing practices. The role of intertextuality in the production of social difference is highlighted in the U.S. legal system, a point that Mertz (1996) makes in showing how law students are socialized into practices of recontextualization in legal argument. This is no less true in policymaking, which also depends on, grows from, and sometimes reframes existing legal discourse, as is the case with the Hazleton ordinance.

I use the term inter*discursivity*, as opposed to intertextuality, to underscore the primacy of discourse—"the processual, real-time, event-bound social action" within which we find textual structures (Silverstein 2005:7). Interdiscursivity is a useful analytic because it is more inclusive: it emphasizes both the forms of intertextuality as well as the participant-role frameworks through which people produce such intertextuality (see also Irvine 1996). This term more accurately conveys the mutually informing relations between texts, producers of texts, and social power. Indeed, Silverstein explains interdiscursivity as "a realizable strategic [and interactional] orientation to achieving" the semiotic effect of intertextuality (2005:9). I focus on two such strategies in the textual analysis below: citation and iconic replication. Such strategic orientations do more than link texts; they alter the social position of producers of texts. The Hazleton ordinance, for example, transforms municipal officials from passive critics of federal immigration policy to immigration lawmakers and, thus, active definers of the national "immigration problem" (cf. Coutin and Pease Chock 1995). This transformation places the processes through which Mexicans are designated as "illegal aliens" at the municipal level—a move that attempts to deputize the population of an entire town as enforcers of immigration law.

Genealogy of Legal Racialization

Ever since the earliest U.S. immigration policies were formulated, the construction of the category "illegal alien" has relied on the racialization of certain groups excluded from "the real America" by virtue of their deviance from a putative white normativity. Even though today legalized racial exclusions are highly covert, they were once quite explicit. In 1790, the first U.S. Congress mandated that access to naturalized citizenship be granted only to "whites"—a provision that remained in effect until 1952 (De Genova 2005:216–217). Although whiteness was at times applied to people of Mexican origin (De Genova 2005:217–220; Haney-López 2006:61–62), the 1790 law nevertheless emerged from and reinforced an association of citizenship, belonging, and whiteness. Racialization, thus, has long been a key way in which the United States negotiates a core tension of liberal democracies—between, on the one hand, defense of national sovereignty, which depends on distinctions between an "us" who is entitled to dwell in the state's territory and a "them" who is not and, on the other, commitments to universal human rights ("all men are created equal"), which erase us/them distinctions and extend rights to all persons "considered moral beings" (Benhabib 2002:86). Since racialized groups are also often criminalized, and are thus morally suspect, their membership even in the category of "moral beings" can become tenuous.

In this article, it is the historical exclusion of people of Mexican descent from forms of national belonging in the United States that is of concern; for it is this history that creates the grounds for the present-day legal racialization of Mexicans and "chiquitafied" people from other parts of Latin America. The association of citizenship, belonging, and whiteness came to exclude people of Mexican descent when it joined forces with another key association: that of Mexicanness with foreignness. These symbolic relationships were a product of the politics of exclusion that unfolded after the Mexican-American War in the present-day U.S. Southwest, the site of the vast majority of Mexican immigration until the late 20th century. The war ended in 1848 with the Treaty of Guadalupe-Hidalgo, in which Mexico ceded to the United States the region that comprises present-day Texas, Arizona, New Mexico, Colorado, and California. In the decades after the war, Anglos in the newly designated "U.S. Southwest" worked to construct Mexicans as foreigners, even though many Anglos were recent immigrants to the area and many Mexicans had been living in the region for generations. Mexican "foreignness" became officialized as the states acquired by the United States in the war often denied Mexican inhabitants U.S. citizenship, which conferred an "opprobrium of illegitimacy and inferiority" that stripped Mexicans and Mexican-American citizens of a legitimate claim to belonging in the region (Ngai 2994:131–133; see also Benton-Cohen 2009).

At the same time, U.S. federal policy left Mexican immigration, though contested in the Southwest, to flow more or less freely across the border; indeed, the U.S. Border Patrol was not created until 1924. Moreover, employers in the Southwest actively recruited labor from Mexico, as the native-born population was too sparse to sustain agricultural production in this nascent part of the United States. The co-occurrence of labor recruitment with the construction of people of Mexican descent as foreigners cultivated a Mexican underclass whose labor was essential to the economic development of the region, but whose members were largely excluded from the polity by law (Ngai 2004:129). By 1930, this segregation of Mexicans from legitimate forms of (white) belonging in the Southwest became codified at the federal level. In this decade, "Mexican" became a distinct, nonwhite racial category (De Genova 2005:221). With the onset of the Great Depression, the U.S. government initiated its first massive deportations of "Mexicans." Tellingly, "illegal aliens" were routinely rounded up by officials who did not bother to verify legal status—as evidenced by the fact that over half of the 1930s deportees were U.S. citizens (Haney-López 2006:38). This suggests that deportation practices relied not only on legal status, but also on the assumption that anyone who "looked or acted Mexican" (i.e., possessed a certain skin tone or bone structure, spoke a certain way, etc.) was foreign, illegal, and deportable.

Then, with the advent of the Bracero Program in 1942, we find an explicit codification of the Southwestern incorporation regime that called Mexicans into the territory with one hand, while marginalizing and excluding them with the other. The Bracero Program, which ran until 1964, was a bi-national accord between the Mexican and U.S. federal governments that recruited Mexicans to work in the United States on temporary labor contracts, first during the labor shortages of World War II and then in response to the labor demands of the post-World War II economic boom. This program augmented the Southwestern politics of exclusion: because it never supplied enough work visas to meet immigrant or employer demand, it created incentives for an increase in undocumented immigration, which went largely unchecked—that is, until the 1950s, when the federal government repeated its indiscriminate deportations in the unhappily named "Operation Wetback," which "repatriated" numerous U.S. citizens to Mexico (Ngai 2004:155–156). Thus, the federal de-authorization of Mexican immigration legitimated at the national level what had started as a regional organization of exclusion, allowing the linkage of "the Mexican immigrant" and the figure of a criminal transient to function as a powerful warrant for segregation in times of national conflict.

Such warrants for segregation act as a covert racializing discourse because they create an indirect social indexicality that allows talk about dangerous forms of "foreignness" to function as code for racial difference for some groups of immigrants. This indirect racial indexicality is revealed by tracking, as I do here, the ways in which concerns about dangerous foreignness are directed, not at all noncitizens, but only at groups positioned as inherently foreign, regardless of actual legal status. Before the 1960s, regulations affecting "undesirable" immigrant groups nominated people for exclusion through direct reference. The plainly named Chinese Exclusion Act (1882–1943), for example, straightforwardly denied entry to Chinese laborers. Such overtly racializing policies were made increasingly untenable, however, by the Civil Rights movement. In response, the Hart-Celler Act of 1965 dismantled openly discriminatory immigration controls and established the foundations of present-day U.S. immigration policy (De Genova 2005:230). Yet the 1965 reform, though it liberalized Asian and European immigration, amplified the covert racialization of Mexican immigrants, a point that can be demonstrated through a consideration of the U.S. system of visa caps.

Prior to 1965, the United States had a quota system that granted visas to a greater number of Western Europeans than Eastern Europeans, Southern Europeans, and Asians. The 1965 law eliminated these caps and created a uniform visa cap for the eastern hemisphere (Europe, Asia, and Africa) of 20,000 visas per country per year. Before the 1965 law, however, there was no visa cap for Mexico. In the early 1960s, the Bracero Program annually granted some 200,000 guest-worker visas to Mexican laborers, in addition to 35,000 regular admissions of Mexican citizens for legal permanent residency (Ngai 2004:261). The Hart-Celler law placed Mexico under visa caps for the first time. It allocated 120,000 visas for the entire western hemisphere (Canada, Mexico, and the rest of Latin America) and, in 1976, the cap of 20,000 visas per country per year was extended to the West (Ngai 2004:258, 261). Thus, the total number of visas granted to Mexicans went from 235,000 per year in the early 1960s to 20,000 per year by 1976.[3] These changes coincided with a period of dramatic increase in Mexican immigration, which began in the 1970s, so that presently Mexicans constitute the largest immigrant group in the United States (Massey et al 2002). Thus, the 1965 law, although it was intended to undo the racializing effects of immigration policy, aggressively racialized Mexican immigrants by transforming Mexican immigration from a once largely legal and unregulated flow to the country's core "illegal immigration problem," making Mexican immigrants more likely than any other group to be designated as "illegal aliens."

Paradoxically, then, it was the 1965 law that solidified the present-day conflation of the legal category "illegal alien" with an image of the Mexican immigrant as a criminal Other. Before the Hart-Celler law, the covert racialization of Mexicans had been largely regional and/or seasonal; after the law's passage, it became comprehensive, national, and constant. This racialization has only become more intense with the trend toward ever more draconian and punitive immigration reforms, most notably the massive militarization of the U.S. southern border, which began in the 1980s but was greatly expanded by policy changes under the Clinton Administration, and then again by the "War on Terror" after September 11, 2001. Since the 1980s, the U.S. Border Patrol has gone from being a "backwater agency" with a budget the size of a municipal police department to the most heavily armed branch of the government after the military (Durand & Massey 2003:237). Relative to the financial investment that it represents, border militarization has been quite ineffective at reducing the flow of undocumented immigrants, but it has rather successfully served as a dramatic spectacle that daily performs the image of the "south-of-the-border" immigrant as a clandestine criminal, an "illegal alien" so threatening to U.S. national security that he makes necessary the multi-million-dollar fortification of the country's southern border (De Genova 2005:242). Notably, border militarization has coincided with an increase in immigration from other parts of Latin America; so it is now not only Mexican immigrants, but immigrants from across the region who are exposed to, and affected by, this spectacle (Menjívar 2000, 2006).

Thus, the criminalization of Mexican immigration, both in its official instantiation and in its presumption in extralegal social life, potentially expands to comprise all unauthorized immigrants from Latin America.

Along with border militarization has come the popularity of a penal logic that views immigration violations as a "facet of 'illegal aliens' [sic] very being" (Coutin 2005:7). This logic of "human illegality" is evident in the discourse of restrictionist immigration reformers, which dehumanizes immigrants as anonymous "illegals" prone to criminal activity (cf. Coutin and Pease Chock 1995; Mehan 1997). Indeed, the presumption of Latin American criminality is evident in the rationalization that Hazleton's Mayor Barletta has given for his ordinance, which he claims became necessary because of a "crime wave" caused by "illegals" (Powell and Garcia 2006). Barletta justifies his assertion that the influx of Latin American immigrants led to an increase in crime by pointing to a single crime in which a nonimmigrant was shot by two undocumented immigrants from the Dominican Republic (Simonich 2007a). Although crime in Hazleton is still overwhelmingly committed by non-immigrant whites and the population of Latin Americans committing violent crime is small relative to the overall population, this one incident of immigrant-initiated crime nevertheless sparked sufficient anti-immigrant sentiment to motivate Hazleton's town counsel to pass Barletta's ordinance (Hopkins 2008:31)—a pattern evident in many of the anti-immigrant municipal ordinances that were proposed throughout the 2000s.

It is reasonable to posit that the willingness on the part of municipal officials to presume that one crime is indicative of an "illegal immigrant crime wave" is motivated by more than the crime itself, regardless of the number of crimes committed by immigrants that subsequently have been documented by the municipality—an activity to which the town has devoted considerable attention since the ordinance was passed, as Barletta reported in a talk that he gave at Temple University in March 2010. The presumption of a "crime wave" was influenced both by a concern for safety and by already-percolating assumptions, rooted in federal immigration law, that Mexicans and other Latin Americans are criminal. In this logic, it is the mere presence of unauthorized immigrants that constitutes the "illegal immigration problem," not the United State's history of policy contradictions and dysfunctions. And if the problem is the immigrants themselves, the "solution" is to exclude them, "whether through deportation, detention, or denying such [im]migrants access to employment, higher education, drivers licenses, public benefits" (Coutin 2005:7). The construction of Mexican criminality, then, justifies denials not only of citizenship, but of human rights. Thus, the tension between human rights and sovereignty is resolved in the case of Mexico-to-United States immigration by a racialization that conflates "illegal alien" with "Mexican immigrant" as well as "personhood" with "citizenship," so that one's humanity depends upon one's right to occupy territory (Collier, et al. 1997:23; Malkki 1992). This nativist personhood creates a disturbing justification for the defense of sovereignty: if unauthorized immigrants are not fully persons, we need not concern ourselves with their humanity in developing policies to eliminate them.

Increasing efforts to also target those who facilitate illegal immigration are part of this penal logic. This legal trend was initiated in the 1986 Immigration Reform and Control Act (IRCA), the first federal law to penalize employers for hiring undocumented immigrants, a provision referred to as the "employer sanction." Although the intent of IRCA's employer sanction was to distribute penalization more fairly by sanctioning both undocumented immigrants as well as the people who provide them with jobs, it has only served to augment legal racialization, an effect felt especially by Mexican immigrants, as they are disproportionately likely to become "illegal aliens." For example, the employer sanction only requires employers to view documents demonstrating legal status, not to verify the validity of those documents; the law has thus created incentives for a boom in the trade of fake documents (Durand and Massey 2003). Therefore, instead of effectively penalizing employers, the law has effectively increased undocumented immigrants' exposure to realms of illegality, such as the trade in fake documents, which justifies and enacts their standing as suspect and criminal.

It is not unreasonable to suggest that Hazleton's landlord sanction would have a similar effect to IRCA's employer sanction. The legal category that racializes immigrants is not only the "illegal alien," but also the illegal immigration facilitator, especially the "immigrant harborer." Initially established in federal law to address human trafficking across U.S. national borders, the Hazleton ordinance broadens the category to include landlords, thereby penalizing persons who, according to the ordinance, facilitate undocumented immigration by renting property to undocumented immigrants. As the ordinance would turn the basic survival activity of finding a safe place to live into a clandestine and illegal endeavor, its landlord sanction, and particularly its expansion of the category "immigrant harborer," exposes immigrants to ever-increasing realms of illegality such as renting property "under the table." Like the other realms of illegality discussed above—engaging in the trade in fake documents, in deportation proceedings, and so on—renting property under the table would racialize immigrants by reinforcing and performing their status as dangerous law-breakers.

Legal Racialization and Interdiscursivity in Hazleton

The genealogy outlined above has created a potent and productive code of exclusion in which the category "illegal alien" allows people to construct racialized difference without mentioning "race." This racialization is rooted in the fact that it is Mexicans, more than any other immigrant group, who are likely to be labeled "illegal aliens," and in the attendant presumption that Mexican immigrants are inherently criminal—a presumption increasingly affecting other Latin American immigrants. The circulation of federal legal categories, including their movement into extralegal life, then creates grounds for further policies, as was the case in Hazleton. Consider Barletta's claims as they appeared in a 2006 article in the *Washington Post*. First, he explains how he decided to propose the ordinance: "I lay in bed and thought: I've lost my city. I love the new legal immigrants; they want their kids to be safe just like I do. I had to declare war on the illegals." Then, regarding the effect of his ordinance, he declares: "I already see progress. I see illegal immigrants picking up and leaving; some *Mexican* restaurants say business is off 75%" (Powell and Garcia 2006, emphasis mine). One wonders how the mayor determined that the people he saw leaving town were "illegal"; and one wonders why the drop in business at *Mexican* restaurants should be considered evidence of the departure of "illegals."

Although studies show that a majority of Mexican immigrant households are "mixed status," containing some members who are citizens and some who are undocumented (Passel 2005),[4] Barletta's declaration of war ontologically separates these groups and associates "illegals" with Mexicans or anyone who appears to be "Mexican." Yet legal contestation of the ordinance has shown that the city has presented scant documentation supporting its presumption of immigrant illegality. Tellingly, pro-Barletta coverage of the ordinance called this demand for evidence a "straw-man argument," an obfuscation of the "real facts:"[5] after all, common sense tells one that "Mexicans" are "illegals," right? The ordinance's linking of Latin American and undocumented immigration relies not on data about the legal status of immigrants in the town, but on its interdiscursivity with federal immigration policy and the ways in which this policy racializes south-of-the-border immigrants. When Hazleton penned an ordinance that criminalizes a Latin American immigration that the town had, in fact, encouraged by courting Cargill Meat Solutions, it created an implied interdiscursivity with federal law. But the Hazleton ordinance does more than implicitly evoke the incorporation regime produced by the politics of contradiction in federal law; it also creates an explicit dialogue with that law, eventually copying its language outright. Through this dialogue, the ordinance makes the federally sanctioned categories that racialize Latin American immigrants applicable to life in Hazleton.

Textual Interdiscursivity with Federal Law

In Hazleton, there were explicit interdiscursive links to the national debate over immigration law that raged in the spring of 2006. With Congress's failure to pass immigration reform in 2006, Barletta began to search for solutions on his own. He found one such solution on the website of a California organization called "Save Our State," headed by a San Bernardino city council member named Joseph Turner (Jordan 2006; Simonich 2006). In May 2006, Turner proposed an ordinance also called the Illegal Immigration Relief Act (IIRA). Although this ordinance was voted down, it lived on thanks to conservative talk radio, which called on like-minded officials in municipalities across the country to pass similar ordinances. Mayor Barletta answered this call in

July 2006 when he proposed his IIRA, which in many respects copies the language of the San Bernardino ordinance. When Hazleton's law passed, it quickly received national attention in the conservative and mainstream media, helping inspire the proposal of similar ordinances in other new-immigrant-receiving areas.

The interdiscursive links among municipal ordinances multiplied as Barletta attempted to "take this fight to Washington," both through his bids for Congress[6], one that failed in 2008 and another that succeeded in 2010, and through his efforts to get the ruling on his ordinance appealed. These efforts led not only to a dramatic shift in Barletta's participant role, but also helped generate what some have called a "grass roots movement" of anti-immigrant activism (Vallis 2006). The mayors of Avon Park, Florida and Valley Park, Missouri, for example, proposed their own Illegal Immigration Relief Acts after hearing Barletta speak on conservative talk radio (Cardenas 2006). Moreover, a website used as a central resource by many anti-immigrant groups (www.illegalaliens.us) has made the Hazleton ordinance available for download, presenting it as a template that other municipalities that are concerned for their nation's sovereignty can copy and propose to their town counsels. Lou Dobbs and other conservative media stars have hosted Barletta on their programs, asking viewers to make donations to support Barletta's ongoing court battles. This "movement" also enjoys the legal and ideological support of national anti-immigrant organizations such as the Federation for American Immigration Reform (FAIR), which was recently listed as a nativist hate group by the Southern Poverty Law Center. FAIR's head legal council, Kris Kobach—famous for his involvement in drafting Arizona's controversial immigration bill (SB 1070), which would require police, in the course of routine police activities, to check the immigration status of people whom they suspect are "illegal"—was Hazleton's defense lawyer in the lawsuit over its constitutionality (Simonich 2007b).

Given the interdiscursive links among municipal ordinances, I have analyzed Illegal Immigration Relief Acts penned in San Bernardino, California; Hazleton, Pennsylvania; and Valley Park, Missouri. I consider how the Hazleton ordinance was revised between its first proposal, in July 2006, and its second, in September 2006. Out of the many Hazleton-like ordinances, I selected the Valley Park ordinance because its final version is a word-for-word copy of the final Hazleton ordinance; and because, unlike the Hazleton ordinance, the Valley Park ordinance has become implemented as law. In total, I have analyzed five documents:[7] the proposed San Bernardino ordinance (SBO), voted down in May 2006; the original Hazleton ordinance (HO-I), passed in July 2006; the revised Hazleton ordinance (HO-II]), passed in September 2006, which is stalled in appeal; the original Valley Park ordinance (VPO-I), passed a week after HO-I; and the revised Valley Park ordinance (VPO-II), passed a week after HO-II.

The San Bernardino ordinance was more innovative than the ordinance in Hazleton. Most notably, it establishes a new legal category: the "day laborer," defined as any person, except those who offer "secretarial, clerical, or professional services," whose employment is "irregular or occasional"; the ordinance would have made this form of labor illegal. By contrast, the Hazleton ordinance was distinguished by a close dialogue with the categories of federal law, drawing on the existing federal employer sanction as well as federal statutes concerning harboring of immigrants. In revising the ordinance from July to September, however, municipal officials in Hazleton transformed its interdiscursivity with federal law from a relationship of replacement to one of expansion, increasingly adopting the terminology of federal law. In doing so, they employed two principle tactics of interdiscursivity: citation of federal code and iconic replication of that code.

Consider the definitions of "illegal alien" in the July and September Hazleton ordinances:

HO-I July 2006	HO-II Sept 2006
An "illegal alien" is—	An "illegal alien" is—
...any person whose initial entry into the United States was illegal and whose current status is also illegal as well as any person who, after entering legally, has failed to leave the United States upon the expiration of his or her visa.	... [any person who] is not lawfully present in the United States, according to the terms of the <u>United States Code Title 8, section 1101 *et seq.*</u>

In HO-I, the law's authors take the general categories of federal immigration law (illegal entrants, visa violators) and rewrite them, laminating the ordinance on top of federal law. This rewriting leads to a definition of "illegal alien" that is so ambiguous that it could be interpreted to include anyone who has ever entered the United States illegally, regardless of current legal status—an ambiguity for which the ordinance was taken to task by opponents of the law, prompting the revision of the definition. Seeking protection from future legal contest, HO-II's definition defers to U.S. Code Title 8, Section 1101 by citing it.

Title 8 is the federal statute on "Aliens and Nationality"; Section 1101 contains the definitions pertinent to interpreting the sections of the law dealing with unauthorized immigration.[8] Citing Title 8 situates the ordinance, and those who penned and passed it, in direct dialogue with federal law, rendering explicit the implicit copying of federal law evident in the first definition. Significantly, Section 1101's definitions are twenty-six single-spaced pages long; the definition of "alien" alone takes up more than nine pages. Unlike other citations of federal code in HO-II, this one does not direct the reader to the particular subsection that is relevant to Hazleton's law; rather, it leaves the person who is interpreting the ordinance to figure this out on his or her own. Thus, while the legal label "illegal alien" is absolute and easily decontextualizable, HO-II leaves highly ambiguous the issue of to whom the label refers. This not only allows the Hazleton ordinance to take cover under federal law, it also creates a space of ambiguity and interpretation in which the pre-existing conflation of "illegal alien" and "Mexican immigrant" can function as the basis for the application of the Hazleton law.

Now consider the sections in HO-I, the San Bernardino ordinance (SBO), and the first Valley Park Ordinance (VPO-I) that outlaw renting property to undocumented immigrants, the original landlord sanctions. The HO-I and VPO-I landlord sanctions produce an implied movement toward the terms of federal law:

SBO May 2006	HO-I July 2006	VPO-I July 2006
Illegal aliens are prohibited from leasing or renting property. Any property owner or renter/tenant/lessee in control of property, who allows an illegalalien to use, rent, or lease their property shall be in violation of this section, **irrespective of such person's intent, knowledge, or negligence, said violation hereby being expressly declared a strict liability offense.**	Illegal aliens are prohibited from leasing or renting property. Any property owner or renter/tenant/lessee in control of property, who **knowingly** allows an illegal alien to use, rent, or lease their property shall be in violation of this section.	Illegal aliens are prohibited from leasing or renting property. Any property owner or renter/tenant/lessee in control of property, who **knowingly** allows an illegal alien to use, rent, or lease their property shall be in violation of this section.

In HO-I and VPO-I, these sections are identical; they also closely replicate SBO, with one key difference: they reduce the category of violation to people who *knowingly* rent property to undocumented immigrants. As this illustrates, SBO served as a template for later ordinances. But HO-I and VPO-I revise SBO through an implied replication of the language of federal law. Here the Hazelton ordinance copies, in particular, the employer sanction of IRCA, which outlaws only the practice of *knowingly* engaging with undocumented immigrants. As in the initial definition of "illegal alien" in HO-I, these early drafts replace the general category of "illegal immigration facilitator" that is established by federal law, creating a new category, "landlords." This pattern changes in later drafts of HO and VPO, whose landlord sanctions rely heavily on the language of federal law, thus constructing an explicit pattern of textual replication.

In the "Findings and Declaration of Purpose" sections that open the ordinances, HO-II and VPO-II identically state that "United States Code Title 8, subsection 1324(a)(1)(A) [note the direct reference to the subsection] prohibits the harboring of illegal aliens. The provision of housing to illegal aliens is a fundamental component of harboring." Here we see an overt effort to expand the federal definition of harboring to include the renting of property. This expansion takes its lead from the 2005 bill HR 4437, which sought to embrace within the category "harborer" any person or organization that aided undocumented immigrants, thereby categorizing churches and pro-immigrant humanitarians together with human traffickers (Chavez 2008:9).

Consider the sections in HO-II and VPO-II regarding the harboring of illegal aliens, which replace the sections on "renting to illegal aliens" discussed above:

HO-II & VPO-II Sept 2006	US Title 8, Subsection 1324 (a)(1)(A)(iii)
It is unlawful for any person or business entity that owns a dwelling unit in the City to harbor an illegal alien in the dwelling unit, <u>knowing or in reckless disregard of the fact that an alien has come to, entered, or remains in the United States in violation of law</u>, unless such harboring is otherwise expressly permitted by federal law.	Criminal penalties [will be levied on] any person who—
For the purposes of this section, to **let, lease, or rent** a dwelling unit to an illegal alien, <u>knowing or in reckless disregard of the fact that an alien has come to, entered, or remains in the United States in violation of law</u>, constitute harboring.	<u>knowing or in reckless disregard of the fact that an alien has come to, entered, or remains in the United States in violation of law</u>, conceals, harbors, or shields from detection, or attempts to conceal, harbor, or shield from detection, such alien in any place, including any building or any means of transportation

Again, one sees a trend toward more explicit replication of text as the terms of federal law are imported through the iconic replication of its content: the use of the word "harbor" and the underlined phrase, lifted from Title 8. The shift from renting to harboring moves HO-II away from the prior effort to replace federal law toward a new effort to work within the terms of federal law. This iconic replication allows the Hazleton ordinance to make manifest the entailments of federal law, extending the definition of "harboring" to include locally salient categories of person and interaction: in particular, the renting of property to undocumented immigrants. Such efforts to make manifest the entailments of federal law are not unique to the Hazleton ordinance. As Urban (2001:97ff) demonstrates in his analysis of the Declaration of Independence, U.S. social movements often use interdiscursivity with established federal discourse to transform society. Sometimes such interdiscursivity is used to extend the referents of the "we of the United States" to include marginalized groups, as seen in the Civil Rights movement. But at other times, this process is used to broaden categories of exclusion from the nation, as seen in Hazleton.

This interdiscursive shift from the replacement of federal categories to their expansion reduces the degree of discursive dissimilarity between federal law and the Hazleton ordinance, closing the "intertextual gap" between them (Briggs and Bauman 1992:149). This closure creates the effect that federal law is merely replicated, and not challanged, by the ordinance. The movement toward federal law re-enacts the hierarchical relationships between federal and municipal policymaking—a re-enactment imposed on municipal lawmakers by legal contestation of the ordinance, which challenged its constitutionality on the basis of its overstepping the boundaries of jurisdiction in policymaking. In this way, the ordinance becomes constrained by existing policy and the established pragmatics of policymaking across scales of sovereignty. At the same time, closing the intertextual gap creates a semiotic unity of forms that allows the ordinance to take on the authority and legitimacy of federal law (Briggs and Bauman 1992:149–159; Philips 1998:28), essentially saying, "We as a country have already agreed to this policy." This unity of forms makes it seem as though lawmakers in Hazleton are not originating immigration law, but merely rearticulating federal law—a move that they hope will allow them to refute accusations of unconstitutionality (Simonich 2007b).

Officials who redrafted the law may have thought that the ordinance, thus revised, would achieve the same policy outcome of "controlling" local immigration that had been intended in the original draft of the ordinance. The interdiscursive shift, however, enacts an important and profound transformation of the politics of exclusion that is expressed through the ordinance. In expanding the federal category of "immigrant harborer" to include landlords, the ordinance attempts to make the violation of town boundaries iconic of the violation of the nation's sovereignty. This move expands the legal racialization of Mexican and other Latin American immigrants. Most broadly, it does this because it is based on an assumption that south-of-the-border immigration is illegal; it thus extends federal policy's conflation of "illegal alien" with "Mexican immigrant" into local policymaking. More specifically, in pushing the category of "immigrant harborer" to include landlords, it establishes another arena of social interaction in which judgments of legality are required: the renting of property. As part of this, the roles of producers of discourse also shift: not only do municipal officials become immigration lawmakers, the ordinance deputizes the population of an entire town to report "illegal aliens" and those who harbor them.[9] Although HO-II states that allegations of illegality made solely "on the basis of national origin, ethnicity, or race shall be deemed invalid," it gives no guidelines for how to determine illegality. This creates further interpretive ambiguities in which the extant criminalization of Latin Americans can become a driving factor in determinations of future illegality as the categories of legal racialization potentially reach more pervasively into the daily lives, and homes, of people in Hazleton.

Conclusion

This article has shown how the Hazleton ordinance relies on interdiscursivity with a history of policy that has criminalized and racialized Latin American immigrants, especially Mexicans or those perceived to be Mexican. The ordinance extends and transforms this history by situating the processes of legal racialization in locally salient categories of person and interaction. The argument presented here also speaks to a fundamental problem in legal and extralegal debates over local immigration policies. It is common for proponents and opponents of these policies to line up along a divide created by the argument over whether or not such laws are racist—an argument that depends on which order of indexicality one takes into account. Champions of local immigration restrictions make recourse to overt indexicality in claiming that the laws are not racist because their denotational content targets illegal aliens and not any specific racial group; in fact, in revising the Hazleton ordinance, officials have taken pains to ensure that this is so (Simonich 2007b). Yet, as we see in this article, the category "illegal alien" does *indirectly* index race, increasingly over time, by disproportionately affecting some immigrant groups and not others—a process of racialization and criminalization that is not evident in the denotational content of the law. Rather, the racializing effects of these laws dwell in the indirect racial indexicality—the conflation of "illegal alien" and "criminal Mexican immigrant"—that can only be established by considering the genealogy detailed here and the forms of intertextuality that extend this genealogy into current law.

Such genealogies are not easily decontextualized, and are therefore difficult to circulate in public debate. By contrast, legal labels are easily removed from contexts of production and thus seem neutral and natural, lending credence to assertions that immigration categories are "colorblind." Such assertions, based as they are on the essentialized categories of immigration law and the ways in which these categories make their racializing effects covert, appear commonsensical and innocent—as promoting the "general good" of defending national sovereignty. The problem for opponents of these laws is that claims that the laws are racist require the unpacking of complex histories of discourse that, relative to putatively natural and innocent legal labels, are difficult to replicate and, thus, harder to circulate. Such claims of racism appear as artificial and constructed—as interested, benefiting only some—and therefore appear illegitimate as foundations for policy (cf. discussion of innocence and interest in Hill 2001; Woolard 1990). This is a complex problem that is experienced especially acutely in the present political moment in the United States, when to talk about race at all is to risk being called racist (see Urciuoli and Blanton, this volume). This one article, obviously, cannot resolve this problem. I can, however, highlight that it is impossible to counter the covert racializing strategies of anti-immigrant ordinances without examining these ordinances, and their interrelationships, as problems of discourse. This means, above all else, moving beyond a focus on denotational content to consider as well the indirect indexicalities that these ordinances construct through interdiscursive relationships with immigration law across time and space.

Notes

Aknowledgments. I am grateful to Kristina Wirtz, whose keen eye helped me see this article's structure, and to Bonnie Urciuoli for her generous feedback. I extend thanks as well to Kathleen D Hall, who served as discussant on the 2008 American Anthropological Association panel (*Racializing Discourses*) on which I first presented this argument. I was fortunate to present this work at the Center for the Humanities at Temple University and to the Anthropology Department of Kutztown University; thanks to Peter Logan and William Donner respectively for inviting me. Thanks also go to the Michicagoan Faculty Seminar group for editorial responses on a late draft of this article. Finally, I thank Susan U. Philips and Judith Goode for helping me think through this piece at an early and awkward stage in my thinking.

1. A note on terminology: First, I am intentionally using the term "anti-immigrant"; proponents of laws like the Hazleton ordinance would have such laws, and the people and organizations that support them, called "anti-*illegal* immigrant." However, I prefer the term "antiimmigrant" because these laws affect all racialized immigrants, regardless of their actual legal status. Second, while it is common in anthropology to refer to the global movement of people with the term "migration" (and related terms, "migrant," "migrate," etc.), in this article, for simplicity's sake, I use "immigration" and related terms, as I am also referring, throughout, to immigration policy, which is never called "migration policy."

2. Seehttp://www.aclu.org/immigrants-rights/report-united-nations-special-rapporteur-human-rights-migrants-dr-jorge-bustamante.

3. In 1990, the U.S. Congress enacted an increase in the number of visas allotted to each country to 25,620 visas per country per year (Greenwood and Ziel 2005).

4. Passel found that 4.7 million children live in the more than 6.3 million households in the United States that are headed by undocumented immigrants, and that 67% of those children are U.S. citizens.

5. See, for example, the Diggers Realm blog at www.diggersrealm.com/mt/archives/003125.html.

6. See usatoday.com fact sheet "Anti-illegal Immigration Mayor Running for Congress."

7. The American Civil Liberties Union (ACLU) website, www.aclu.org, has links to the full texts of these ordinances.

8. See www.law.cornell.edu/uscode/uscode08/usc_sup_01_8.html for a complete rendition of Title 8.

9. The September draft of the ordinance calls on residents to submit signed complaints to the municipal code enforcement office, detailing the identity of the offender, the actions of offense, and their date and location.

References

Agha, Asif
  2005 Introduction: Semiosis Across Encounters. Journal of Linguistic Anthropology 15(1):1–5.
  2007 Language and Social Relations: Studies in the Social and Cultural Foundations of Language. Cambridge, UK: Cambridge University Press.

Bauman, Richard, and Charles L. Briggs
  1990 Poetics and Performance as Critical Perspectives on Language and Social Life. Annual Review of Anthropology 19:59–88.

Benhabib, Seyla 2002 Citizens, Residents, and Aliens in a Changing World: Political Membership in the Global Era. *In* The Postnational Self: Belonging and Identity. U. Hedetoft and M. Hjort, eds. Pp. 85–119. Minneapolis: University of Minnesota Press.

Benton-Cohen, Katherine
  2009 Borderline Americans: Racial Division and Labor War in the Arizona Borderlands. Cambridge, MA: Harvard University Press.

Briggs, Charles L., and Richard Bauman
  1992 Genre, Intertextuality, and Social Power. Journal of Linguistic Anthropology 2(2):131–172.

Brubaker, Rogers
  2009 Ethnicity, Race, and Nationalism. Annual Review of Sociology 35:21–42.

Cardenas, Jose 2006 Grass Roots Groups Challenge Illegals. *In* St. Petersburg Times. LexusNexus. St. Petersburg, FL.

Chavez, Leo 2001 Covering Immigration: Popular Images and the Politics of the Nation. Berkeley: University of California Press.

    2008 The Latino Threat: Constructing Immigrants, Citizens, and the Nation. Stanford: Stanford University Press.

Collier, Jane F., Bill Maurer, and Liliana Suárez-Navaz
    1997 Sanctioned Identities: Legal Constructions of Modern Personhood. Identities 2(1–2):1–27.

Coutin, Susan Bibler 2005 Contesting Criminality: Illegal Immigration and the Spatialization of Legality. Theoretical Criminology 9(1):5–33.

Coutin, Susan Bibler, and Phyllis Pease Chock
    1995 "Your Friend, the Illegal": Definition and Paradox in Newspaper Accounts of U.S. Immigration Reform.
        Identities 2(1–2):123–148.

De Genova, Nicholas
    2002 Migrant "Illegality" and Deportability in Everyday Life. Annual Review of Anthropology 31:419–47.
    2005 Working the Boundaries: Race, Space, and "Illegality" in Mexican Chicago. Durham: Duke University Press.

De Genova, Nicholas, and Ana Y. Ramos-Zayas 2003 Latino Racial Formations in the United States: An Introduction. Journal of Latin American Anthropology 8(2):2–17.

De Jesús, José 2006 Employees at Meatpacking Plant Allege Mistreatment. Des Moines Register. April 12.

Degnen, Chris 2007 Documentary: Immigration on Main Street. *In* NOW. PBS, October 18.

Durand, Jorge, and Douglas S. Massey 2003 The Costs of Contradiction: US Border Policy 1986–2000. Latino Studies 1:233–252.

El Nasser, Haya, and Brad Heath
    2007 Hispanic Growth Extends Eastward. USA Today. August 9.

Fleury-Steiner, Benjamin, and Jamie Longazel
    2010 Neoliberalism, Community Development, and Anti-Immigrant Backlash in Hazleton, Pennsylvania. In Taking
        Local Control: Immigration Policy Activism in U.S. Cities and States. Monica W. Varsanyi, ed. Stanford: Stanford
        University Press.

Flores, William V.
    2003 New Citizens, New Rights: Undocumented Immigrants and Latino Cultural Citizenship. Latin American
        Perspectives 30(2):295–308.

Flores, W.V., and R. Benmayor
    1997 "Constructing Cultural Citizenship." *In* Latino Cultural Citizenship: Claiming Identity, Space, and Rights.
        Edited by W. V. Flores and R. Benmayor. Boston: Beacon Press. 1–23.

Greenwood M.J., and F.A. Ziel
    2005 The Impact of the Immigration Act of 1990 on U.S. Immigration. Davis: University of California, Davis.

Hagan, Jacqueline Maria
    1994 Deciding to be Legal: A Maya Community in Houston. Philadelphia: Temple University Press.

Hall, Kathleen D.
    2004 The Ethnography of Imagined Communities: The Cultural Production of Sikh Ethnicity in Britain. The Annals
        of the American Academy of Political and Social Science 595:108–121.

Haney-López, Ian
    2006 White by Law: The Legal Construction of Race. New York: New York University Press.

Hill, Jane H. 2001 Mock Spanish, Covert Racism, and the (Leaky) Boundary between Public and Private Spheres. *In* Languages and Publics: The Making of Authority. S. Gal and K.A. Woolard, eds. Pp. 83–102. Manchester: St. Jerome.
    2005 Intertextuality as Source and Evidence for Indirect Indexical Meanings. Journal of Linguistic Anthropology
        15(1):113–124.

2008 The Everyday Language of White Racism. Malden: Wiley-Blackwell.

Hopkins, Daniel J.
2008 Threatening Changes: Explaining Where and When Immigrants Provoke Local Opposition. Center for the Study of American Politics, Yale University, 2008.
2010 Politicized Places: Explaining Where and When Immigrants Provoke Local Opposition. American Political Science Review 104(1):40–60.

Huntington, Samuel P.
2004 Who Are We?: The Challenges to America's Identity. New York: Simon & Schuster.

Irvine, Judith T.
1996 Shadow Conversations: The Indeterminancy of Participant Roles. *In* Natural Histories of Discourse. M. Silverstein and G. Urban, eds. Pp. 131–159. Chicago: University of Chicago Press.

Jordan, Miriam
2006 In Immigrant Fight, Grass-Roots Groups Boost Their Clout. *In* Wall Street Journal, September 28, 2006. http://online.wsj.com/article/SB115940950734176279.html?mod=googlenews_wsj, accessed May 4, 2009.

Lee, Benjamin 1997 Talking Heads: Language, Metalanguage, and the Semiotics of Subjectivity. Durham, NC: Duke University Press.

Malkki, Liisa 1992 National Geographic: The Rooting of Peoples and the Territorialization of National Identity among Scholars and Refugees. Cultural Anthropology 7(1):24–44.

Massey, Douglas S., Jorge Durand, and Nolan J. Malone.
2002 Beyond Smoke and Mirrors: Mexican Immigration in an Age of Economic Integration. New York: Russell Sage Foundation.

Massey, Douglas S.
2007 Categorically Unequal: The American Stratification System. New York: Russell Sage Foundation.

Matoesian, Greg
2000 Intertextual Authority in Reported Speech: Production Media in the Kennedy Smith Rape Trial. Journal of Pragmatics 32(7):879–914.

Mehan, Hugh
1996 The Construction of an LD Student: A Case Study in the Politics of Recognition. *In* Natural Histories of Discourse. M. Silverstein and G. Urban, eds. Pp. 253–276. Chicago: University of Chicago Press.
1997 The Discourse of the Illegal Immigration Debate: A Case Study in the Politics of Representation. Discourse and Society 8(2):249–270.

Mendoza-Denton, Norma
2008 Homegirls: Language and Cultural Practice among Latina Youth Gangs. Malden: Blackwell.

Menjívar, Cecilia
2000 Fragmented Ties: Salvadorean Immigrant Networks in America. Berkeley: University of California Pres.
2006 Liminal Legality: Salvadoran and Guatemalan Immigrants' Lives in the United States. American Journal of Sociology 111(4): 999–1037.

Mertz, Elizabeth
1996 Recontextualization as Socialization: Text and Pragmatics in the Law School Classroom. *In* Natural Histories of Discourse. M. Silverstein and G. Urban, eds. Pp. 229–249. Chicago: University of Chicago Press.

Ngai, Mae M.
2004 Impossible Subjects: Illegal Aliens and the Making of Modern America. Princeton: Princeton University Press.

Ochs, Elinor
1990 Indexicality and Socialization. *In* Cultural Psychology. J. Stigler, R. Shweder, and G. Herdt, eds. Pp. 287–308. Cambridge: Cambridge University Press.

Passel, J.S.

    2005 Unauthorized Migrants: Numbers and Characteristics. Washington, DC: Pew Hispanic Center, pewhispanic.org

Philips, Susan Urmston

    1998 Ideology in the Language of Judges: How Judges Practice Law, Politics, and Courtroom Control. New York: Oxford University Press.

Powell, Michael, and Michelle Garcia

    2006 PA City Puts Illegal Immigrants on Notice. *In* Washington Post, August 22, 2006. www.washingtonpost.com/wp-dyn/content/article/2006/08/21, accessed November 10, 2008.

Roediger, David

    1991 The Wages of Whiteness. New York: Verso.

Sacks, Karen Brodkin

    1994 How Did Jews Become White Folks? *In* Race. S. Gregory and R. Sanjek, eds. Pp. 78–102. New Brunswick: Rutgers University Press.

Santa Ana, Otto.

    2002 Brown Tide Rising: Metaphors of Latinos in Contemporary American Discourse. Austin: University of Texas Press.

Silverstein, Michael

    2005 Axes of Evals: Token versus Type Interdiscursivity. Journal of Linguistic Anthropology 15(1):6–22.

Silverstein, Michael, and Greg Urban

    1996a The Natural Histories of Discourse. *In* Natural Histories of Discourse. M. Silverstein and G. Urban, eds. Pp. 1–17. Chicago: University of Chicago Press. eds. 1996b Natural Histories of Discourse. Chicago: University of Chicago Press.

Simonich, Milan

    2006 Hazleton Ordinance Aimed at Illegal Immigrants Puts Mayor at Center Stage. *In* Pittsburgh Post-Gazette, August 27, 2006. http://www.post-gazette.com/pg/06239/716707-85.stm, accessed October 22, 2008.

2007a Witnesses Back off on Immigrant Law. *In* Pittsburgh Post-Gazette, March 13, 2007. http://www.post-gazette.com [LexusNexus], accessed April 22, 2010.

2007b Hazleton Immigrant Law Being Reworked Again. *In* Pittsburgh Post-Gazette, March 4, 2007. http://www.post-gazette.com [LexusNexus], accessed April 22, 2010.

Soysal, Yasemin Nuho glu

    1994 Limits of Citizenship: Migrants and Postnational Membership in Europe. Chicago: University of Chicago.

Stephen, Lynn

    2004 The Gaze of Surveillance in the Lives of Mexican Immigrant Workers. Development 47(1):97–102.

Thompson, Heather Ann

    2010 Why Mass Incarceration Matters: Rethinking Crisis, Decline, and Transformation in Postwar American History. Journal of American History 97(3):703–758.

Tilove, Jonathan

    2007 Immigration Debate Rages in Coal Town. Lexus Nexus. Star-Ledger.

Urban, Greg

    2001 Metaculture: How Culture Moves through the World. Minneapolis: University of Minnesota Press.

Urciuoli, Bonnie

    1996 Exposing Prejudice: Puerto Rican Experiences of Language, Race, and Class. Boulder: Westview Press.

Vallis, Mary

    2006 U.S. Cities Taking Illegal Immigration into Own Hands: Businesses to be Fined. *In* National Post, July 13, 2007. http://www.nationalpost.com [LexusNexus], accessed October 15, 2008.

Varsanyi, Monica W.

2010 Immigration Policy Activism in U.S. States and Cities: Interdisciplinary Perspectives. In Taking Local Control: Immigration Policy Activism in U.S. Cities and States. Monica W. Varsanyi, ed. Stanford: Stanford University Press.

Woolard, Kathryn A.

1990 Voting Rights, Liberal Voters, and the Official English Movement: An Analysis of Campaign Rhetoric in San Francisco's Proposition "O." *In* Perspectives on Official English: The Campaign for English as the Official Language of the USA. K.L. Adams and D.T. Brink, eds. Pp. 125–138. New York: Mouton de Gruyter.

Wortham, Stanton E.F., Enrique G. Murillo, and Edmund T. Hamann

2002 Education in the New Latino Diaspora: Policy and the Politics of Identity. Westport: Ablex.

Zentella, Ana Celia

1995 The "Chiquita-fication" of U.S. Latinos and Their Languages, or, Why We need an Anthropolitical Linguistics. *In* Proceedings of the Third Annual Symposium About Language and Society at Austin (Texas Linguistic Forum 36). Risako Ide, Rebecca Parker, and Yukako Sunaoshi, eds. Pp. 1–18. Austin: University of Texas Department of Linguistics.

Discussion Questions

1. How is racialization a form of social differentiation? Provide specific examples.
2. Throughout U.S. history, immigrant groups have variably been seen both as desirable (as enhancing "who we are") and as undesirable (a threat to sovereignty and national security). How have changing social conditions (both in the U.S. and worldwide) changed national attitudes about immigrants?
3. How does the language used in the immigration debate contribute to Americans' attitudes about immigrants? Is this helpful or hurtful? Provide specific examples.
4. Do U.S. immigration policies tend to target a specific group of people? What are the risks and benefits of this? Make sure to provide reasoning for your statements.
5. Can a nation's – *any* nation's – immigration policies be a form of ethnocentrism? Why or why not?

Chapter 5

"Better to Be Hot than Caught": Excavating the Conflicting Roles of Migrant Material Culture

Jason De León

Department of Anthropology, University of Michigan,
Ann Arbor, MI 48109–1107;
jpdeleon@umich.edu

D ue to increased border security in the United States, an intricate smuggling network has formed in Mexico—the ultimate goal is for migrants to cross boundaries undetected. In this article, Jason De León examines the culture of this clandestine activity, blending the experiences of the migrants with material culture and archaeological data left behind during border crossings. Material culture is more than just tangible objects—what stories can these items tell?

Abstract

Since the mid-1990s, heightened U.S. border security in unauthorized crossing areas near urban ports of entry has shifted undocumented migration toward remote regions such as the Sonoran Desert of Arizona, where security is more penetrable but crossing conditions are more difficult. Subsequently, a complex smuggling industry has developed in Northern Mexico that profits from helping migrants cross the desert on foot to enter the United States undetected. Desert crossing is now a well-established social process whereby items such as dark clothes and water bottles have been adopted as tools used for subterfuge and survival by migrants. This article highlights ethnographic data on the experiences of migrants and archaeological data collected along the migrant trails that cross the Arizona desert to illustrate the routinized techniques and tools associated with the violent process of border crossing, as well as the dialectical and often oppressive relationship that exists between migrants and objects. [*material culture, undocumented migration, border crossing, U.S.–Mexico, archaeology of the contemporary*]

Resumen

Desde los 1990s, el augmento de seguridad fronteriza de EE.UU. en áreas cerca de puertos oficiales de entrada ha desplazado la migración indocumentada a regiones remotas como el desierto de Sonora en Arizona donde la seguridad es más penetrable, pero las condiciones para cruzas son más dificiles. Posteriormente, una industria para ayudar los migrantes a cruzar la frontera illegalmente ha desarrollado en el Norte de México. Hoy cruzando el desierto es un proceso social bien establecido. Los migrantes utilizan herramientas como ropa negra y bottelas de agua para eluden la Patrulla Fronteriza y sobrevivir el desierto. Este artículo presenta datos etnográficos de las experiencias de migrantes y datos arqueológicos hubo collectado en los caminos de migrantes en el desierto. Ha demonstrado que las técnicas y instrumentos associado con el proceso violento de cruce son normalizados, tambien la relación entre los migrantes y sus objetos son dialéctica y a veces opresivo.

I'm watching Victor and Miguel pack.[1] We have just returned from a shopping trip where they bought four gallons of water, three cans of beans, 11 cans of tuna, two cans of sardines, half a kilo of limes, two bags of tortillas, a loaf of bread, a bulb of garlic (to rub on their clothes as a defense against snakes), and a can of chiles. They are both trying to cram two gallons of water into their backpacks that are already overloaded with food and clothes. Miguel tells me he has an extra pair of socks in case his feet get wet or he starts to get blisters from his uncomfortable knock-off Adidas sneakers. He has also packed a couple of black T-shirts that he says will help him avoid *la migra* [Border Patrol]. "It makes it harder for them to see us at night," he says. I ask about the discomfort from the extra heat generated by wearing black in the scorching desert, and he says, "It's better to be hot than caught." Victor then jokes that he should make some room in his small pack to take a couple of *caguamas* [one-quart bottles of beer]. We laugh at the ridiculous idea but deep down no one is laughing about the fact that the two gallons of water they are each carrying are not even close to what they will need to survive a multiday hike across the desert where recent temperatures have been in the low 100s. They will have to find water along the way and will likely end up drinking the green liquid from the bacteria-laden cattle tanks that dot the southern Arizona desert. These men, who I met several weeks prior while working in a migrant shelter in Nogales, have struggled for almost two weeks to come up with the 30 dollars needed to buy enough food to last them both on a multiday crossing. They have attempted this trip several times before and will undertake this one without a paid guide. There is no point in asking them questions like why they don't wear hiking boots or take a compass with them. Hiking boots are an unfamiliar and unattainable commodity to these working-class men. A compass is too expensive and something that Border Patrol would use to classify them as smugglers. If they get caught and labeled as smugglers, they face harsher punishment in the form of long-term jail time. I don't ask them if the few meager goods they are carrying are going to be sufficient to get across the border. I just sit and imagine the unforeseen perils that no one wants to talk about. Later, we hop on a bus and silently ride to the outskirts of Nogales where they will enter the desert on foot. Out of nowhere Victor turns to me and says "A lot of things are going through my head right now. I'm thinking about my family and I'm scared that I am going to die out there. Each time is different; you never know what is going to happen. . . . The *bajadores* [armed border bandits] should be out partying tonight because it's Saturday. We should be able to avoid them. We have food and water and God willing we will get across." The three of us get off the bus and walk toward a tunnel that leads out of town. We hug and say goodbye, and Victor walks away jokingly saying he brought the beer after all. I watch them disappear into the darkness of the tunnel and I wonder to myself how anyone can possibly try to prepare for something like this.

Introduction

This article is about the materiality and technologies of undocumented border crossing between Sonora, Mexico, and Southern Arizona. It is an analysis of seemingly ordinary items such as clothes, shoes, and water bottles that over the last 20 years have been shaped by the institutionalized border enforcement practices of the U.S. government, the human smuggling industry in Mexico, and by undocumented migrants into a unique set of tools used for subterfuge and survival. For people like Victor and Miguel, and the thousands of other women, men, and children who attempt crossings each year, these common items take on new functions and meaning once brought into the desert and deposited along the many trails that lead from Mexico into Arizona. These items are the tools of the undocumented, and they are relied on to avoid detection by Border Patrol and to survive the Sonoran Desert that has claimed the lives of thousands of people since the mid-1990s (Rubio-Goldsmith et al. 2006). Those who characterize the artifacts left behind by migrants as mere "trash" (see discussion in Sundberg [2008]) fail to recognize the historical, political, and global economic forces that have shaped border crossing into a well-structured social process (Singer and Massey 1998) with a distinct archaeological fingerprint.

Migrants like Victor choose to wear dark clothing because they have been told (and believe) it will help camouflage them in the desert. Although many migrants know that dark clothing raises the body's core temperature and signals to law enforcement that one is a border crosser, this technique continues to be used by thousands of people each year. In this article I demonstrate that while migrant technology and material culture have become somewhat standardized over the last 20 years, it does not necessarily mean that these tools and techniques are effective or even safe. I focus my analysis on three artifact classes (water bottles, shoes, and clothes) to illustrate that a dialectical relationship between border crossers and these objects exists whereby material culture is adopted and employed to achieve a social goal (i.e., successful crossing) and that material culture simultaneously acts on people's bodies, shapes their behavior, and becomes a medium that produces and projects social distinctions (Tilley 2006:61). Material culture is not just a reflection of the social process of border crossing, it actively constitutes and continuously shapes it. I illustrate that the use of these items is determined by a complex and culturally shaped set of processes influenced by many factors including economic constraints, folk logic, enforcement practices, migrant perceptions of Border Patrol, and the human smuggling industry. Moreover, the techniques used during crossings, both individually and collectively, can often have unintended negative consequences. By focusing on the complex and conflicting roles of the deceptively simple objects used by border crossers, I demonstrate how routinized the violent social process of border crossing and its associated tool kit has become, how people mediate their experiences in the desert through everyday objects, and how objects and technologies can create oppressive consequences through both somatic trauma and by marking people as vulnerable migrants.

I draw on ethnographic and archaeological data from the Undocumented Migration Project (UMP), a long-term study of border crossing along the U.S.–Mexico border (see Figure 1) that I have directed since 2008. This project was conceived in an effort to better understand various elements of border crossing, deportation, and the human smuggling industry in Latin America, as well as demonstrate the effectiveness of using an archaeological approach to understand an ongoing and clandestine social process. Archaeological surveys of migrant trails and ad hoc resting areas known as *migrant stations* were conducted in the Arizona deserts northwest of Nogales during the summers of 2009 and 2010. These surveys occurred in the Border Patrol jurisdiction known as the Tucson Sector, extending from the New Mexico state line to the Yuma, Arizona county line. Migrant stations are places where people rest, eat, change clothes, and leave items behind while crossing into the United States (see Figure 2). To date, the UMP has mapped dozens of migrant stations and collected thousands of artifacts, including water bottles, clothing, and other materials. The ethnographic data were collected in the Mexican towns of Nogales and Altar (see Figure 1) in the summers of 2009 and 2010. Semistructured and informal interviews were conducted in Spanish with hundreds of migrants either before crossing or immediately following deportation. In addition, hundreds of hours of observational data on the day-to-day experiences of deported people in Nogales were collected. Several migrants were also given disposable cameras and asked to photograph their crossing for anonymous publication (see Adler et al. [2007] for similar project), some of which are included here. Although migrants attempt to cross the Sonoran Desert at all times of the year, I focus on the summer months because this is the period when people face the highest risk of death from exposure. Although undocumented migration has slowed over the last several years (see Table 1), summer fatalities have risen suggesting that desert crossings are more dangerous and violent than ever before (McCombs 2011a). The interviews that I collected with migrants during this time of year provide important insight into how people experience the summer desert and the role that material culture plays in surviving this process.[2]

"Prevention through Deterrence"

Since the mid-1990s, heightened U.S. border security in unauthorized crossing areas near urban ports of entry has shifted undocumented migration toward remote regions such as the Sonoran Desert of Arizona, where security is more penetrable but crossing conditions (e.g., geography and environment) are more difficult. This federal enforcement strategy is known as *Prevention through Deterrence* (PTD) (Government

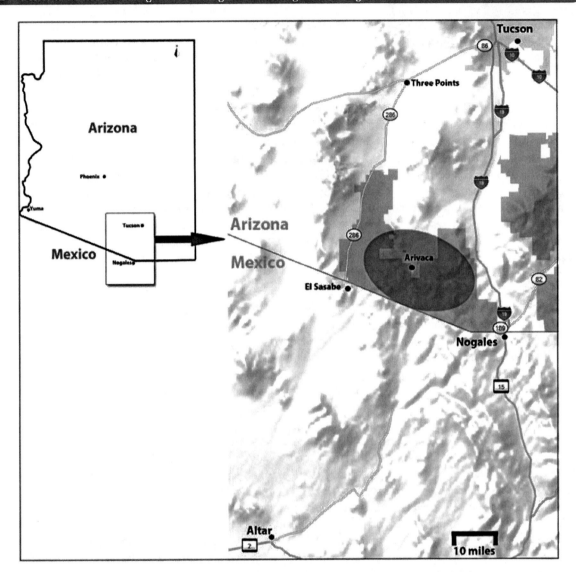

FIGURE 1. Map of study area with major towns and cities mentioned in text. The light gray rectangular areas designate national forest and federal nature reserve lands. The dark shaded circle around the town of Arivaca represents the approximate boundaries of the archaeological survey area.

Accountability Office [GAO] 1997:64–65). PTD along with ever-evolving technologies of enforcement control have increasingly turned the U.S.–Mexico border into a militarized zone where Border Patrol practice a strategy modeled on the Pentagon's Low-Intensity Conflict Doctrine, a policy first designed to suppress domestic insurgencies in the "Third-World" (Dunn 1996). The rampant unofficial racial profiling of Latinos, the impenetrable fencing surrounding ports of entry, the surveillance technologies (e.g., motion sensors), and the desert itself all contribute to a hostile and oppressive environment for migrants.

Initially it was thought that the desert would act as a natural deterrent to migration (Cornelius 2001), but over a decade of research has shown PTD to be ineffective (e.g., Cornelius and Salehayan 2007). This is especially true in Arizona, where despite hundreds of migration-related deaths annually, hundreds of thousands still attempt to cross the vast desert on foot each year to enter the United States without authorization. Rather than deterring, the strategies and policies associated with PTD have helped shape border crossing

FIGURE 2. A) Resting at a migrant station. B) Over the course of repeated use, migrant stations can develop into sizeable archaeological sites.

into a well-organized, dangerous, and violent social process. In Arizona, the busiest crossing point along the southern border, migrants must negotiate a rugged and inhospitable landscape characterized by extreme environmental conditions (e.g., summer temperatures exceeding 115 °F) and few water sources. In the summer, injuries and death are common, and many fail to successfully cross after running out of water, becoming dehydrated, or sustaining an injury. Adding to these environmental factors, migrants must also contend with bajadores who assault them and *coyotes* [human smugglers] who may abandon them in the desert. If migrants are able to overcome these obstacles, they must still evade Border Patrol who employ sophisticated ground and aerial surveillance technology to detect and capture people.

It is important to note that the data presented here were collected during a moment when major shifts in undocumented migration began to occur. This included a decrease in migration levels linked to the economic crisis of 2008, increased anti-immigrant sentiment sparked by Arizona State Bill 1070 that sought to give state police the authority to check the legal status of suspected undocumented people, increased federal spending to secure the Arizona border, and new deportation strategies that were initiated to deter multiple crossing attempts (De León in press; Slack and Whiteford 2011). Recent apprehension statistics (see Table 1), a notoriously problematic measure of undocumented migration (Andreas 2009:85–112), suggest that border crossing is at its lowest level in decades. Despite this slowing of migration and the fact that the Tucson Sector is now one of the most heavily monitored regions with the

TABLE 1 Southwest border apprehension statistics (2000–2010).

Southern border sectors	2000	2001	2002	2003	2004	2005	2006	2007	2008	2009	2010
San Diego, CA	151,681	110,075	100,681	111,515	138,608	126,909	142,122	152,459	162,392	118,712	68,565
ELCentro, CA	238,126	172,852	108,273	92,099	74,467	55,726	61,469	55,881	40,962	33,520	32,562
Yuma, AZ	108,747	78,385	42,654	56,638	98,060	138,438	118,537	37,994	8,363	6,952	7,116
Tucson, AZ	**616,346**	**449,675**	**333,648**	**347,263**	**491,771**	**439,090**	**392,104**	**378,323**	**317,709**	**241,667**	**212,202**
EL Paso, TX	115,696	112,857	94,154	88,816	104,399	122,689	122,261	75,464	30,310	14,998	12,251
Marfa, TX	13,689	12,087	11,392	10,319	10,530	10,536	7,517	5,537	5,390	6,357	5,288
Del Rio, TX	157,178	104,875	66,985	50,145	53,794	68,510	42,634	22,919	20,761	17,082	14,694
Laredo, TX	108,973	87,068	82,095	70,521	74,706	75,342	74,843	56,715	43,659	40,571	35,287
Rio Grande Valley, TX	133,243	107,844	89,927	77,749	92,947	134,188	110,531	73,430	75,476	60,992	59,766
Total Southwest apprehensions	1,643,679	1,235,718	929,809	905,065	1,139,282	1,171,428	1,072,018	858,722	705,022	540,851	447,731

Southern border sectors	2000	2001	2002	2003	2004	2005	2006	2007	2008	2009	2010
San Diego, CA	0.09	0.09	0.11	0.12	0.12	0.11	0.13	0.18	0.23	0.22	0.15
EL Centro,CA	0.14	0.14	0.12	0.10	0.07	0.05	0.06	0.07	0.06	0.06	0.07
Yuma, AZ	0.07	0.06	0.05	0.06	0.09	0.12	0.11	0.04	0.01	0.01	0.02
Tucson, AZ	**0.37**	**0.36**	**0.36**	**0.38**	**0.43**	**0.37**	**0.37**	**0.44**	**0.45**	**0.45**	**0.47**
EL Paso, TX	0.07	0.09	0.10	0.10	0.09	0.10	0.11	0.09	0.04	0.03	0.03
Marfa, TX	0.01	0.01	0.01	0.01	0.01	0.01	0.01	0.01	0.01	0.01	0.01
Del Rio, TX	0.10	0.08	0.07	0.06	0.05	0.06	0.04	0.03	0.03	0.03	0.03
Laredo, TX	0.07	0.07	0.09	0.08	0.07	0.06	0.07	0.07	0.06	0.08	0.08
Rio Grande Valley, TX	0.08	0.09	0.10	0.09	0.08	0.11	0.10	0.09	0.11	0.11	0.13
Total Southwest apprehensions	1.00	1.00	1.00	1.00	1.00	1.00	1.00	1.00	1.00	1.00	1.00

Note: Despite an overall slowing of migration, the Tucson Sector continues to have the highest crossing rate. Data from www.cbp.gov

highest fatality rate, Arizona continues to be the preferred crossing point for those who would rather risk the desert than attempt to cross elsewhere along the border where drug cartel violence toward migrants has been escalating (Slack and Whiteford 2011:11). Recent research by Slack and Whiteford (2011) suggests that increased attacks against migrants, high death rates, and anti-immigrant sentiment have done little to deter those still desperate enough to undertake an Arizona crossing in hopes of finding work in a failing and hostile U.S. economy. Others have shown that deportation programs such as the Alien Transfer and Exit Program may be transporting people to Sonora where crossing the desert is the only option (De León in press).

This analysis centers on the act of crossing from Northern Sonora into Arizona. It is, however, important to highlight that undocumented migration is a complex process that extends far beyond the border region. There are key planning stages and social networks involved, which often include contracting a coyote from a person's home community (usu. through kinship networks) and relying on money from relatives already in the United States to pay for the cost of transport (Spener 2009:166–171). Spener's (2009) work on the relationship between coyotes and migrants in south Texas provides insight into both the complexities of the human smuggling business and the strategies that people use to find a reliable guide. Although Spener and others (e.g., Parks et al. 2009) have shown that in many instances coyotes are important resources for undertaking a safe and successful crossing, these analyses have not focused on Arizona where the natural environment and social conditions are more difficult and increasingly more dangerous (Slack and Whiteford 2011:16). In addition, the relationship between migrants and coyotes has been recently complicated by the increasing involvement of drug cartels in human smuggling, coyotes who work in cahoots with bajadores, a rise in migrants from some of the poorest parts of Central America and Southern Mexico who cannot afford to contract more expensive community-based coyotes, and systematic attempts by Bor der Patrol to use lateral deportation to separate migrants from their previously contracted coyotes. More than ever before, it is common to see migrants arrive in Nogales (either through lateral deportation or by choice) and contract a local guide who is more likely to rob or abandon them in the desert.

Given the rising anti-immigrant sentiment currently being felt across the United States, it seems unlikely that comprehensive immigration reform will somehow precede improvements in the domestic economy. Moreover, the strategies of border control that are currently in place will likely continue (or escalate) as we approach an election year when politicians often pander to the recurring public perception held by many that the borders of the United States are "out of control" (Nevins 2002:62–94). This emphasis on border security has long been an effective political smoke screen that diverts attention away from economic and foreign policy issues (Andreas 2009). In 2011, the Obama administration deported 396,906 people, the most in Immigration and Customs Enforcement history (McCombs 2011b). Many of these deportees were nonviolent offenders, people with long histories in the United States, and those brought to the country as children. While visiting Nogales in the summer of 2011, I was struck by the number of people I encountered who had been deported after many years of living in the United States and who were now about to undertake a first desert crossing. This rise in deportations of long-time undocumented residents and young adults raised in the United States indicates that immigration enforcement policies are now creating a new type of undocumented migration stream that is fundamentally different from previous generations in terms of life histories, as well as general awareness and preparedness for a desert crossing. My focus on the relationship between migrants and the meager tools at their disposal to survive the desert thus has important implications for understanding the day-to-day experiences of the thousands of people who, despite the current U.S. economic crisis, are still attempting to cross the desert (see Table 1) and how their experiences are linked to and continuously shaped by broad-scale forms of immigration enforcement policy. The hypersuffering that now characterizes the crossing process is likely to continue even once the U.S. economy improves and migration flows increase, suggesting that for the next several years, hundreds of thousands of people will continue to enter the desert and experience many of the difficulties described in this article.

Migrant Material Culture

As the PTD strategy began to shift undocumented migration toward the deserts of Arizona in the 1990s, the human smuggling industry in Northern Mexico grew to deal with the influx of migrants to the region. Sleepy agricultural towns such as Altar soon became major staging areas for hundreds of thousands of border crossers who arrived each year. Subsequently, coyotes, vendors, and local manufacturers began to capitalize on migrants who needed guide services, temporary housing, food, and equipment. In Altar, smuggling has become a major industry, and many outdoor vendors and convenience stores now specialize in the goods used by migrants (see Figure 3). Crossings are typically chaotic, and people often have very little control over what will happen to them. One of the few things they can control is what they choose to carry into the desert. Vendors exploit migrant fears and anxieties by selling them a variety of goods at elevated prices under the promise that they are essential for a safe crossing. In this case, desperation, folk logic, and predatory entrepreneurism play major roles in shaping consumer decisions about what to purchase. I refer to the complex of smugglers, criminals, vendors, and manufacturers who profit by robbing and selling products and services to migrants as the *Border Crossing Industry*. This industry and its associated goods are constantly evolving as migrants, smugglers, and vendors attempt to adjust to changes in enforcement practices and surveillance technology.

Over the years, desert crossing has become associated with a material culture that includes a codified set of darkly colored (sometimes camouflage) clothing (see Figure 3), cheaply made sneakers and hiking boots, consumables, and other accessories. Consumables include bottled water, electrolyte beverages, and high

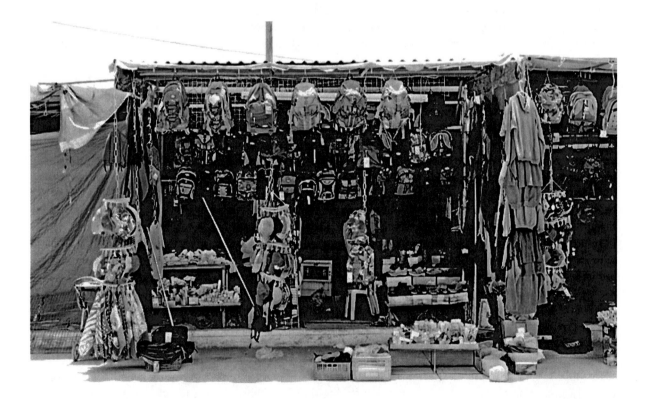

FIGURE 3. Vendor in Altar, Sonora, Mexico that specializes in migrant goods. Photograph by Michael Wells.

salt content foods (e.g., canned tuna and salted crackers). Additionally, people equip themselves with first-aid and utilitarian items such as gauze, pain relievers, and pocket mirrors used to signal Border Patrol in case a rescue is needed. These items are carried in small darkly colored or camouflage backpacks that once filled can weigh upward of 50 pounds. These goods foremost reflect technological attempts to avoid Border Patrol and cope with the dangerous conditions in the desert. However, these items can also create physical and social problems for those who use them. To illuminate the complex (and often-contradictory) aspects of migrant goods, I use a theoretical framework that emphasizes the role of technology, as well as the dialectical and somatic relationships between people and objects. This approach allows for a better understanding of the forces that have shaped migrant technology, the techniques associated with different objects, how these objects "act" in personal and public domains, and how these items come to be embedded with the traces of human suffering. Below, I briefly discuss each of these components of my approach.

Technology is a fundamental aspect of the human condition that is interwoven into the very fabric of our lives and implicated in all forms of cultural development (past, present, and future) (Mackenzie and Wajcman 1999:3–27). Reductionist views of technology have tended to focus either on the tools themselves or their "effectiveness" relative to other technologies (Lemmonier 1986:150). Some of the most innovative studies of techniques (i.e., technology or technical processes) have shown that material objects are but one (and not always necessary [Downing 2007]) element of complex technical systems that also include action and cognition (Lemmonier 1986:147–148). To understand how objects are appropriated and employed in the context of border crossing, I draw on technological studies by Alfred Gell (1988) and Bryan Pfaffenberger (1992). Gell points out that minimally "technology not only consists of the artefacts which are employed as tools, but also includes the sum total of the kinds of knowledge which make possible the invention, making, and use of tools" (1988:6). Analyses should thus neither focus primarily on an object's characteristics or its effectiveness at achieving a particular task. Tools cannot be studied in isolation because the knowledge needed to materialize them and employ them in set tasks is fundamentally connected to (and shaped by) the specific social context in which they exist (1988:6). This means that migrant technology may involve commonly found objects such as shoes and water bottles, but their exact use can only be understood in the context of clandestine crossings. Pfaffenberger (1992:497) refers to these distinct contexts of technological activity as *sociotechnical systems* and argues that they derive from the linkage of techniques (e.g., operational sequences, behavioral patterns, knowledge) and material culture to the social coordination of labor. In this case, the technology and social coordination of labor are directed at helping migrants cross the desert undetected. In addition to contextualizing technological activity to understand how people make decisions about what to use and how to use it, I also draw on theories that focus on techniques of the body (e.g., Mauss 1973; Wacquant 1995) and the relationship between the body and objects (e.g., Bordieu 1977:72–95; Downey 2007:215). Pfaffenberger acknowledges that a key aspect of any sociotechnical system is human action, but his approach is missing a more detailed analysis of the physical techniques involved in object use. My framework gives equal footing to the context and underlying factors that create a sociotechnical system, as well as the bodily techniques involved in the technological deployment of objects in the system. This allows not only for a better understanding of how technologies arise but also the dynamic relationship between objects and the human body. I use *Border Crossing Sociotechnical System* (BCSS) to refer to the nexus of social, economic, legal, political, and scientific factors that have shaped the BCI as well as the subsequent social processes, technologies, and bodily techniques of desert crossing.

In the following discussion, I demonstrate that the decisions to adopt particular techniques and objects result from the influence and logic of the BCSS. For migrants, it is often the perceived efficacy (i.e., folk logic) that drives the selection of certain types of goods, which can sometimes be ineffective or detrimental. However, my point is not that migrant technology is illogical. As Pfaffenberger points out:

> That a sociotechnical system develops does not imply that it is a logical system, or the only possible system, that could have developed under the circumstances; social choice, tactics, alternative techniques, and the social redefinition of needs and aspirations all play a role in the rise of sociotechnical systems. [1992:499]

Instead, my focus on technology and its impacts on migrants allows for a better understanding of the social dimensions of how this particular set of techniques is used in the context of crossing and how these techniques are assessed by migrants. Similar to Wacquant's (1995:85) finding that the boxing universe has its own internal logic that may appear irrational to outsiders, the migrant techniques presented here can neither be judged or subject to critical evaluation that blames individuals for using what often appear to be contradictory or somatically damaging practices. Although I am interested in how material culture (mis) functions at the individual level of use and how collectively these goods have the unintended (or at least unwanted) consequence of serving as markers of illegality, my intent is to highlight the dialectical relationship between people and objects and to examine the blurry line between the two (Keane 2006b).

Two decades of research on material culture has demonstrated that objects have social lives (e.g., Appadurai 1986), agency (e.g., Hoskins 2006), and can oppress users (e.g., Latour 1992). My analysis draws on the concept of objectification (Tilley 1996), which posits a dialectical relationship between people and material culture whereby we create objects to improve our capacity as humans and these objects can develop their own autonomy, which may eventually come to oppress us (Miller 2010:59). Whether it is the high fencing and cameras at urban ports of entry that shift migrant streams toward more remote border regions, the motion sensors and unmanned aerial drone planes that detect migrants, or the harsh desert that is used as a geographic deterrent, the bulk of the surveillance and deterrent technologies used along the U.S.–Mexico boundary are inherently oppressive to the flow of undocumented people. Like the panopticon, these specific technologies require very little human input to do their jobs effectively. However, it is not just law enforcement technologies that oppress migrants. The seemingly ordinary objects that have been co-opted for crossings have also come to negatively impact migrants but in more subtle, less obvious manners. This objectification is visible in the ways that migrants try to use objects to improve their personal capacity to avoid detection and survive the desert while simultaneously adopting a uniform set of goods that increases stress on their bodies and publicly marks them as vulnerable and "illegal" to others.

An analysis of the personal and public qualities of migrant material culture allows us to understand both how people conceptualize border surveillance technology and how their adoption of certain goods "makes possible or inhibits new practices, habits, and intentions" (Keane 2006a:193). This framework provides insight into why material culture (e.g., dark clothing) that has negative impacts on people's bodies and social interactions continues to be used by migrants over time. Karen Hansen notes:

> The subjective and social experiences of dress are not always mutually supportive but contradict one another or collide. The contingent dynamic between these two experiences of dress gives rise to considerable ambiguity, ambivalence, and, therefore, uncertainty and debate over dress. Dress becomes a flash point of conflicting values, fueling contests in historical encounters, in interactions across class, between genders and generations, and in recent global cultural and economic exchanges. [2004:372].

Focusing on the conflicting role of migrant material culture is fertile ground for improving our knowledge about the social process of border crossing, as well as the embodied experiences of migrants. As part of this analysis, I argue that migrant-specific habitus (Spener 2009:226–229) in the form of routinized physical suffering can be gleaned from detailed studies of migrant artifact classes and how they were used or modified. In particular, I employ the archaeological concept of "use-wear" (i.e., modifications made to objects as a result of usage) to provide a more intimate understanding of the somatic relationship between people and objects. Studies of artifact use-wear and discard show how the repeated patterning of empty water bottles, worn out shoes, and sweat-drenched clothes reflect years of individual and collective suffering in the desert. Migrant habitus is not only represented in the traces of human activity embedded in individual artifacts but also in the long-term systematic use of particular objects associated with the alleviation of suffering that derives from exposure to the desert environment (e.g., pain medication, gauze). In the following sections, I describe three classes of commonly used artifacts (water bottles, shoes, and clothes), highlight the technique and logic behind their use, and document the somatic and social effects these goods have on people.

Water Bottles

By far the most ubiquitous artifact type found at migrant stations is the water bottle. This is no surprise given that the leading cause of migration-related injuries and death are now linked to hyperthermia (failed thermoregulation caused by exposure to excessive temperature) (GAO 2006:15). Outside of avoiding heat and exposure to the sun (often an impossibility in the desert), the only way to combat this problem is through the continued consumption of water and other hydrating liquids. In no uncertain terms, bottled water is what keeps people alive.

Most of the water purchased by migrants is bottled locally in one of the many plants in Northern Mexico that cater primarily to this transitory population. In Altar alone (population approx. 9,000) there are at least six water bottling plants, all of which produce the typical plastic one gallon rounded jug that is commonly used by migrants (see Figure 4a). Migrants favor this style because its large handle and thick walls make it durable and easier to carry on long walks. This vessel style is not typically used by U.S. water companies, making it easy to distinguish country of manufacture based on bottle shape alone. Prior to 2009, all of the one gallon Mexican bottles were manufactured using either clear or white opaque plastic. For many years migrants either painted these bottles black or fashioned covers out of plastic, burlap, or cloth (see Figure 4b-c) in an attempt to camouflage the object from Border Patrol. A common assumption is that white bottles are a disadvantage. As one person stated: "We got caught on the first night of our trip because Border Patrol saw the light reflecting off of a water bottle." Toward the end of 2009, companies began to produce one gallon bottles out of black plastic (see Figure 4d), a sign that technological changes at the factory level were the direct result of migrant preferences. However, agents working on the ground primarily rely on sign cutting (i.e., foot tracking), ground sensors, infrared cameras, and sound to locate people, suggesting that it is unlikely that darkly colored bottles provide a strong tactical advantage. The insistence by migrants (and border vendors) that camouflaged bottles help you avoid detection probably reflects a combination of people's lack of understanding about current surveillance technology, as well as entrepreneurial attempts to capitalize on migrant folk logic. In

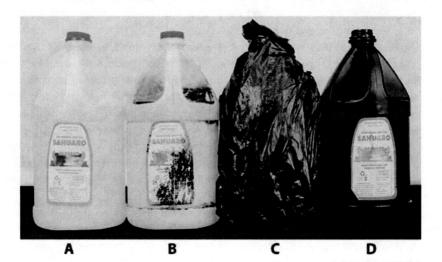

FIGURE 4. A) One gallon white bottle. B) Bottle with plastic cover. C) Bottle that was once painted black with shoe polish. D) Black plastic bottle.

FIGURE 5. A) Santo Niño de Atocha is a Latino version of the Christ child who is thought to assist travelers on journeys. B) A bottle from the Santo Niño de Atocha factory in Altar, Sonora, Mexico.

addition to specialized color and shape, many company brand names overtly target migrant consumers and their religious beliefs. For example, one company in Altar is called "Santo Niño de Atocha" and their label features a drawing of the Latino version of the Christ child believed to assist pilgrims on dangerous journeys (Thompson 1994; see Figure 5). To an observer familiar with the BCI (incl. Border Patrol), the shape, color, and labels on these bottles are easily recognized as both being manufactured in Northern Mexico and linked to undocumented migration.

Technique and Logic

Although human water needs range widely depending on metabolism, climate, diet, clothing, and activity level (Sawka et al. 2005:31–33), estimates of the average U.S. Adequate Intake (AI) (i.e., the level of daily water consumption needed to prevent the deleterious effects of dehydration) are approximately 3.7 liters and 2.7 liters for middle-age men and women, respectively (Institute of Medicine 2004:73).[3] However, this AI is likely insufficient for desert environments where studies have shown male soldiers losing an average of 4.9 liters of water a day from sweating alone (2004:4–11). Some postulate that active adults in warm climates have a daily water need of six liters (Sawka et. al 2005:32), a conservative estimate for those doing intense desert hiking. If we use six liters as a minimum AI for adults walking several miles a day during hot summer months, a person would need to consume approximately 1.6 gallons a day to prevent dehydration. If someone walks for three days, which is the approximate time it takes to get from the border to one of the common rendezvous locations in southern Arizona (e.g., Three Points) (see Figure 2), they minimally need to carry 4.8 gallons. A gallon of water weighs 8.35 pounds, which means that someone carrying four gallons starts their trip with 33.4lbs of liquid. This weight would be augmented by food, extra clothes, and other supplies. Based on my observations and interviews, the maximum amount of water an adult can carry is four gallons, with many opting to bring between one and two (see Figure 6a).

Migrants typically never carry enough water to sustain themselves on a multiday crossing, and this is influenced by several factors. First, many crossers are unfamiliar with desert environments and greatly underestimate how much water they will need to consume to avoid hyperthermia or dehydration. This is often exacerbated by conflicting information they may be told by their coyote (who almost always underestimates the actual distance that will be walked), stories they have been told by other migrants who crossed

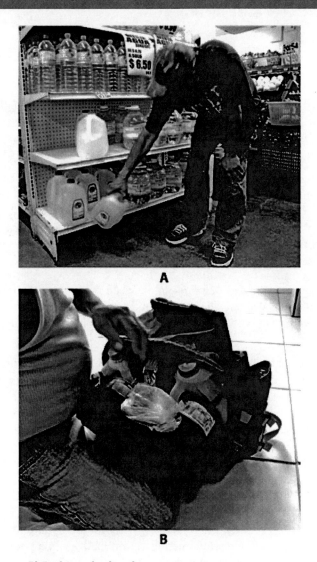

FIGURE 6. A) Shopping for water. B) Packing a backpack.

with little water, or a person's inability to purchase water. The amount of water a person carries is also influenced by their physical (in)ability to carry multiple gallons, the size of their backpack, and how much other gear they are carrying (see Figure 6b). In an excerpt from a typical interview with a person preparing to cross, they talk about the difficulty of carrying water:

> I'm bringing one gallon of water. I know it is not enough, but water is really heavy. I can't carry more than one gallon. Look at my bag [points to a small duffel bag] . . . I don't want to drink too much water before I leave . . . I don't want to get a cramp . . . I just take little sips of my bottle and hope that I find more water along the way if I run out.

Those who find gallon bottles too heavy or expensive will opt for smaller sizes (ranging from 500 milliliters to 1.5 liters). It is common to see people traveling with less than one gallon of water in their packs, and the high density of small bottles found at migrant stations suggests that this is a widespread trend.

Somatic Impacts

Having insufficient water for a crossing inevitably creates physiological stress, and the majority of people I interviewed who spent more than a day in the desert described suffering from various effects of hyperthermia:

> I thought I was going to die out there . . . I couldn't take it. My heart was pounding and I started to see things. I was delirious. I was hallucinating. I was looking at the trees but I was seeing houses and cities all around me . . . I would stop and take a small drink of water but five minutes later I would see things again . . . I only brought a gallon of water with me. [Raul, 36 years old]

Additional water sources for those who run out are limited in the desert. Although some humanitarian groups maintain permanent water tanks and water drop locations for migrants, these sites are few and far between. Those who run out of water often rely on stagnant ponds or bacterialaden water tanks used for livestock, if they are "lucky" enough to encounter one (see Figure 7a). This practice is archaeologically visible via use-wear on refilled bottles (see Figure 7b). Moreover, many commented that drinking this water causes intestinal illness and increased dehydration:

> We crossed with another man who was 62 years old. He couldn't handle it. He drank some water from a cattle tank that made him sick. Well, we all drank it but he got an infection. The water had little animals swimming in it but we were so thirsty. . . . He started vomiting and had diarrhea so we took him back into Mexico.

Even if you have enough water to stay hydrated, it may heat to a temperature that renders it virtually undrinkable. During the summer of 2010, as part of the UMP field school, University of Washington undergraduate student Steven Ritchey conducted an experiment to test the temperature differential between white and black bottles. He filled both types with water and exposed them to direct sunlight over the course of a typical summer day. Measurements of the internal temperature of the water in each bottle were taken at one hour intervals, along with the corresponding external air temperature (see Figure 8). The results showed that within the first hour, the black bottle's temperature eclipsed both ambient temperature and the white bottle. By 12:30 p.m., the temperature differential between bottles reached 15 degrees (black bottle = 121.8 °F, white bottle = 106.8 °F). The black bottle would eventually heat to 126.3 °F, 6.3 degrees higher than the recommended temperature setting for a domestic water heater. Drinking hot water raises a person's core temperature forcing the body to expend additional energy to cool the hot liquid. This can increase exhaustion levels even if the liquid is consumed while resting. Additionally, gulping hot water in the desert is not only unpleasant but also sometimes physically difficult.

A   **B**

FIGURE 7. A) Filling up bottles at a cattle tank. B) Recovered bottle filled with green cattle tank water.

Water Bottle Temperature Comparison

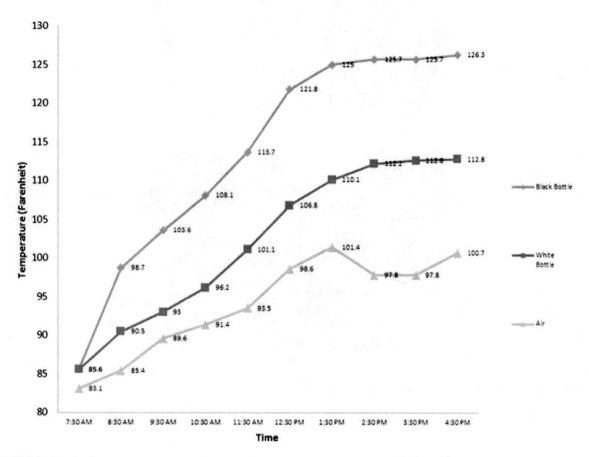

FIGURE 8. Results from an experiment comparing the water temperature in white and black plastic bottles (Courtesy of Steven Ritchey).

Shoes

Because of their close connection to the body and their ability to maintain shape even when the wearer is absent, shoes are an artifact class whose physical properties are strongly tied to those who once wore them. For example, in museum contexts they are often used as "stand-ins" for those who cannot be physically present. However, making shoes metonyms for people or their embodied experiences can be ethically questionable (Jones 2001) and theoretically reductionistic. I argue that the hundreds of shoes recovered by the UMP that belonged to women, children, and men are an important artifact class. However, instead of functioning as metonyms for migrants, these objects provide phenomenological insight (via use-wear) into the dialectical relationship between people (in this case their feet) and the desert.

The shoes most commonly worn by migrants are inexpensive Chinese-or Mexican-made sneakers, usually replicas of higher priced U.S. models (see Figure 9). These shoes are often ill-fitting, poorly constructed, and generally not wellsuited for rugged desert hiking (see Figure 10). They offer little ankle support, have hard rubber bottoms that easily wear through, and have soles that frequently detach from their leather or plastic uppers. It is common for people to carry an extra pair of shoes (in case their first pair breaks) and

FIGURE 9. New pairs of men and women sneakers typically worn by migrants.

FIGURE 10. Climbing over rocky terrain in sneakers.

super glue for ad hoc repairs. Sneakers are common, but those who cannot afford them or who choose to wear something more familiar will attempt to cross the desert in styles including cowboy boots, dress shoes, cheap hiking boots, and traditional sandals.

Technique and Logic

Most migrants cannot afford high-end hiking boots, but their preference for sneakers is not a simple economic issue. Individuals may be familiar with hiking boots, but opt for sneakers because they have never worn hiking boots, they believe that sneakers are more appropriate for the desert, or they choose to wear the shoe style they think will both get them through the desert and stylistically help them blend in once in the United States. It is not uncommon to see Mexican and Central Americans crossing the desert with fresh haircuts and new sneakers. Many undocumented migrants assume that the best way to avoid detection is to "not look poor," a strategy that can backfire. I once observed a Mexican immigration official board a bus in Chiapas and single out and remove a group of Central American migrants whose new wardrobes, fresh haircuts, and shiny sneakers caused them to stand out against the rest of the passengers who appeared to be working-class, underdressed Mexicans. Although sneakers may be the most accessible and culturally preferred type of footwear for migrants, their use in the desert has harmful impacts on people's feet.

Somatic Impact

Friction blisters are subdermal pockets of fluid caused by forceful rubbing. After hyperthermia-related injuries, blisters on feet are the most common physical trauma experienced by migrants (see Figure 11). During normal long-distance hiking these injuries can be caused by poorly conditioned feet, ill-fitting shoes and socks, improper footwear, heat, and moisture, all of which are typical conditions for border crossers. Migrant blister problems are exacerbated by cheaply made shoes (esp. if they are not "broken in"), a person's failure to recognize and adequately treat the early stages of a blister, and unhygienic desert conditions that can lead to infection. Migrants who employ a guide are often at the mercy of their coyote who typically dictates if and

FIGURE 11. A woman having her blisters bandaged after a failed desert crossing.

when the group can stop and rest. Additionally, Border Patrol's relentless pursuit of migrants by air and land, combined with a person's desperation to cross the border, may lead people to ignore foot and other injuries until they can no longer walk. By the time people get a chance to change their shoes, socks, or apply first-aid, their blisters may have become severe. Indirect evidence of this foot trauma is visible archaeologically in the bloody socks, gauze, and worn out shoes (see Figure 12) that are often recovered at migrant stations located several days walk from the border. Those who develop severe blisters sometimes only stop walking once they are captured by Border Patrol or when their feet literally give out. This extreme walking behavior is logical if one considers that many who undertake crossings are escaping some of the most impoverished communities in Latin America (and beyond) or trying to return home to their families in the United States at any cost, even death. I've witnessed this desperation when I have encountered people in the desert who were suffering from extreme dehydration, excruciating blisters, and life-threatening injuries but had to be thoroughly convinced to go to the hospital to avoid impending death.

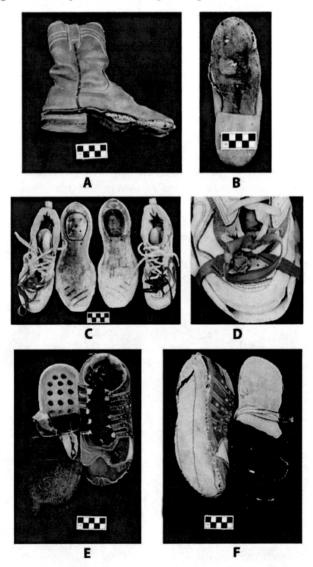

FIGURE 12. Shoes with use-wear. A-B) A child's cowboy boot with hole worn through the sole. C-D) A woman's sneaker with detached soles. A red bra strap was used to refasten the two parts. E-F) Shoe with detached sole that the user has attempted to re-connect with a sock and binding from a t-shirt.

Clothing

Recent anthropological studies of clothing have focused on the dialectical relationship between people and the objects with which they adorn their bodies (Miller 2010:12–41). Moving beyond previous semiotic studies of clothing that tended to emphasize the ways in which these items represented differences (e.g., class), these new analyses highlight the active and substantial role that dress plays in creating and shaping peoples experiences and determining what constitutes the self (e.g., Banerjee and Miller 2003). For example, in her study of sarongs in Eastern Indonesia, Catherine Allerton (2007:25–37) found that they are intimately tied to the wearer's body and bodily substances while also projecting messages that are interpreted by the outside world. Here I demonstrate a similar pattern whereby the clothing adopted by migrants for clandestine crossings impacts their bodies and simultaneously sends messages to others about their social and juridical status.

Migrants typically wear darkly colored clothes, usually black T-shirts, dark denim jeans, and dark sweatshirts (see Figure 13b). These items either come from a person's wardrobe or are bought from border vendors. Unlike specialty hiking clothes that are designed with lightweight fabric for optimal ventilation and quick drying, most migrants wear clothes constructed with thick cotton, synthetic fibers, or denim. These clothes are heavy, absorb heat and moisture, and are not well-suited for desert environments or hiking. This apparel is usually supplemented with dark socks and shoes, as well as black, blue, or camouflage backpacks (see Figure 13a).

Technique and Logic

Similar to black bottles, dark clothing is thought to be an effective form of camouflage, especially when walking at night or when resting in shaded areas during the day. However, as previously noted, most of the methods Border Patrol uses to detect migrants rely on remote sensing, signcutting, and infrared. A description of the infrared thermal imaging used by Border Patrol suggests that dark clothing is useless against (and may actually assist) this surveillance technology:

> All objects that are not at absolute zero temperature emit various types of electromagnetic radiation including infrared. The hotter an object gets, the more infrared radiation is emitted.... Blacker colors and duller surfaces usually have a higher emissivity and radiate infrared energy more effectively.... Due to their own levels of infrared heat energy, people are easily seen 24 hours a day. [Mesenbrink 2001]

Somatic Impacts

Dark clothes absorb more heat, which can raise a person's core temperature and increase the rate of dehydration and heat-related exhaustion. Compounding the issue of heat absorption is the added weight of thick insulated clothes and a heavy backpack along with the low moisture permeability of material such as denim. Together, these factors contribute to increased physiological strain in the form of more wetted skin, higher skin temperatures, and greater general discomfort. This stress is often seen in the recovered clothes and backpacks that emit intense perspiration odor and display large, crystalline sweat stains.

The physical stress caused by wearing dark clothes impacts people individually, but for migrants as a group these clothes create the unwanted signal that a person is a border crosser. Border Patrol agents I have spoken with commented that when using remote cameras or visual spotting techniques they can easily distinguish among hikers, narco-traffickers, and migrants based on a combination of phenotype, clothing style, backpacks, water bottles, and behavior. In essence, walking through the desert wearing dark clothing arouses suspicion. My personal tendency to wear dark clothes and a large backpack while conducting archaeological surveys has repeatedly caused me to be *dusted* by Border Patrol helicopters and stopped and questioned by agents on the ground.[4] It is not just agents who read signals from migrant clothing. Both the bajadores who assault migrants in the desert and the criminals who prey on recently deported people at ports of entry use clothing as an indentifying characteristic when selecting their victims (De León in press).

FIGURE 13. A) and B) Migrants wearing dark clothes.

Discussion

Despite repeated use over many years, the migrant techniques and goods described here are at best minimally effective at helping someone avoid detection and at worst somatically and socially injurious. In essence, the paradox of objectification (Miller 2010:59) is visible in the contradictions created by the reliance on particular types of water bottles, shoes, and clothing that often do more harm than good: the black water bottles that marginally help someone avoid being seen while simultaneously heating up its life-saving contents to an almost undrinkable temperature; the cheap sneakers that migrants assume will be suitable for hiking but eventually rip apart while traversing a rocky and thorny terrain, but not before causing excruciating blisters; the dark clothing that is supposed to provide camouflage but is useless against Border Patrol's sophisticated technologies and instead raises the body's core temperature and helps speed up the dehydration process. Close inspection of these objects shows how each betrays their user in different ways. When examined collectively as an archaeological assemblage that goes back as far as the 1990s, a pattern of use-wear emerges that is indicative of routinized and intense human suffering resultant from millions of systematic attempts to overcome institutionalized enforcement practices. If we look at migrant material culture from the perspective of those who encounter border crossers and read the messages encoded in their quasi-uniforms, we see that the clothes, water bottles, and cheap sneakers further betray people by broadcasting their vulnerability to those seeking to either apprehend or assault them.

In their seminal paper on border crossing, Singer and Massey argued that border crossing is a "well-defined social process whereby migrants draw upon various sources of human and social capital to overcome barriers erected by U.S. authorities" (1998:562). People accrue *migration-specific capital* (i.e., the human and social capital gained from the crossing experience such as where, when, and how to cross) during each attempt, and as this capital increases so does one's likelihood of success (1998:569). Others have since confirmed these findings (e.g., Spener 2009). The question then arises: If migrants accumulate knowledge during each crossing attempt, why do the seemingly negative or ineffective techniques described here continue to be replicated? The answer to this question is not straightforward and requires a dissection of the many factors that shape the BCSS.

Border crossers, even first-timers, are often aware of the general obstacles involved in the process. Still, this phenomenon is chaotic and rife with physical and emotional difficulties that can make focusing on the minutia of material culture quite challenging. The tendency to downplay or ignore material culture in this setting relates to what Miller calls the "humility of things":

> Objects are important, not because they are evident and physically constrain or enable, but quite the opposite. It is often precisely because we do not *see* them. The less we are aware of them, the more powerfully they can determine our expectations, by setting the scene and ensuring our appropriate behavior, without being open to challenge. They determine what takes place to the extent that we are unconscious of their capacity to do so. [2010:50].

Among those facing injury and death, the failure to recognize the negative impact of black water bottles or cheap sneakers is not only excusable but also expected.

Additionally, the ineffectiveness of different types of techniques can be subtle and difficult to disentangle from the general chaos, violence, and suffering of border crossing. Migrants already expect the process to be miserable, and the fact that one technique might add additional discomfort can be easily overlooked. Moreover, the ephemeral nature of border crossing communities and the diversity of individuals involved in the process (e.g., migrants from different ethnic and economic backgrounds) means that there is often little regulation of folk knowledge and a great deal of mythology about what the process is like. One only needs to spend an hour talking with a group of recently deported migrants to hear a wide range of crossing techniques that range from "rational" (e.g., drinking a lot of water) to preposterous (e.g., a person once told me he almost evaded Border Patrol in the dark by walking on all fours and pretending to be a wild animal). Migrants often lack the means to critically evaluate and test different techniques in the desert, and many will often accept that certain technologies are effective (even if they are not) because they see others using them. The BCSS has its own internal logic that is difficult to critique from within the system. Furthermore, the BCSS is not strongly regulated, and misinformation can both easily be incorporated into and perpetuated by the system. A migrant's crossing success is strongly determined by tenacity and luck (Cornelius et al. 2008), which means many have been able to cross despite their use of seemingly harmful techniques.

Conclusion

This article provides insight into the complexities and conflicts of the material culture and techniques that hundreds of thousands of undocumented migrants rely on each year during dangerous border crossings. This material culture has been shaped by 20 years of institutionalized enforcement practices that have funneled people toward the Sonoran Desert, by the human smuggling industry that profits by responding to and overcoming changes in border security strategies, and by the migrants who for many years only needed to evade Border Patrol and survive the lethal desert gauntlet before being welcomed through the literal and figurative backdoors of low-wage labor markets in the United States. The recent rise in deportations and state-based anti-immigration laws directed at policing the undocumented labor force suggest that things are going to get worse for migrants before they get better, and it remains to be seen whether the rate of border crossings will rise if and when the U.S. economy improves. Although apprehensions are at an all-time low, there are still thousands of both impoverished migrants and recently deported long-time undocumented residents who are entering the desert. This dynamic nexus of suffering, politics, economics, and contradictions continues to shape the BCSS today.

My analysis has focused on the dialectical relationship between migrants and their material culture to highlight that these objects and technology: (1) are fundamentally connected to (and shaped by) the BCSS, (2) are formalized and have a clear technological purpose, (3) are logical within the context of the BCSS but often have conflicting somatic impacts, and (4) emit social messages at every stage of the crossing process. I have shown that people's perceptions about the functionality and efficacy of particular goods are often in direct conflict with the social and somatic impacts associated with the use of those of objects. In many instances, migrant material culture is profoundly oppressive and often runs counter to the goals of avoiding detection and surviving the desert. However, migrants have limited economic means to purchase equipment that would make their trip more bearable. People make conscious decisions to purchase and use certain goods because they are relatively affordable, they are rational based on the collective knowledge associated with the crossing process (influenced by vendors, coyotes, and previous migrants), and the sometimes dysfunctional nature of different techniques is camouflaged by a host of factors that make the crossing experience a chaotic setting where no one particular object or behavior will ensure success. Many have either been caught or lost their lives because of ineffective or harmful techniques, but millions of others have successfully crossed with little water and cheap sneakers.

I have focused on the techniques, as well as the oppressiveness of migrant material culture. My intent has not been to provide evidence that all undocumented migrants are easily identifiable based on what they wear and carry but, rather, that in the Sonoran Desert, one can expect to find a relatively uniform collection of material culture that reflects a specific group's set of techniques used to overcome border enforcement. To declare that migrants can somehow be identified solely on shoes or clothes foolishly ignores the complex and dominant role that racial profiling plays in border enforcement. Simply put, the primary measure Border Patrol uses to identify suspected undocumented migrants is phenotype. You only need to ask "documented" Latinos who live in southern Arizona what arouses suspicion at immigration checkpoints to understand that one's skin color, last name, and accent supersede clothing or shoes. The study presented here should also not be seen as an attempt to offer insight into how to avoid detection. No technology that is readily accessible to impoverished border crossers could ever hope to match the level of sophisticated machinery that is used to detect and capture people. The best that any migrant technique can hope to accomplish is assuage some of the suffering experienced in the desert and possibly help someone avoid an untimely death. Although I have highlighted some of the conflicts associated with migrant techniques, future research will need to address the contradictions of Border Patrol surveillance technologies that are relatively ineffective in "deterring" people from migrating but highly successful in making the crossing process more miserable and dangerous.

Intensified border enforcement, increases in violence associated with border crossing, and more punitive measures directed at apprehended migrants have all made it more difficult for undocumented Latinos to work in the United States on a temporary or seasonal basis over the last two decades. As a result, the undocumented Latino work force is now more permanently settled (Massey et al. 2002) and less likely to voluntarily return to Mexico periodically. Today those who successfully cross the desert are well aware of the magnitude of this accomplishment. Two months after I watched him and Miguel walk into a dark tunnel on the outskirts of Nogales, I caught up with Victor and asked him how he finally entered the United States (see Figure 14):

> We walked for five days. . . . We ran out of food and spent the last two days without anything to eat. . . .
> I got very sick from walking so far. My blood pressure dropped very low while I was trying to climb out of a

FIGURE 14. Victor and his backpack. Photograph by Michael Wells.

wash. . . . We ran out of water but were able to find a cattle tank. . . . The water was very dirty but we drank it anyways. . . . We ended up throwing away our backpacks and our extra clothes on the fourth day. We put all our water into one backpack and took turns carrying it for a few hours at a time. . . . In the end I think we walked more than 60 miles. This was my fifth time trying to cross the desert and I finally made it. . . . I keep this backpack as a memento of that last trip.

Notes

Acknowledgments. Parts of this research were funded by the National Science Foundation (Award # 0939554), the University of Washington's Royalty Research Fund, and the University of Michigan. I wish to thank Bob Kee, Michael Wells, Jackson Hathorn, Aaron and Madeline Naumann, Ran Boytner and the Institute for Field Research, Consuelo Crow, Robyn Dennis and the Center for Advanced Spatial Technology at the University of Arkansas, and all of the students who participated in the 2010 field school. Special thanks to Steven Ritchey whose data on water bottle temperatures were used in the article and Michael Wells for Figures 3 and 14. In addition, Hannah DeRose-Wilson, Emma Duross, Anna Forringer, Sarah Rybak, and Joia Sanders assisted with the laboratory analysis and photography of artifacts. María Inclán proofread the Spanish abstract. The archaeological field work could not have been carried out without the help and support of the many residents of Arivaca including Fern Robinson, Penny and Steve Shepard, Maggie and Rich Milinovitch, Shaun Quintero, Ronnie, Uncle Jojo, and everyone at the La Gitana Cantina. The ethnographic fieldwork could not have been carried out without the support of Doña Hilda and Don Paco Loureido at the Albergue Juan Bosco migrant shelter in Nogales. I am indebted to my friends Chapo, Chava, Eric, Polo, Netchy, Fernando, and Panchito who introduced me to La Linea and whose stories are interwoven into this narrative. This article has greatly benefited from feedback from several people. First, I am indebted to my wonderful wife, Abigail Bigham, who read many drafts of this article from start to finish. Kirk French, María Elena García, Anthony Graesch, and José Antonio Lucero provided comments on an early draft of this article. University of Michigan graduate students and faculty provided feedback on this article through the Anthro-History Program's writing workshop. I wish to thank the four anonymous reviewers whose insightful comments and critiques significantly improved the quality and coherence of this piece. I also want to thank Tom Boellstorff at *American Anthropologist* for all of the editorial comments and assistance in translating the reviewer comments into major themes that made the revising process immensely easier. Any mistakes or omissions in the final product are my own. Finally, this work would not have been possible without the help and trust of the many people I have met along the border who have graciously shared their powerful stories with me. Although I cannot name them here, I have tried to repay their generosity by doing my best to accurately document what they experience on a daily basis. Gracias.

1. All names are pseudonyms.
2. Conditions during other seasons such as winter can also be extreme and many people have died from exposure to freezing temperatures. Compared to the summer, the experiences of those crossing during the winter are less known and warrant further research.
3. One liter equals 0.26 gallons.
4. Dusting is a tactical maneuver whereby helicopters descend on migrants in the desert and attempt to blind and disorient them by kicking up dust with their propeller blades.

References Cited

Adler, Rudy, Victoria Criado, and Breet Hunneycutt
    2007 Border Film Project: Photos by Migrants & Minutemen on the U.S.-Mexico Border. New York: Abrams.

Allerton, Catherine
    2007 The Secret Life of Sarongs: Manggarai Textiles as Super-Skins. Journal of Material Culture 12(22):22–46.

Andreas, Peter
    2009 Border Games: Policing the U.S.-Mexico Divide. New York: Cornell University Press.

Appadurai, Arjun, ed.
    1986 The Social Life of Things: Commodities in Cultural Perspective. Cambridge: Cambridge University Press.

Banerjee, Mukulika, and Daniel Miller
    2003 The Sari. Oxford: Berg Publishers.

Bourdieu, Pierre
    1977 Outline of a Theory of Practice. Cambridge: Cambridge University Press.

Cornelius, Wayne
    2001 Death at the Border: Efficacy and Unintended Consequences of US Immigration Control Policy. Population and Development Review 27(4):661–685.

Cornelius, Wayne, Scott Borger, Adam Sawyer, David Keyes, Clare Appleby, Kristen Parks, Gabriel Lozada, and Jonathan Hicken
    2008 Controlling Unauthorized Immigration from Mexico: The Failure of "Prevention through Deterrence" and the Need for Comprehensive Reform. Technical report. La Jolla: Immigration Policy Center.

Cornelius, Wayne, and I. Salehyan
    2007 Does Border Enforcement Deter Unauthorized Immigration? The Case of Mexican Migration to the U.S. of America. Regulation & Governance 1:139–153.

De León, Jason
    In press The Alien Transfer and Exit Program: Migrant Perspectives from Nogales, Sonora, Mexico. International Migration.

Downey, Greg
    2007 Producing Pain: Techniques and Technologies in No-Holds-Barred Fighting. Social Studies of Science 37(2):201–226.

Dunn, Timothy
  1996 The Militarization of the U.S.-Mexico Border. 1978–1992: Low-Intensity Conflict Doctrine Comes Home. Austin: University of Texas Press.

Gell, Alfred
  1988 Technology and Magic. Anthropology Today 4(2):6–9.

Government Accountability Office
  1997 Report to the Committee on the Judiciary, U.S. Senate and the Committee on the Judiciary, House of Representatives, Illegal Immigration: Southwest Border Strategy Results Inconclusive; More Evaluation Needed. http://www.gao.gov/archive/1998/gg98021.pdf, accessed March 1st, 2011.

  2006 Report to U.S. Senate; Illegal Immigration: Border Crossing Deaths Have Doubled Since 1995; Border Patrol's Efforts Have Not Been Fully Evaluated. http://www.gao.gov/new.items/d06770.pdf, accessed March 1st, 2011.

Hansen, Karen
  2004 The World in Dress: Anthropological Perspectives on Clothing, Fashion, and Culture. Annual Review of Anthropology 33:369–392.

Hoksins, Janet
  2006 *Agency, Objects* and Biography. *In* Handbook of Material Culture. C. Tilley, W. Keane, S. Küchler, M. Rowlands, and P. Spyer, eds. Pp. 74–85. London: Sage

Institute of Medicine
  2004 Dietary Reference Intakes for Water, Potassium, Sodium, Chloride, and Sulfate. Washington, D.C.: National Academies Press.

Jones, Ellen Carol
  2001 Empty Shoes. *In* Footnotes on Shoes. S. Benstock and S. Ferriss, eds. Pp. 197–232. New Brunswick: Rutgers University Press.

Keane, Webb
  2006a Signs Are Not the Garb of Meaning: On the Social Analysis of Material Things. *In* Social Analysis of Material Things. Daniel. Miller, eds. Pp. 182–205. Durham: Duke University Press.
  2006b Subjects and Objects. *In* Handbook of Material Culture. C. Tilley, W. Keane, S. Küchler, M. Rowlands, and P. Spyer, eds. Pp. 197–202. London: Sage.

Latour, Bruno
  1992 Where Are the Missing Masses?: The Sociology of a Few Mundane Artifacts. *In* Shaping Technology/Building Society: Studies in Sociotechnical Change. W. Bijker and J. Law, eds. Pp. 225–258. Cambridge: MIT Press.

Lemonnier, Pierre
  1986 The Study of Material Culture Today: Toward an Anthropology of Technical Systems. Journal of Anthropological Archaeology 5:147–186.

MacKenzie, Donald and Judy Wajcman (eds)
  1999 The Social Shaping of Technology. Buckingham: Open University Press.

Mauss, Marcel
  1973 [1934] Techniques of the Body. Economy and Society 2:70–87.

Massey, Douglas, Jorge Durand, and Nolan Malone
  2002 Beyond Smoke and Mirrors: Mexican Immigration in an Era of Economic Integration. New York: Russell Sage Foundation.

McCombs, Brady
  2011a Border-Crosser Deaths Reach a Low, But Still 182 People Died. Arizona Daily Star, October 12. http://azstarnet.com/news/local/border/article_97e908b4–5cb9–54a9-a03e-49341f85dcb6.html, accessed November 30, 2011.

2011b US Deportations Set Record Even as Those from Arizona fall. Arizona Daily Star, October 19. http://azstarnet.com/news/local/border/us-deportations-set-record-even-as-those-from-arizona-fall/article_bee8c9d0-cdfa-5890-b8fe-7a033d482c4d.html, accessed November 30, 2011.

Mesenbrink, Johh
  2001 Protecting Borders with Thermal Imaging. http://www.securitymagazine.com/articles/protecting-borders-with-thermal-imaging-1, accessed July 25, 2011.

Miller, Daniel
  2010 Stuff. Cambridge: Polity Press.

Nevins, Joseph
  2002 Operation Gatekeeper: The Rise of the "Illegal Alien" and the Making of the U.S.-Mexico Boundary. New York: Routledge Press.

O'Leary, Anna
  2009 The ABCs of Migration Costs: Assembling, Bajadores, and Coyotes. Migration Letters 6(1):27–35.

Parks, K., G. Lozada, M. Mendoza, and L. García Santos
  2009 Strategies for Success: Border Crossing in an Era of Heightened Security. In Migration from the Mexican Mixteca: A Transnational Community in Oaxaca and California. W. Cornelius, D. Fitzgerald, J. Hernández-Díaz, and S. Borger, eds. Pp. 31–61. San Diego: Center for Comparative Immigration Studies.

Pfaffenberger, Bryan
  1992 Social Anthropology of Technology. Annual Review of Anthropology 21:491–516.

Rubio-Goldmsith, Raquel, Melissa McCormick, Daniel Martinez, and Inez Duarte
  2006 "The Funnel Effect" and Recovered Bodies of Unauthorized Migrants Processed by the Pima County Office of the Medical Examiner 1990–2005. http://immigration.server263.com/indexphp?content=B070201, accessed October 10, 2010.

Sawka, M., S. Cheuvront, and R. Carter III
  2005 Human Water Needs. Nutrition Reviews 63(6):30–39.

Singer, Audrey and Douglas Massey
  1998 The Social Process of Undocumented Border Crossing Among Mexican Migrants. International Migration Review 32(3):561–592.

Slack, Jeremy and Scott Whiteford
  2011 Violence and Migration on the Arizona-Sonora Border. Human Organization 70(1):11–21.

Spener, David
  2009 Clandestine Crossings: Migrants and Coyotes on the Texas-Mexico Border. Ithaca: Corne ll University Press.

Sundberg, Juanita
  2008 'Trash-Talk' and the Production of Quotidian Geopolitical Boundaries in the USA-Mexico Borderlands. Social & Cultural Geography 9(8):871–890.

Thompson, John
  1994 Santo Niño de Atocha. Journal of the Southwest 36(1): 1–18.

Tilley, Christopher
  2006 Objectification. In Handbook of Material Culture. C. Tilley, W. Keane, S. Küchler. M. Rowlands, and P. Spyer, eds. Pp. 60–73. London: Sage.

Wacquant, Loïc
  1995 Pugs at Work: Bodily Capital and Bodily Labour among Professional Boxers. Body & Society 1:65–93.

For Further Reading

(These selections were made by the American Anthropologist *editorial interns as examples of research related in some way to this article. They do not necessarily reflect the views of the author.)*

Dorsey, Margaret E
    2010 Miguel Diaz-Barriga Beyond Surveillance and Moonscapes: An Alternative Imaginary of the U.S.–Mexico Border Wall. Visual Anthropology Review 26(2):(128–135)

Sandell, David P.
    2010 Where Mourning Takes Them: Migrants, Borders, and an Alternative Reality. Ethos 38(2):179–204

Susan, Bibler Coutin
    2003 Legalizing Moves: Salvadoran Immigrants' Struggle for U.S. Residency. pp. 228 Ann Arbor: University of Michigan Press.

Discussion Questions

1. It has been suggested that the items left behind by migrants are not artifacts, but trash. What do you think? Are these items truly material culture or just more litter? Explain your reasoning.
2. What can the items left behind by migrants tell us about the migrants themselves? Is this useful information? Why or why not?
3. What is the common theme in the items migrants choose for the journey? In other words, why do migrants choose the items they do?
4. What is the relationship between the people and artifacts they leave behind? Use examples from this article in your answer, but feel free to use examples from elsewhere.
5. Why do you think the author wrote this article? What knowledge do we gain from information on the material culture of migrants?

Chapter 6

The Worst Mistake in the History of the Human Race

Jared Diamond

W hat we eat is important, and not just for the nutritional value – much of the food we consume is also significant in a cultural way. In this article, Jared Diamond suggests that the introduction of agriculture and the eventual abandonment of a foraging lifestyle have been detrimental to humans. We know it takes less effort to simply open a kitchen cupboard and have food waiting, but we often forget about other important connections between culture and agriculture.

What we eat and how we eat are important both nutritionally and culturally. This selection suggests that how we get what we eat—through gathering and hunting versus agriculture, for example—has dramatic consequences. This seems pretty obvious. We all imagine what a struggle it must have been before the development of agriculture. We think of our ancestors spending their days searching for roots and berries to eat, or out at the crack of dawn, hunting wild animals. In fact, this was not quite the case. Nevertheless, isn't it really better simply to go to the refrigerator, open the door, and reach for a container of milk to pour into a bowl of flaked grain for your regular morning meal? What could be simpler and more nutritious?

There are many things that we seldom question; the truth seems so evident and the answers obvious. One such sacred cow is the tremendous prosperity brought about by the agricultural revolution. This selection is a thought-provoking introduction to the connection between culture and agriculture. The transition from food foraging to farming (what archaeoloists call the Neolithic revolution) may have been the worst mistake in human history or its most important event. You be the judge. But for better or worse, this cultural evolution has occurred, and the world will never be the same again.

To science we owe dramatic changes in our smug self-image. Astronomy taught us that our earth isn't the center of the universe but merely one of billions of heavenly bodies. From biology we learned that we weren't specially created by God but evolved along with millions of other species. Now archaeology is demolishing another sacred belief: that human history ever the past million years has been a long tale of progress. In particular, recent discoveries suggest that the adoption of agriculture, supposedly our most decisive step toward a better life, was in many ways a catastrophe from which we have never recovered. With agriculture came the gross social and sexual inequality, the disease and despotism, that curse our existence.

At first, the evidence against this revisionist interpretation will strike twentieth-century Americans as irrefutable. We're better off in almost every respect than the people of the Middle Ages, who in turn had it easier than cavemen, who in turn were better off than apes. Just count our advantages. We enjoy the most abundant and varied foods, the best tools and material goods, some of the longest and healthiest lives, in history. Most of us are safe from starvation and predators. We get our energy from oil and machines, not from our sweat. What neo-Luddite among us would trade his life for that of a medieval peasant, a caveman, or an ape?

For most of our history we supported ourselves by hunting and gathering: we hunted wild animals and foraged for wild plants. It's a life that philosophers have traditionally regarded as nasty, brutish, and short. Since no food is grown and little is stored, there is (in this view) no respite from the struggle that starts anew each day to find wild foods and avoid starving. Our escape from this misery was facilitated only 10,000 years ago, when in different parts of the world people began to domesticate plants and animals. The agricultural revolution gradually spread until today it's nearly universal, and few tribes of hunter-gatherers survive.

From the progressivist perspective on which I was brought up, to ask "Why did almost all our hunter-gatherer ancestors adopt agriculture?" is silly. Of course they adopted it because agriculture is an efficient way to get more food for less work. Planted crops yield far more tons per acre than roots and berries. Just imagine a band of savages, exhausted from searching for nuts or chasing wild animals, suddenly gazing for the first time at a fruit-laden orchard or a pasture full of sheep. How many milliseconds do you think it would take them to appreciate the advantages of agriculture?

The progressivist party line sometimes even goes so far as to credit agriculture with the remarkable flowering of art that has taken place over the past few thousand years. Since crops can be stored, and since it takes less time to pick food from a garden than to find it in the wild, agriculture gave us free time that hunter-gatherers never had. Thus it was agriculture that enabled us to build the Parthenon and compose the B-minor Mass.

While the case for the progressivist view seems overwhelming, it's hard to prove. How do you show that the lives of people 10,000 years ago got better when they abandoned hunting and gathering for farming? Until recently, archaeologists had to resort to indirect tests, whose results (surprisingly) failed to support the progressivist view. Here's one example of an indirect test: Are twentieth-century hunter-gatherers really worse off than farmers? Scattered throughout the world, several dozen groups of so-called primitive people, like the Kalahari Bushmen, continue to support themselves that way. It turns out that these people have plenty of leisure time, sleep a good deal, and work less hard than their farming neighbors. For instance, the average time devoted each week to obtaining food is only 12 to 19 hours for one group of Bushmen, 14 hours or less for the Hadza nomads of Tanzania. One Bushman, when asked why he hadn't emulated neighboring tribes by adopting agriculture, replied, "Why should we, when there are so many mongongo nuts in the world?"

While farmers concentrate on high-carbohydrate crops like rice and potatoes, the mix of wild plants and animals in the diets of surviving hunter-gatherers provides more protein and a better balance of other nutrients. In one study, the Bushmen's average daily food intake (during a month when food was plentiful) was 2,140 calories and 93 grams of protein, considerably greater than the recommended daily allowance for people of their size. It's almost inconceivable that Bushmen, who eat 75 or so wild plants, could die of starvation the way hundreds of thousands of Irish farmers and their families did during the potato famine of the 1840s.

So the lives of at least the surviving hunter-gatherers aren't nasty and brutish, even though farmers have pushed them into some of the world's worst real estate. But modern hunter-gatherer societies that have rubbed shoulders with farming societies for thousands of years don't tell us about conditions before the agricultural revolution. The progressivist view is really making a claim about the distant past: that the lives of primitive people improved when they switched from gathering to farming. Archaeologists can date that switch by distinguishing remains of wild plants and animals from those of domesticated ones in prehistoric garbage dumps.

How can one deduce the health of the prehistoric garbage makers, and thereby directly test the progressivist view? That question has become answerable only in recent years, in part through the newly emerging techniques of paleopathology, the study of signs of disease in the remains of ancient peoples.

In some lucky situations, the paleopathologist has almost as much material to study as a pathologist today. For example, archaeologists in the Chilean deserts found well preserved mummies whose medical conditions at time of death could be determined by autopsy. And feces of long-dead Indians who lived in dry caves in Nevada remain sufficiently well preserved to be examined for hookworm and other parasites.

Usually the only human remains available for study are skeletons, but they permit a surprising number of deductions. To begin with, a skeleton reveals its owner's sex, weight, and approximate age. In the few cases where there are many skeletons, one can construct mortality tables like the ones life insurance companies use to calculate expected life span and risk of death at any given age. Paleopathologists can also calculate growth rates by measuring bones of people of different ages, examining teeth for enamel defects (signs of childhood malnutrition), and recognizing scars left on bones by anemia, tuberculosis, leprosy, and other diseases.

One straightforward example of what paleopathologists have learned from skeletons concerns historical changes in height. Skeletons from Greece and Turkey show that the average height of hunter-gatherers toward the end of the ice ages was a generous 5'9" for men, 5'5" for women. With the adoption of agriculture, height crashed, and by 3000 B.C. had reached a low of only 5'3" for men, 5' for women. By classical times heights were very slowly on the rise again, but modern Greeks and Turks have still not regained the average height of their distant ancestors.

Another example of paleopathology at work is the study of Indian skeletons from burial mounds in the Illinois and Ohio river valleys. At Dickson Mounds, located near the confluence of the Spoon and Illinois Rivers, archaeologists have excavated some 800 skeletons that paint a picture of the health changes that occurred when a hunter-gatherer culture gave way to intensive maize farming around A.D. 1150. Studies by George Armelagos and his colleagues then at the University of Massachusetts show these early farmers paid a price for their new-found livelihood. Compared to the hunter-gatherers who preceded them, the farmers had a nearly 50 percent increase in enamel defects indicative of malnutrition, a fourfold increase in iron-deficiency anemia (evidenced by a bone condition called porotic hyperostosis), a threefold rise in bone lesions reflecting infectious disease in general, and an increase in degenerative conditions of the spine, probably reflecting a lot of hard physical labor. "Life expectancy at birth in the pre-agricultural community was about twenty-six years," says Armelagos, "but in the post-agricultural community it was nineteen years. So these episodes of nutritional stress and infectious disease were seriously affecting their ability to survive."

The evidence suggests that the Indians at Dickson Mounds, like many other primitive peoples, took up farming not by choice but from necessity in order to feed their constantly growing numbers. "I don't think most hunter-gatherers farmed until they had to, and when they switched to farming they traded quality for quantity," says Mark Cohen of the State University of New York at Plattsburgh, co-editor, with Armelagos, of one of the seminal books in the field, *Paleopathology at the Origins of Agriculture*. "When I first started making that argument ten years ago, not many people agreed with me. Now it's become a respectable, albeit controversial, side of the debate."

There are at least three sets of reasons to explain the findings that agriculture was bad for health. First, hunter-gatherers enjoyed a varied diet, while early farmers obtained most of their food from one or a few starchy crops. The farmers gained cheap calories at the cost of poor nutrition. (Today just three high-carbohydrate plants—wheat, rice, and corn—provide the bulk of the calories consumed by the human species, yet each one is deficient in certain vitamins or amino acids essential to life.) Second, because of dependence on a limited number of crops, farmers ran the risk of starvation if one crop failed. Finally, the mere fact that agriculture encouraged people to clump together in crowded societies, many of which then carried on trade with other crowded societies, led to the spread of parasites and infectious disease. (Some archaeologists think it was crowding, rather than agriculture, that promoted disease, but this is a chicken-and-egg argument, because crowding encourages agriculture and vice versa.) Epidemics couldn't take hold when populations were scattered in small bands that constantly shifted camp. Tuberculosis and diarrheal disease had to await the rise of farming, measles and bubonic plague the appearance of large cities.

Besides malnutrition, starvation, and epidemic diseases, farming helped bring another curse upon humanity: deep class divisions. Hunter-gatherers have little or no stored food, and no concentrated food sources, like an orchard or a herd of cows: they live off the wild plants and animals they obtain each day. Therefore, there can be no kings, no class of social parasites who grow fat on food seized from others. Only in farming populations could a healthy, non-producing elite set itself above the disease-ridden masses. Skeletons from Greek tombs at Mycenae *c.* 1500 B.C. suggest that royals enjoyed a better diet than commoners, since the royal skeletons were two or three inches taller and had better teeth (on the average, one instead of six cavities or missing teeth). Among Chilean mummies from *c.* A.D. 1000, the élite were distinguished not only by ornaments and gold hair clips but also by a fourfold lower rate of bone lesions caused by disease.

Similar contrasts in nutrition and health persist on a global scale today. To people in rich countries like the U.S., it sounds ridiculous to extol the virtues of hunting and gathering. But Americans are an élite, dependent on oil and minerals that must often be imported from countries with poorer health and nutrition. If one could choose between being a peasant farmer in Ethiopia or a Bushman gatherer in the Kalahari, which do you think would be the better choice?

Farming may have encouraged inequality between the sexes, as well. Freed from the need to transport their babies during a nomadic existence, and under pressure to produce more hands to till the fields, farming women tended to have more frequent pregnancies than their hunter-gatherer counterparts—with consequent drains on their health. Among the Chilean mummies, for example, more women than men had bone lesions from infectious disease.

Women in agricultural societies were sometimes made beasts of burden. In New Guinea farming communities today I often see women staggering under loads of vegetables and firewood while the men walk empty-handed. Once while on a field trip there studying birds, I offered to pay some villagers to carry supplies from an airstrip to my mountain camp. The heaviest item was a 110-pound bag of rice, which I lashed to a pole and assigned to a team of four men to shoulder together. When I eventually caught up with the villagers, the men were carrying light loads, while one small woman weighing less than the bag of rice was bent under it, supporting its weight by a cord across her temples.

As for the claim that agriculture encouraged the flowering of art by providing us with leisure time, modern hunter-gatherers have at least as much free time as do farmers. The whole emphasis on leisure time as a critical factor seems to me misguided. Gorillas have had ample free time to build their own Parthenon, had they wanted to. While post-agricultural technological advances did make new art forms possible and preservation of art easier, great paintings and sculptures were already being produced by hunter-gatherers 15,000 years ago, and were still being produced as recently as the last century by such hunter-gatherers as some Eskimos and the Indians of the Pacific Northwest.

Thus with the advent of agriculture an élite became better off, but most people became worse off. Instead of swallowing the progressivist party line that we chose agriculture because it was good for us, we must ask how we got trapped by it despite its pitfalls.

One answer boils down to the adage "Might makes right." Farming could support many more people than hunting, albeit with a poorer quality of life. (Population densities of hunter-gatherers are rarely over one person per ten square miles, while farmers average 100 times that.) Partly, this is because a field planted entirely in edible crops lets one feed far more mouths than a forest with scattered edible plants. Partly, too, it's because nomadic hunter-gatherers have to keep their children spaced at four-year intervals by infanticide and other means, since a mother must carry her toddler until it's old enough to keep up with the adults. Because farm women don't have that burden, they can and often do bear a child every two years.

As population densities of hunter-gatherers slowly rose at the end of the ice ages, bands had to choose between feeding more mouths by taking the first steps toward agriculture, or else finding ways to limit growth. Some bands chose the former solution, unable to anticipate the evils of farming, and seduced by the transient abundance they enjoyed until population growth caught up with increased food production. Such bands outbred and then drove off or killed the bands that chose to remain hunter-gatherers, because a hundred malnourished farmers can still out-fight one healthy hunter. It's not that hunter-gatherers abandoned their life style, but that those sensible enough not to abandon it were forced out of all areas except the ones farmers didn't want.

At this point it's instructive to recall the common complaint that archaeology is a luxury, concerned with the remote past, and offering no lessons for the present. Archaeologists studying the rise of farming have reconstructed a crucial stage at which we made the worst mistake in human history. Forced to choose between limiting population or trying to increase food production, we chose the latter and ended up with starvation, warfare, and tyranny.

Hunter-gatherers practiced the most successful and longest-lasting life style in human history. In contrast, we're still struggling with the mess into which agriculture has tumbled us, and it's unclear whether we can solve it. Suppose that an archaeologist who had visited us from outer space were trying to explain human history to his fellow spacelings. He might illustrate the results of his digs by a 24-hour clock on which one hour represents 100,000 years of real past time. If the history of the human race began at midnight, then we would now be almost at the end of our first day. We lived as hunter-gatherers for nearly the whole of that day, from midnight through dawn, noon, and sunset. Finally, at 11:54 p.m., we adopted agriculture. As our second midnight approaches, will the plight of famine-stricken peasants gradually spread to engulf us all? Or will we somehow achieve those seductive blessings that we imagine behind agriculture's glittering façade, and that have so far eluded us?

Discussion Questions

1. Diamond begins by saying that "human history over the past million years has been a long tale of progress." What do you think he means by this?
2. How might the adoption of agriculture have encouraged inequality between the sexes?
3. What is the relationship between health and nutrition? How does one affect the other? Use examples from the discussion on Dickson Mounds to support your answer.
4. Anthropologists often claim that the development of "civilization" gave our ancestors enough leisure time to develop different types of art and craft specialization, but Diamond disputes this claim. How do you feel about this issue? Provide specific examples to support your reasoning.
5. Would it be possible reduce the scale of agriculture as it is practiced worldwide? Could agriculture be eliminated altogether? Why or why not? Provide reasoning for your statements.

Would you feel comfortable identifying as genderless? The strong reaction many will have to this question reveals the strong connection between our own gender and identity. In the United States, many social policies strive for equality, calling into question whether factors like gender should really matter in the public sphere. Would moving toward an end of gender eliminate problems – or create them? Could society ever really be gender neutral?

Look closely and you may see signposts.

- Kathy Witterick and her husband, David Stocker, are raising their 4-month-old child, Storm, without revealing the child's gender. According to the birth announcement from the Toronto couple: "We've decided not to share Storm's sex for now—a tribute to freedom and choice in place of limitation, a stand up to what the world could become in Storm's lifetime (a more progressive place?)"
- Andrej perjic, an androgynous Australian model, worked both the male and female runways at the Paris fashion shows earlier this year.
- A recent J. Crew catalog drew national attention when it featured a young boy with his toenails painted pink.

Could we be heading toward the end of gender?

And by "gender" we mean, according to Merriam-Webster, "the behavioral, cultural, or psychological traits typically associated with one sex." In other words, the cultural expectations that go along with saying that someone is a boy or a girl. In other words, not someone's sex—the person's *gender*.

"Sex differences are real and some are probably present at birth, but then social factors magnify them," says Lise Eliot, an associate professor of neuroscience at the Chicago Medical School and author of *Pink Brain, Blue Brain: How Small Differences Grow Into Troublesome Gaps and What We Can Do About It.* "So if we, as a society, feel that gender divisions do more harm than good, it would be valuable to break them down."

As history shows, one enterprise in which Americans excel is the breaking down of divisions.

Gender Neutrality

Perhaps you have a friend or family member who is more comfortable with a new gender. Or maybe you have had dealings with someone of indeterminate gender in the checkout line. Maybe you have seen the old "It's Pat" routines from *Saturday Night Live.*

Because there is a growing societal awareness of gender consciousness and of a certain blurriness of genders, the question "Is it a boy or a girl?" may not just be for expectant parents anymore.

And so what? Does gender matter? In a country with the ideal of treating everyone fairly and equitably, do we really need to know if someone is a boy or a girl? These questions are driving decisions and actions around the country.

- In Muskegon, Mich., officials at Mona Shores High School declared this year's prom court would be gender-neutral—with no "kings" and "queens"—after denying a transgender student the homecoming-king crown last year.
- In Johnson City, Tenn., East Tennessee State University recently announced that it is exploring gender-neutral housing for students—following the lead of Stanford University, the University of Michigan, Rutgers University and other colleges. These are not just coed dorms, but dorms for anyone regardless of how they express their gender. The roommate you choose can be gay or straight or whatever.
- Around the beginning of this year, the State Department began using gender-neutral language on U.S. passports—replacing "father" and "mother" with "Parent One" and "Parent Two"—to make it simpler for nontraditional parents, beyond the male/female combination, to get passports for their children.

Everywhere you turn, it seems, there is talk of gender-neutral this and gender-free that: baby bedding (Wild Safari by Carousel); fashion (Kanye West in a Celine women's shirt); Bibles (the New International Version).

Gender neutrality, writes one blogging parent, is the new black.

'High-Stakes Social Constructions'

A female-to-male transsexual and advocate for transgender rights, Dean Spade writes often about gender issues. Spade is an assistant professor at Seattle University School of Law and founder of the Sylvia Rivera Law Project in New York City, which offers free legal guidance to transgender, intersex and gender-nonconforming clients.

In a 2008 paper, "Documenting Gender," Spade examines the gender reclassification polices of public agencies and departments in the United States. In the past 40 years, Spade observes, society has come to recognize the existence of a group of people, currently known as "transgender," who identify with and live as a different gender than the one assigned to them when they were born.

In an interview, Spade makes a passionate pitch for the elimination of gender categorization in most government record-keeping. "I really don't think that data needs to be on our IDs or gathered by most agencies and institutions," Spade says. Tagging someone as female or male "enforces binary gender norms and it pretends that gender is a more stable category of identity than it actually is."

Spade says, "I can see why we might want institutions to be aware of gender at a general level in order to engage in remediation of the sexism and transphobia that shape our world."

For example, Spade says, gender-based affirmative action—that rectifies discrimination against women—might be called for in certain programs and institutions "so we might want institutions to do an analysis of who is getting to participate." But, Spade adds, in order to gain a general idea of the gender makeup of a particular population, it is not necessary to then turn around and post that information on a particular participant's personal record.

Developing policies to counter the impact of sexism and transphobia, Spade adds, does not require a belief that gender categories are "real—stable, unchangeable, natural. We can engage such strategies while understanding that gender categories are high-stakes social constructions deployed in ways that endanger and harm socially determined groups."

Why Gender Still Matters

Gender matters to Leonard Sax, a family physician, psychologist and founder and executive director of the National Association for Single Sex Public Education. Sax has written several books on gender, including *Why Gender Matters* and *Girls on the Edge*.

When NPR asked Sax whether he sees signs of the end of gender in contemporary society, he responded with a lively defense of gender distinctions, an edited version of which appears here:

The tidbits you mention—the Toronto couple, or the J. Crew fashion catalog—are of interest only to a small segment of media people, and without resonance in the larger society.

As opposed to the tidbits you cited, I would observe:

- The new head of New York City Public Schools, Dennis Walcott, has called for more single-sex public schools in New York City.
- The newly elected mayor of Chicago, Rahm Emanuel, has called for more single-sex public schools in the city of Chicago.
- Tampa public schools are opening a girls' public school and a boys' public school this fall. Not charter schools, but regular public schools under the authority of the district.

Ignoring gender won't make it go away. On the contrary: Ignoring gender has the ironic consequence of exacerbating gender stereotypes.

The determined tack of awareness of gender difference which you describe ... puts both girls and boys at risk—but in different ways. Not merely academically, but physically—increasing girls' risks of knee injury and concussion—and spiritually—increasing girls' risks of drug and alcohol abuse; increasing boys' risk of disengagement and apathy.

If you don't think gender matters in the classroom, you haven't been in a third-grade classroom recently. I have visited more than 300 schools over the past 11 years.

You will find that white, black, Spanish-speaking doesn't matter on this parameter; affluent or low-income doesn't matter; urban or rural doesn't matter. Gender is far more important, more fundamental, than any of those other parameters. On many parameters relevant to education, such as attention span, a white boy from an affluent home in Bethesda or McLean has more in common with an African-American mate from a low-income home in Southeast D.C. than he has in common with his own sister, a white girl.

Many third-grade boys today in the United States have told me "school is a stupid waste of time." I have never heard such a comment from a third-grade girl in this country. Do you think that doesn't matter?

—Linton Weeks

Boychicks

To chronicle her adventures in gender-neutral parenting, Arwyn Daemyir writes a blog called Raising My Boychick. She describes herself as "a walking contradiction: knitting feminist fulltime parent, Wiccan science-minded woowoo massage therapist, queer-identified male-partnered monogamist, body-loving healthy-eating fat chick, unmedicated mostly-stable bipolar."

She describes her boychick, born in March 2007, as a "male-assigned at birth—and so far apparently comfortable with that assignment, white, currently able-bodied, congenitally hypothyroid, cosleeper, former breastfed toddler, elimination communication graduate, sling baby and early walker, trial and terror, cliched light of our life, and impetus for the blog. Odds are good he will be the most privileged of persons: a middle class, able bodied, cisgender, straight, white male."

The adjective cisgender—as opposed to transgender—describes someone who is at peace with the gender he or she was assigned at birth.

Daemyir lives in Portland, Ore. She and her straight male partner are expecting another baby in September.

For Daemyir, gender-neutral parenting is not an attempt to eliminate gender, "because the 70s'-era gender neutral parenting movement proved that's not possible."

But, she adds, she has concerns about the ways we designate and segregate gender in public, "starting with the idea that there are two-and-only-two genders—a construction, and a myth, in our society that excludes many."

To that end, Daemyir supports, among other changes, non-gender-designated single-stall bathrooms and an option for unisex washrooms and locker rooms. "Right now, when an establishment only has one toilet stall, of course it is non-gendered. Why, when there is room for two, must they arbitrary be designated for 'Men' and 'Women'? When a place has room enough for several large rooms of toilets and free-standing single-stalls, why must they *all* be gendered, when it would be as easy to make some single-gendered and some not, giving people the ability to make choices that are most comfortable or convenient for them?"

Daemyir does not think that eliminating all single-gender areas "is beneficial or safe either, necessarily, but ... we over-designate many of these things when it's simply not necessary, and actively harms a particularly marginalized population—people with non-binary genders."

Eliot, the neuroscience professor, is not so sure about total change. "Perhaps I'm too old-school—or fussy—to argue for the elimination of men's and women's bathrooms," Eliot says," but certainly employment forms and loan applications should not require gender information. Also, if parents did not buy into the gender stereotyping of children's toys and clothes, kids would stay open-minded longer during childhood. The goal is to keep girls physically active, curious and assertive, and boys sensitive, verbal and studious."

Discussion Questions

1. Lise Eliot is quoted as saying "sex differences are real and some are probably present at birth, but then social factors magnify them." What does this statement mean? Do you agree? Why or why not?
2. The author says that Americans excel at breaking down divisions. Do you agree with this statement? Provide examples in your answer.
3. Physician Leonard Sax has stated that "ignoring gender won't make it go away." Is a gender-neutral society one that ignores gender?
4. Is it necessary for a society to become gender-neutral in order for all citizens to be considered equal? Why or why not?
5. Are we moving toward an end of gender? Why or why not?

Chapter 8

Child Survival in Community Contexts

Nancy Andes

Department of Sociology, University of Alaska Anchorage

I n this article, Nancy Andes argues that "so much of the cost of social transformation and disease in transitional populations is borne by infants and children" and that "education of women is among the strongest, most persistent, and consistent explanatory factors for infant mortality." Women's status as disadvantaged in developing (and often patriarchal) societies is strongly tied to infant and child survival outcomes, though, as the author points out, rapidly changing cultural practices related to child survival need further, careful study.

Abstract

Characteristics of community contexts important to child survival in Third World countries are reviewed. The type of economic production and stratification system, women's position, medical care and public health services, and cultural practices constrain and provide resources to individuals living within a community. Child survival viewed within the community context expands upon structural forces affecting mortality differentials.

> ...salt packets are not breastmilk, nor are they a sufficient substitute for weaning food, clean water, attentive care, adequate housing, fair wages, free and available education and health care, and sexual equality, all of which are prerequisites for optimum child health, development, and survival. Nancy Scheper-Hughes (1987:21)

> Health institutions and folk society are not cultures in contact.... They share their personnel, their social roles and their political economic context. Paradoxically but unsurprisingly Western social scientists have usually rejected the social process in favor of the individual attribute. Ronald Frankenberg (1980:206)

Explanations for child survival in countries under development have shifted from an emphasis on individual-level factors to broader socioeconomic changes in the standards of living, status of women, public health systems, and medical care within communities. Since the 1950s researchers have observed a connection between an increased standard of living, economic development, and superior sanitation for reducing mortality rates (Dubos 1968; McKeown 1976). This emphasis on structural, community contexts is evident in anthropology (see Swedlund and Armelagos 1990 and Scheper-Hughes 1987; Orubuloye and Caldwell 1975), demography (Smith 1989; Casterline 1987; Jain 1985; Haines and Avery 1981), nutrition (DaVanzo 1988; Mata 1978), sociology (LaVeist 1992; Andes 1989; Entwisle, Casterline and Sayed 1989), and medicine (Braithwaite and Lythcott 1989; Mosley and Chen 1984).

The goal of this paper is to integrate literature on structural characteristics within the community context as they relate to infant and child mortality. This perspective investigates the contributions sociology, demography, and anthropology have made to understanding macro-level social and economic effects on survival. A structuralist approach to social organization is taken in an effort to place the study of child survival within the community context while at the same time expanding upon underlying forces affecting child mortality differentials.

Community Structure and Mortality

Economic, social, public health, medical care, cultural, and environmental differences are ever-present factors affecting human health and well-being. In Third World countries material deprivation and scarcity within the economic, medical care and public health systems highlight the challenges women and families face under rapidly changing circumstances. Societies under transition due to modernization pressures, cultural trauma, or dependency relations face extreme poverty, social disorganization, brakedown of traditional support systems, and confusion about available services and care for childrearing. Some groups within a society are more vulnerable than others.

Structuralist perspectives have tended to focus on the larger economic, social, and cultural contexts that constrain the behavior and opportunities of individuals living within them. Whether following structuralist theories on universalistic patterns of human analogical thinking of Levi-Strauss, the collective rules and resources associated with the structuration of market capacities, reproduction, and consumption (Giddens 1973), relations of domination and social positions common to the political economy tradition (Waitzkin 1991; Roseberry 1988), or lawlike regularities among social facts associated with an ecological framework (McElroy and Townsend 1989), a structralist perspective draws from fundamental insights that the structure of economic, social, and cultural systems have a systematic impact on individual's lives.

While I am not arguing for an amalgamation, my focus is on investigating structuralist ideas and research across the anthropological/sociological divide in order to stimulate a fresh reassessment on health prospects for societies undergoing transformation. Economic, social, and environmental structures form a core that can greatly explain patterns of survival and health among Third World populations.

Community structure is broadly comprised of the <u>social organization</u> (economic, social, and gender structures and relations that maintain and reproduce inequities), <u>institutions and services</u> (schools, medical care, and public health), and <u>culture</u> (ideas, practices, and beliefs). Since various programs to reduce infant mortality are implemented at the macro level, usually defined by geographic boundaries, the community becomes important in mortality studies to evaluate their impact (Jain and Visaria 1988:51).

Infant mortality is generally viewed as an indicator of a society's capacity to care for its members, and it reflects the effects of personal health and hygiene, diet, public health and sanitation programs, and the quality and availability of medical services (Scheper-Hughes 1987; Mosley and Chen 1984). A significant change in the study of child survival is the shift toward viewing the social structure of communities as consisting of (a) type of economic production and stratification system, (b) social conditions affecting the position of women, (c) medical care and public health institutions providing services, and (d) cultural practices constrains and provides resources to individuals living within a community. The original view of socioeconomic factors affecting infant mortality was restricted to individual-level characteristics (such as parental education and income) influencing probabilities for survival. Mosley and Chen (1984) argue that this conception of socioeconomic factors is too limiting, and researchers must include the community context as part of the morbidity and mortality process.

The more recent anthropological, demographic, and sociological formulations of community structure view the social organization of communities as having a spatial distribution of institutional resources, structural arrangements, and behavioral patterns. Communities often act as effective agents, laying economic and social foundations that foster health and well-being (see the "healthy towns" literature in Ashton and Seymour 1988). There is, however, the possibility that community structure can be the source of insults. The existence (or lack of) and access to the primary resources of society may create structural disadvantages that deprive the basic needs and well-being of the entire population. For example, people who have personal wealth could not always translate that into better health if the town did not have a hospital, health center, or sanitary facilities. A structural model of the community context can serve as a general framework for organizing the major elements in the mortality-community interaction.

Economic Production and Social Stratification

Socioeconomic forces leading to poverty and hence to deprivation of basic needs remain as perhaps the most difficult problem to address for populations undergoing transition today (Swedlund and Armelagos 1990). Characteristics of the labor and commodity markets have potential impact on the standard of living and subsequent mortality risks for infants and children. Of particular relevance in Third World countries is the extent to which communities are dominated by a particular sector of the economy, especially the commercialization and mechanization of agriculture. The composition of the labor market is also important with the fluidity of the occupational system levels of under- and un-employment and income distribution. Mosley and Chen (1984), Scheper-Hughes (1987), and others increasingly insist that significant efforts to reduce morbidity and mortality must deal with these political and economic factors in order to be truly effective.

In my research in two communities in Peru (Andes 1989), levels of economic development and the type of economy, including market diversity and stratification systems, were quite different. In Pisco, a coastal community with lower then expected infant mortality given its level of development, the economy is diversified across agricultural, fishing, manufacturing, and tourist industries. In the community with higher than expected infant mortality, Ilo, the economy is monopolized by two copper companies. Consequently, in Ilo the stratification system is quite rigid, with little opportunity to enter permanent, stable jobs. Pisco's stratification system is more fluid; both women and men follow different occupations as the seasonal and economic cycles require. Most members of the working and poor classes in Pisco float in and out of the formal economy, relying on subsistence activities to provide a low but marginally adequate nutritional base. But these options are not available in Ilo due to economic monopolization.

Economic resources and fluidity of the stratification system are reflected in labor and commodity markets (Wood and Magno 1988; Portes 1985; Entwisle, Casterline, and Sayed 1989). Communities monopolized by a few industries seem especially vulnerable to those levels of capitalization, resources, and job opportunities. Families are economically dependent on the type of industry in a community. The ability of workers to control the resources affecting their lives and obtain a decent standard of living depends on the diversity in the economy and an openness in the stratification system. Insofar as mortality is connected to adults having the resources to make independent decisions, infant survival chances are enhanced.

Position of Women

Education of women is among the strongest, most persistent, and consistent explanatory factors for infant mortality (Grosse and Auffrey 1989). Higher levels of women's education are translated into lower infant mortality. But several researchers argue that mother's education is an easily measured variable that in actuality stands for a broader range of factors (Mason 1986, Caldwell1986, Bourque and Warren 1981). They note that women's status and position within the community are crucial determinants for child survival. Women's status and power are related to the type of work they do, the income received for that work, the respect received, and the capacities women have to use the resources at her disposal.

Gender inequality may be one of the more important factors explaining differentials in infant mortality because women's ability to make independent decisions and garner resources has real and immediate effects on child survival. Respect for women and their right to independent work changes the balance of power within the family, increases the likelihood that she will actively seek out adequate medical care, and reinforces her right to proper treatment. In social settings where women have higher status, infant mortality rates are lower.

In Peru economic autonomy is important for women. Pisco's economic diversity afforded occupational positions for women in agriculture, fishing, industry, and tourism. Both women and men participate in the harvesting and marketing of fish. The division of labor is such that men fish and women sell in the market. In Pisco both genders have integral roles in the fishing industry, thus women have a relatively stable source of independent income. In Ilo, however, women's access to the labor market was limited. With the air and sea polluted due to copper emissions, marketing agricultural and fishing products was closed to women. Additional occupations were limited to industrial jobs in copper, typically men's jobs.

While health and education of women are the common result of the social and economic context (see Mason 1986), autonomy of women remains an important component for child survival. Women's resources and knowledge lead to activities beneficial to child survival including market productivity, higher expenditures on food, housing and medical care household hygiene and removing children from school during outbreaks of disease. They also raise the demand for community health services. Economic resources, including food and medical care, are more likely to be shared. These actions may come about from increased knowledge or, as Caldwell (1986) has noted, because the status of literate mothers changes the structure of the family. Ware (1984) suggests that education has an impact not only through the characteristics of the individual mother but also through the educational level of society as a whole. Gendered inequities, and ultimately death, due to the system of patriarchy can be reduced within a community structure that facilitates women's autonomy and status.

Medical Care and Public Health Services

Despite some successes (Merrick 1985; Flegg 1982), the role of public health and medical care is not clearly related to mortality reductions (Mosley 1984). The inability of medical care and public health programs to explain much of the decrease in mortality is partially due to their limited coverage of the population. In addition, large medical services are magnets for dying children, existence of services do not insure use of services, and the composition of the social classes using the medical or public health facilities affects mortality. The poorest members of a community who may be the largest proportion of a population may not have access to facilities.

McKeown (1976) points out that changes in mortality did not begin in the industrializing West until the majority of the population had an adequate standard of living. If a community does not have an adequate source of food or income to purchase food and shelter, having access to medical care does little to change the living conditions of those on the margins of subsistence. Mortality may be the ultimate consequence of a cumulative series of biological insults related to the socioeconomic conditions of communities rather than the outcome of a single disease event (Mosley and Chen 1984). Public health and medical care services may not be effective at certain levels of economic subsistence.

In Peru the effects of medical care make more difference in larger cities. The two smaller towns I studied had somewhat similar medical care facilities. They each had hospitals, health centers and first aid "sanitary posts" available to the community. In Ilo, however, more medical outreach, nutritional, and social services were available, but their infant mortality was rather high. The greater number of services may reflect a greater need rather than any negative impact of the health care system.

The key is to identify under what socioeconomic conditions do public health and medical care systems make significant differences in child survival. Continued mortality decline may not be a matter of increasing literacy but of providing a sufficient density of medical and public health services of reasonable caliber. The importance of public health and medical care is embedded within the context of other community factors important to child survival. The multifaceted, multivariate consideration of the interrelations informs a more detailed understanding of the forces playing with human survival.

Cultural Practices

Caldwell's (1986) study of four societies that are superior health achievers given their health expenditures (Sri Lanka; Costa Rica; Kerala, a state in south India; and China) concluded that ethnic, religious, and cultural differences help explain why these societies have such low infant mortality relative to their expenditures. The findings in DaVanzo (1988) show that a consistent difference between poor health achieving states and superior health achievers was religion; the former were almost all Muslim states and many of the latter were Buddhist. Among Malaysia's ethnic groups, the Malays are Muslim and many of the Chinese are Buddhist. In Peru infant mortality varies between the coast, mountain, and rain forest regions. Higher infant mortality exists in the mountains where the Quechuas predominately live (Young, Edmonston, and Andes 1983). These ethnic differences in infant mortality persist even when education is controlled.

Overt ethnic or regional differences may be masking underlying cultural practices and beliefs that vary among ethnic groups. If culture can be defined as a design for living that a particular group of people follows, then much ambiguity remains. Some cultural differences are more pragmatic and revolve around ways of doing things (for example, whether water is boiled); while other differences emerge from an interaction between a worldview that guides behavior and the actuality of how the world works in people's lived experience (see infant feeding practices in Scheper-Hughes 1987, and nurturing practices in Scrimshaw 1978). This latter emphasis implies that a group is actively learning and creating strategies for survival. In both respects, cultural responses to child care practices in harsh contexts interact with fundamental economic and political structures that exogenously control patterns and resource priorities within society.

What needs to be untangled are the effects of cultural practices within different economic and social community contexts. What portion of mortality differences among groups within a population is due to cultural differences? What portion is due to cultural trauma accompanying social disorganization of societal transition? What portion is due to differential access to societal resources? A refined exploration of these questions within specific socioeconomic contexts can lead to a more detailed understanding of the multiple layers of factors that affect child survival.

Conclusion

So much of the cost of social transformation and disease in transitional populations is borne by infants and children (see Swedlund and Armelagos 1990). Community structures can cause significant variability and complexity for child survival. Many simultaneous processes are going on in the Third World today that do not fit what occurred historically in Western Europe (Palloni 1990). Currently, large-scale investments attempt to integrate the economic and health care systems in Third World countries to the capitalist, biomedical systems prevalent in the First World. These transitions are occurring within economic and social circumstances that frequently skew Third World societies toward greater internal inequities. Women's status drawn from their disadvantageous positions within patriarchy can further change probabilities for child survival. But specific cultural and behavioral forms can positively affect the well-being of infants and children.

The interface between society, biomedicine, and sanitation is also broad. Health care systems include not only doctors, nurses, midwives, and pharmacists but also medicines distributed through local markets, medical practitioners, and health aides. The impact of formal and informal medical systems with the particular economic and cultural structures of communities creates simultaneous improvements and declines in mortality risks. The positive effects of improved sanitation services may occur within a socioeconomic context where the poorer social classes have the most means for access.

Societal destabilization, community support structures, and rapidly changing cultural practices related to child survival need careful study. Anthropological, demographic, and sociological studies on the kinds of efforts necessary to improve the social and health conditions important to child survival have no doubt been accompanied by some progress. But without consideration of the community context and the effects it can have independent of the actions of individuals or organizations, our expectations for more rapid reduction in mortality levels in Third World countries will have to be tempered. Underlying mortality reductions in Third World countries is the development of healthy towns.

Research needs to show within specific community contexts how infant mortality is dependent on a community's structural arrangements. Some contexts lead to healthy outcomes, others not.

It will be valuable knowing which mixtures of community characteristics form structural foundations for healthy communities. Unidimensional possibilities include reducing differences between the poorest and richest social classes, improving the autonomy and resource control patterns of women, and democratizing access to medical care and public health services. An additional challenge for the future is to identify the multidimensional confluence of community conditions that draws from economic resources, social ties, cultural strengths, and institutional bases to maximize probabilities for child survival.

Acknowledgements

Ideas were developed while Visiting Professor at the Universidad Peruana Cayetano Heredia, Lima, Peru. I wish to thank the Comisión Fulbright for financial support. Elsa Alcántara, Luis M. Sobrevilla, and Roger Guerra García graciously offered their support to this research. Janardan Subedi and anonymous reviewers provided suggestions and comments, and I am indebted to them.

References Cited

Andes, Nancy
 1989 Socioeconomic, Medical Care, and Public Health Contexts affecting Infant Mortality: A Study of Community-Level Differentials in Peru. *Journal of Health and Social Behavior* 30:386–97.

Ashton, John and Howard Seymour
 1988 *The New Public Health: the Liverpool Experience*. Philadelphia: Open University Press.

Bourque, Susan C. and Kay B. Warren
 1981 *Women of the Andes*. Ann Arbor: University of Michigan Press.

Braithwaite, Ronald L. and Ngina Lythcott
 1989 Community Empowerment as a Strategy for Health Promotion for Black and Other Minority Populations. *Journal of the American Medical Association* 261:282–283.

Caldwell, John C.
 1986 Routes to Low Mortality in Poor Countries. *Population and Development Review* 12:171–220.

Casterline, John B.
 1987 The Collection and Analysis of Community Data. *In The World Fertility Survey: An Assessment*, John Cleland and Chris Scott in collaboration with David Whitelegge, eds. pp. 882–905. Oxford: Oxford University Press.

DaVanzo, Julie
 1988 Infant Mortality and Socioeconomic Development: Evidence from Malaysian Household Data. *Demography* 25:581–95.

Dubos, René J.
 1968 *Man, Medicine, and Environment*. New York: Praeger.

Entwisle, Barbara, John B. Casterline, and Hussien A.-A. Sayed.
 1989 Villages as Contexts for Contraceptive Behavior in Rural Egypt. *American Sociological Review* 54:1019 34.

Flegg, A.T.
 1982 Inequality of Income, Illiteracy and Medical Care as Determinants of Infant Mortality in Underdeveloped Countries. *Population Studies* 36:441–57.

Frankenberg, Ronald
    1980 Medical Anthropology and Development: A Theoretical Perspective. *Social Science and Medicine* 14B:197–207.

Giddens, Anthony
    1973 *The Class Structure of the Advanced Societies*. New York: Harper & Row.

Grosse, Robert N. and Christopher Auffrey
    1989 Literacy and Health Status in Developing Countries. *Annual Review of Public Health* 10:281–97.

Haines, Michael R. and Roger C. Avery
    1981 Differential Infant and Child Mortality in Costa Rica: 1968–1973. *Population Studies* 36:31–43.

Jain, A.K.
    1985 Determinants of Regional Variations in Infant Mortality in Rural India. *Population Studies* 39:407–24.

Jain, Anrudh K. and Pravin Visaria
    1988 Infant Mortality in India: An Overview. *In Infant Mortality in India: Differentials and Determinants*, Anrudh K. Jain and Pravin Visaria, eds. pp. 23–64. New Delhi: Sage.

LaVeist, Thomas A.
    1992 The Political Empowerment and Health Status of African-Americans: Mapping a New Territory. *American Journal of Sociology* 97:1080–1095.

Mason, Karen Oppenheim
    1986 The Status of Women: Conceptual and Methodological Issues in Demographic Studies. *Sociological Forum* 1:284–300.

Mata, Leonardo J.
    1978 *The Children of Santa María Cauqué: A Prospective Field Study of Health and Growth*. Cambridge: The MIT Press.

McElroy, Ann and Patricia K. Townsend
    1989 *Medical Anthropology in Ecological Perspective*. Boulder: Westview Press.

McKeown, Thomas
    1976 *The Modem Rise of Population*. New York: Academic Press.

Merrick, Thomas W.
    1985 The Effect of Piped Water on Early Childhood Mortality in Urban Brazil, 1970 to 1976. *Demography* 22:1–23.

Mosley, W. Henry
    1984 Child Survival: Research and Policy. *In Child Survival: Strategies for Research*, W. Henry Mosley and Lincoln C. Chen, eds. pp. 3–23. *Supplement to Population and Development Review,* Vol.10.

Mosley, W. Henry and Lincoln C. Chen
    1984 An Analytical Framework for the Study of Child Survival in Developing Countries. *In Child Survival: Strategies for Research*, W. Henry Mosley and Lincoln C. Chen, eds. pp. 25–45. *Supplement to Population and Development Review*, Vol. 10.

Orubuloye, I.O. and John C. Caldwell
    1975 The Impact of Public Health Services on Mortality: A Study of Mortality Differentials in a Rural Area of Nigeria. *Population Studies* 29:259–72.

Palloni, Alberto
    1990 Fertility and Mortality Decline in Latin America. *The Annals* 510:126–44

Portes, Alejandro
    1985 Latin American Class Structures: their Composition and Change during the Last Decades. *Latin American Research Review* 20:7–39.

Roseberry, William
    1988 Political Economy. *Annual Review of Anthropology* 17:161–185.

Scheper-Hughes, Nancy

1987 The Cultural Politics of Child Survival. *In Child Survival*, Nancy Scheper-Hughes, ed. pp. 1–29. Dordrecht: Reidel.

Scrimshaw, Susan

1978 Infant Mortality and Behavior in the Regulation of Family Size. *Population Development Review* 4:383–403.

Smith, Herbert L.

1989 Integrating Theory and Research on the Institutional Determinants of Fertility. *Demography* 26:171–184.

Swedlund, Alan C. and George J. Armelagos

1990 Introduction. *In Disease in Populations in Transition: Anthropological and Epidemiological Perspectives*, Alan C. Swedlund and George J. Armelagos, eds. pp. 1–15. New York: Bergin and Garvey.

Waitzkin, Howard

1991 *The Politics of Medical Encounters: How Patients and Doctors Deal with Social Problems*. New Haven: Yale University Press.

Ware, Helen

1984 Effects of Maternal Education, Women's Roles, and Child Care on Child Mortality. *In Child Survival: Strategies for Research*, W. Henry Mosley and Lincoln C. Chen, eds. pp. 191–214. *Supplement to Population and Development Review*, Vol. 10.

Wood, Charles H. and José Alberto Magno de Carvalho

1988 *The Demography of Inequality in Brazil*. Cambridge: Cambridge University Press.

Young, Frank W.., Barry Edmonston and Nancy Andes

1983 Community-Level Determinants of Infant and Child Mortality in Peru. Social Indixators Research 12:65–81

Discussion Questions

1. The author says infant mortality is generally viewed as an indicator of a society's capacity to care for its members – do you agree with this statement? Why or why not?
2. How are economic production and social stratification related to community survival, in a broad sense?
3. How is women's status in a community related to the work they do? What other factors influence women's status?
4. The article points out that changes in mortality did not begin in the industrializing West until the majority of the population had an adequate standard of living. Why do you think this was?
5. Why do children often bear the brunt of social transformation? Will this ever change? Why or why not?

Chapter 9

Blood and Desire: The Secret of Heteronormativity in Adoption Narratives of Culture

Sara Dorow
Amy Swiffen
University of Alberta

Ve all have an identity, and for the most part, we do not think about what it is or how it was created. This article explores the pervasive heteronormativity that exists in Western culture and the significant impact of this cultural practice on identity creation, specifically in relation to our kin identity. The authors also examine *cultural kinship*, which can be changing and flexible. How can we examine all facets of identity from an anthropological point of view?

The last 15 to 20 years has seen interesting developments in kinship theory. One of these was the arrival of "new kinship studies," an often-referenced and sometimes-maligned attempt to retheorize kinship relations beyond the assumptions of the heterosexual, biologically reproduced nuclear family. A second development was in transnational–transracial adoption scholarship, which in the 1990s stretched beyond the question of the adopted child's psychosocial identity to focus on adoptive kinship as situated within a globalized political economy, racialized national projects, and gendered cultural constructions. These two branches of analysis have met and interacted in various ways, their interlocution perhaps most pronounced in studies focused on the decentering and recentering of blood ties, gay and lesbian parenting, and the hybridization of racial and cultural family identities (see, e.g., the *AE* Forum: Are Men Missing? in *American Ethnologist* 32[1]; Toby Alice Volkman's 2005 edited volume *Cultures of Transnational Adoption;* and Sarah Franklin and Susan McKinnon's 2001 edited volume *Relative Values*).

In this article, we develop what remains an underexplored conversation between the critiques of heteronormativity found in some of the new kinship studies and the scholarship of transnational–transracial adoption. The adoption literature has certainly taken up new kinship studies' central concern with nonnormative family formations: Some scholars have examined if and how adoptive kinship moves beyond the bounds of heterosexual biological reproduction, for example, in queer and single parenting (Eng 2003; Shanley 2001; Sullivan 2004), and others have interrogated the "trans" of racial and cultural kin relations (Dorow 2006; Volkman 2005; Watkins 2004). But we are interested in how these two domains are linked— in how the negotiation of nonbiological adoptive kinship happens in and through the question of cultural identity. Specifically, we examine the "culture question" as taken up in interviews with parents in the United States who have adopted children from China. Indeed, we hyphenate *Chinese-culture* to emphasize its currency in the social enactment of kinship. We find that, across the narratives of single-parent, straight, and queer families, Chinese-culture works as a socially intelligible sign that mediates blood and social family origins. But more than this, narrative labor around Chinese-culture leads us to rethink how ideas of blood origin and social desire operate in the construction of socially intelligible kinship in general: Each does not so much collapse into the other as require the other in particular ways. Thus, specific operations of race and culture in adoption offer insights into new kinship studies' theorization of heteronormativity, in particular how it might be reproduced "even" amidst hybrid, multiple family forms.

Interviews with U.S. parents of Chinese children catalyze our analysis. In the late 1990s, as China became the top sending country in international adoption, coauthor Sara Dorow devoted several years to a study of the cultural economy of the process, focusing on raced and gendered exchanges in the formation of adoptive kinship (Dorow 2006). Several years later, when we together revisited a selection of 15 of the interviews Dorow had conducted with adoptive parents in the United States, we were struck by the parents' sometimes-implicit grappling with heteronormative ideas of kinship. We noticed a series of conflations and slippages around questions of blood, race, and cultural origins of the child and family. These questions prompted significant narrative labor by adoptive parents, which, in turn, prompted us to explore the questions further. Our interest was also piqued by the occurrence of similar questions about origin across single-parent, straight, and queer families. Although each family had a unique narrative, there were points of commonality among them, especially in moments in which the lack of correspondence between blood and social family origins seemed to be accompanied by the sign "Chinese-culture" and its race correlatives.

This article is the product of our interactions as we pursued the line of inquiry that emerged out of our collaborative reading of Dorow's interviews with adoptive parents. In her original research, Dorow interviewed a broad representation of some forty adoptive families in the San Francisco, California, Bay Area and the Twin Cities of Minneapolis and St. Paul, Minnesota, placing their negotiations of their children's racial and cultural identities in the context of adoption as a set of transnational exchanges. In going back to the interviews several years later with a new set of questions about heteronormativity and kinship, we took up Malin Åkerström and colleagues' methodological insight that "a return to dusty [ethnographic] material from the past ... may not only be fruitful but also intellectually stimulating" (2004:344). We selected the 15 interviews to which we "returned" from across the straight two-parent, queer single-parent, and single-mother participants in the original study.

In the first part of the article, we review relevant feminist arguments in new kinship studies, especially Judith Butler's notion of "intelligible kinship." We then turn to exploring the interplay of blood and social family origins in adoptive kinship, especially around the figures of mother and father. In the second half of the article, we move to a discussion of how, within adoptive-parent narratives, the sign "Chinese-culture" becomes a means to manage the heteronormative demand for social intelligibility.

A few words are in order about the characteristics of the China–U.S. adoption program from 1994 to 2006, the period during which it grew into the most popular adoption program in the United States (parents interviewed for the study had adopted mostly in the mid-1990s). First, we note the fact of abandonment and its attendant unknowns: Nearly all children adopted from China had been found in public places and then brought to orphanages. There was little or no information about their birth families and preadoptive biographies. This lack of information was nevertheless accompanied by a plethora of professional and popular narratives addressing it, whether in the form of children's stories on adoptive mother love or advice on preserving adoptee birth heritage. Second, the fact of abandonment in China was also the fact of desire on the part of U.S. parents. Many of the Chinese children available for adoption were healthy girls, desirable to many prospective adoptive parents.[1] Third, compared with most other international adoption programs, the China Center of Adoption Affairs in Beijing put relatively generous parameters on the age, health, and marital-status requirements of adoptive parents when it officially opened to international adoptions in the early 1990s. New restrictions were imposed in 2001 and again in 2007: Adoptions by lesbian and gay prospective parents were officially prohibited, adoptions by single people were curtailed and then stopped, and new regulations regarding health, age, and income were put on all prospective adopters of Chinese children.[2] We finally note that, although its numbers have dropped in recent years, China–U.S. adoption remains the largest of contemporary intercountry adoption migrations. Each year, some six thousand Chinese children are adopted into the United States alone. Most adoptive parents are relatively well-off, well educated, and white (Dorow 2006; Tessler et al. 1999).

One Father, Two Mothers: Social Intelligibility and Adoptive Kinship

A key feature of new kinship studies is criticism of the heteronormative assumptions that underpin anthropological concepts of kinship, a critique that, instead, foregrounds the social flexibility and historical particularity of kinship forms (Campbell 2002; Wade 2005). For example, Louise Lamphere (2005) urges researchers not to treat heteronormative kinship as an ideal type but as one possible configuration among many: "Anthropologists should assume no basic units and propose no universals; rather, they should work for a plurality of models" (2005:34). Butler (2000, 2002) is eloquent on the subject, arguing that cultural ideas of kinship do not correspond to natural structures in the ways expressed by politicians and social scientists but, instead, are norms regulated through ideological grids of intelligibility. Heteronormativity constitutes this grid for cultural ideas of kinship, and the result is the conflation of heteronormativity and kinship under the rubric of "culture," in which kinship is taken as always already heteronormative and heteronormativity is taken as natural. In Butler's hands, the idea that "stable kinship norms support our abiding sense of culture's intelligibility" (2000:71) is turned on its head, and, instead, cultural intelligibility of kinship assumes a blood relation, which is constructed as essential and teleological and is a matter of politics.

This grid of intelligibility, asserts Evelyn Blackwood, still continues to underpin much anthropological and ethnographic study of kinship. The absent presence of the "patriarchal man" even structures concepts intended to capture alternative kinship arrangements; for example, the concept "matrifocal" depends on heteronormative ideas of kinship because the patriarchal man (who in the matrifocal case is "missing") is still the organizing term. The "patriarchal man" assumes the center or origin of kinship in two main ways: biologically "activating" kinship and culturally "controlling" kinship (Blackwood 2005:6). Whereas the mother is the biological site of origin, the father is the biological and social agent of reproduction. The cultural production of socially intelligible kinship rides on the ideological conflation of biological and social origins. Blackwood and Butler thus take a truism most explicitly articulated by Claude Lévi-Strauss, that kinship is the simultaneity of a blood and social origin, and expose it as an ideological construct (Borneman 1996; Schneider and Gough 1984).

We explore the presupposition of blood suggested by Butler and Blackwood using adoptive parents' narratives of Chinese-culture as leverage. Peter Wade (2005), drawing on the work of Marilyn Strathern, has argued that, in practice, Western notions of kinship do not operate within the heteronormative limits that have been assigned to such relatedness, but, rather, kinship is a process in which the social and biological interact in multiple ways. Scholars such as Janet Carsten (2007) and Barbara Yngvesson (2007) have used adoptee narratives as evidence of this interplay, focusing especially on shifting meanings of biology that occur in the "web of intertwinings, separations, and rejoinings between what is apparently inherited from the past, and what is created anew" (Carsten 2007:403).

The attention to what Wade calls "kinship as hybridity" provides a cautionary footnote to the suggestion that a kind of biological foundationalism automatically reproduces the dominance of heteronormativity. But, at the same time, there is a striking absence in many of these more "optimistic" works of a concerted analysis of gender, patriarchy, or sexuality. And so we approach our China–U.S. adoption narratives interested in a tension that has not been fully addressed in new kinship studies between, on the one hand, hybridity scholarship (including some of the adoption literature) that emphasizes flexible and newly formulated relations between blood and social kinship, and, on the other hand, critical feminist scholarship that foregrounds how kinship continues to be made socially intelligible through the conflated and gendered relationship between blood and social family origins. Even as the contingency and uncertainty of this relationship is increasingly exposed in contemporary formations of parenthood (see, e.g., Stacey 2006),[3] the relationship of socially intelligible kinship with blood remains. Some recent scholarship, for example, has demonstrated how disaggregating biological and social fatherhood results in "confusion" that seems to require some kind of management. Rosanna Hertz (2002) notes in her study of single women who use sperm banks that the sperm-donating father tends to figure as a stand-in until a "real" social father comes along, and Deborah

Dempsey (2004) finds in a legal study of custody claims involving children in lesbian-parented families in Australia that courts face the dilemma of either recognizing a biological father or recognizing a "fatherlike" social relationship (see also Lewin 1993). If such an inextricable relation of social and biological origins underpins intelligible kinship, then adoptive parents' narratives foreground the kind of labor required when the gap in that origin is brought into focus.

In new kinship studies, adoption is often interpreted as a "no" to normalized kinship in that it creates family outside and often independent of blood lineage (Weston 2001). Indeed, some scholars have argued that adoptive kinship potentially calls attention to and challenges several hegemonic discourses of family: that is, that it is blood based, and prepolitical (Modell 2002; Volkman 2003). Butler points out how the critique of a formal notion of kinship within anthropology that is centered on "the fiction of bloodlines" (2000:74) has not led to "a dismissal of kinship altogether" (2002:15). She cites *Families We Choose,* by Kath Weston (1991), as an example of research that attends to kinship formation by replacing the centrality of blood with that of choice. Adoption literature often focuses on the idea of "chosen" family, suggesting that adoptive kinship helps to unmask normative assumptions of the family in general.

Focusing on the idea of "choice" is a move away from the conventional assumption of blood that has underpinned kinship studies, but we argue that the idea proves inadequate. As Corinne P. Hayden points out, the very idea of "chosen families" only becomes meaningful "in the context of the cultural belief in the power of blood ties" (1995:45). But more than this, privileging choice might mask other modes in which heteronormativity operates. In this article, we draw on the narratives of parents with children adopted from China to consider how the connection of blood and social origins persists in adoptive kinship as desire, even if it has been rejected in much of new kinship theory. We have already suggested that the desire of adoptive parents connects with the fact of abandonment and a nonconsensual relocation of the child from the country and family of birth. Desire for intelligible kinship is caught up with cultural difference. For adoptive families with whom Dorow spoke, their choice in having a family comes along with their child's Chinese-culture, the meaning of which is overdetermined—including by blood—but operative in discernibly varying ways. In the next section, we demonstrate that the question of origins for China–U.S. adoptive families is a site of tensions between biological and socially chosen kinship and that these tensions are palpable in narratives of cultural heritage. The continued centrality of blood is still experienced in adoption in the gap between origins of the child and social desire (choice) of parents, which includes the desire for social intelligibility.

The circumstances under which individual children in China have been made available for adoption are usually not known. For the adoptive parents with whom Dorow spoke, anxiety was often attached to a lack of knowledge about blood origins, and it was often manifested in forms of narrative labor on the complicated social causes of adoptive kinship, including biological parents' reasons for abandoning their children and their own desire for parenthood or for particular kinds of children. The anxiety of uncertainty functioned as a source of frustration and sometimes of fear, both before and after the adoption. As adoptive father Fred Coombs put it, "I think the hard part is the decision that the biological parents had to leave their child. But I think the words I just said are as far as we can go with it." When Dorow asked single mother Nan Heinman whether she had talked with her daughter about birth parents and abandonment, she replied, "Yeah, that whole subject—I don't even know how … that scares the hell out of me, that whole subject. I don't know how or when to even go there. And I have to say, that I've been to a number of lectures on parenting of these girls and how to talk about the adoption thing." The anxiety over blood origin as neither known, shared, nor chosen by their daughters was also, in the same moment, an expression of the adoptive parents' desire for a family and a social origin of the family.[4]

Some have pointed out that, in its popular imaginary, this anxiety focuses on the mother(s).[5] Adoption narratives conjure a child exchanged between two women (Berebitsky 2000; Clark 1998). As adoptive mother Ginger Adley lamented, "What makes me the most sad is that I can't find her mother. And her mother—and father, I shouldn't be sexist—have no idea that their child is safe." The mention of the birth father is an afterthought; it is the birth mother who mediates between one (birth) family and another (social) family.[6]

This spectacle of exchange suggests that one mother takes up at the point at which the other left off. It is the social notion of motherhood—of nurturance and motherly love—that is the basis for understanding why one woman can be seen to "stand in" for another. Acknowledging two mothers at once might be difficult, but we consider how this idea of exchange alone does not unravel the tension around origins but, instead, compares to the question of unresolved fatherhood.

In Dorow's interviews, adoptive parents' narratives were marked often by silence regarding the blood father; he was an afterthought who came in and out of conversation. Jennifer Bartz noted that she and her daughter periodically played a game in which they imagined what her daughter's birth mother might be like, and then she added, "Hmmm, I don't think I've ever played the game with her about who her father is, quite honestly."[7] In general, parents appeared to be nonchalant toward the father question. However, the fragility of the social father's position was not far under the surface. For example, questions of racial difference seemed especially likely to raise anxiety about fatherhood, which is not to say that they were a problem for all parents. Adoptive father Terry Schlitz, gay and white, took some pleasure in remembering how one of the straight white fathers in his travel group was "outed" as nonnormative, made particular and suspect as he stood on a street corner in China with a Chinese child in his arms:

> You know, when you're gay and have kids and people realize it, you're just always on display.... So what I laughed at is when we were in China, all these [straight white] parents would be saying, "God, we went to the bus stop and people just stared at us!" ... And the ignorant bossy white male in our group, he hated it the most. And I just secretly savored that. [Terry Schlitz, gay white father]

For Terry and his partner, Matt, anxiety when traveling to China hinged not on racial markers of blood difference but, rather, on the always-present danger that they might not get their child if authorities discovered they were gay. The anxiety for the adoptive straight white father of a baby from China is another thing altogether: He will get his child, but can she really ever be "his"—that is, how is kinship enacted—if the link between biological and social fatherhood no longer holds (something Terry said he had "grieved" when he came out years before)?

Race anxieties often signal the fragility of socially intelligible kinship, and for adoptive families of Chinese children, those anxieties are narrated most often through the question of culture. Dorow (2006), Ann Anagnost (2000), and others have argued that anxiety over how and to what extent a child's birth culture should or can be embraced and integrated is in some ways a displaced anxiety over motherhood. But we explore the possibility that it also functions, albeit differently, to displace anxiety over fatherhood. It just might be that, in adoptive parents' constructions of their cultural identity, one begins to discern heteronormative imperatives in regard to fatherhood. The next section, which considers interview material, is devoted to fleshing out this idea.

Our treatment of the interviews has three unique qualities. First, we do not offer a conventional ethnographic analysis of the field data. Rather, we mine the narratives of Chinese-culture in the interview material as a way to think through this theoretical tension in the relations of blood and social desire. Second, given that most popular and scholarly work on adoption focuses explicitly or implicitly on absent–present birth mothers or on the construction of adoptive motherhood in relation to birth motherhood (Anagnost 2001; Berebitsky 2000; Dorow 2006; Rapp 1999), we quite deliberately plumb the question of fatherhood. This is a process of "reading between the lines" rather than making generalizations about the experience of adoptive families. And, finally, we found our analysis hindered by treating families by "structural type" (e.g., straight, queer, single parent) and, instead, follow Butler in understanding kinship to be "a kind of doing ... [that] can only be understood as an enacting practice" (2002:34). In this sense, we look at single, straight, and queer parents in turn, but with the assumption that heteronormativity operates in all of their enacting practices. Put another way, we understand each parental form as a singular relation to the demand of socially intelligible kinship.

Adoption Narratives: Kinship and "Chinese-Culture"

In a heteronormative North American context, adoption narratives respond to a demand and desire for social intelligibility by somehow negotiating the discontinuity between social and blood origins. Françoise-Romaine Ouellette and Héléne Belleau (2001) have argued that, because kinship is largely defined first through blood and because distinct cultural origins are reminiscent of bloodlines, adoptive parents must negotiate their family's relation to their children's cultural heritage. Often, archives of photographs and souvenirs serve to contain and manage the Otherness of culture that might pose a threat to the family's own social and legal claims to kinship. When blood origins are tied to particular national, cultural, or racial spaces, as is the case in China–U.S. adoption, "culture" figures in especially complicated ways.

Ouellette and Belleau's insights are important, but our own reading of adoptive parents' narratives bears them out only partially. Some parents do, indeed, try to contain or normalize the origin of their family, but some of the adoptive parents Dorow spoke with were enthusiastic about exposing their child to "her" Chinese culture, and others wanted their children to interact with people from similar "backgrounds." What is important for our purposes is that, in all the narratives, Chinese-culture mediated constructions of kinship by functioning as something that could be narrated, which in itself promises some degree of mastery over the knowledge gaps and racial difference that threaten social intelligibility. We think that Chinese-culture understood in this way is a powerful entrée to theorizing kinship and the persistence of heteronormative desire precisely because it is performed at the (dis)juncture of blood and social origins.

The connection between fatherhood and culture was perhaps most explicit for many of the single mothers with whom Dorow spoke. Theirs were families for whom the absence of a father seemed to leave in suspension, or at least to defer, the question of family intelligibility and, connectedly, cultural identity. The question of the social intelligibility of their family was left open, leaving a space between blood and desire. For example, Sharon Anderson could play with rather than against the discontinuous origins of her family to make intelligible both the absent father and the racial– cultural difference of her kinship:

> You know, you have some interesting encounters around, reactions to a Caucasian woman with a Chinese baby. . . . I remember getting into the parking ramp elevator at the hospital [in California] with her when she was a baby. And there was a Japanese woman who got on the elevator with me, and she looked at me, and she said, "Oh, is your husband Asian?" "Oh, no, no" [I replied]. "Is the baby's father Asian?" And I said, "Yes." (Sharon laughs.) The doors open on the bottom floor, and she says, "The baby certainly looks like her father." [Sharon Anderson, single white mother]

Many single mothers seemed to find enjoyment and perhaps comfort in this ambiguity, in which an absent father is also the suggestion that there is one. This is an evocative space in which heteronormalized ideas of kinship have not been realized, but neither have they been disappointed. Perhaps this is why the figure of the father seemed to haunt the future in the narratives of single mothers, as they imagined how their children might be affected in various ways by the absent social father and what he represents.

> I think this single parent thing will loom a lot larger, actually, in the future. My daughter is very clearly aware of it now, and it bugs her. You know, she said, "Why didn't you take care of that [i.e., find a father] before you got me?" It'll loom a lot larger than it does now in terms of what she didn't have, and therefore does that cause her to want to, maybe more than some other kids, try and figure out what she would have had in China that she didn't get: two parents, siblings, the whole nine yards. [Nan Heinman, single white mother]

> I hope in the future my daughter is very secure, that she's very loved and that there's a lot of people that care about her. And I think that being from a single family, that's different. This suburb is a very family—single families aren't real common in this area. So she's gonna be different because of that, too.... I guess I'm going to

have to be very adamant about making sure that she understands that she is—that she knows that she is Chinese, but that she's here because she's very loved and cared for. [Laura Vigdahl, single white mother]

Laura and Nan both stressed a desire for their daughters to have a sense of their Chinese cultural identity; Nan had hired a Chinese nanny to teach her daughter language and culture, to give her as much as possible what she "would have had in China but didn't get." This function of Chinese-culture responds to a string of differences, including the absent presence of a father into the child's future. Unlike Nan and Laura, Hannah Carter acquired a male partner after she adopted her daughter; she suggested that the presence of socially recognized fatherhood would fulfill her daughter's (future) belonging. When Dorow asked her if she was involved with the local Chinese cultural and adoption support group, Hannah's reply indicated a correlation:

I've been reading their newsletter on the web. I think it's good. One of the things—one reason I haven't gotten involved in things like I thought I would is that after I came back I met this really wonderful guy, who is wonderful with Rose, and just always wanted to have kids. And so I haven't had the time that I might have otherwise. And for me, I had to make a decision that this was the best thing for her, for her future, was if I do find somebody, she'll have a dad. I mean he would definitely be her dad, and we've already talked about that. [Hannah Carter, single white mother]

In the narratives of several single mothers, the sign Chineseculture signaled the family's kinship as "unfinished" and was seen as partially making up for the absence of a father. The discontinuity of origins to which it referred might threaten or supplement the adoptive kinship of single mother and adopted child, leaving in suspension the question of intelligibility. Narrations of Chinese-culture by single-parent families suggest that demands for social intelligibility act on single mothers' adoptive kinship not so much through anxiety over the discontinuity of blood and social origins but through the ambiguity of their relationship.

One might assume straight couples who adopt to have less of a conflict with the question of social intelligibility, but the "almost but not quite,"[8] usually made visible in racial difference, makes the discontinuity ever present. Even, and perhaps especially, for white heterosexual couples, the visibility of race materialized in narrative labor on Chineseculture. When it is the equivalence of blood and social origins that makes kinship intelligible, in a variety of ways Chinese-culture is a vehicle for managing the gap held open by the "almost but not quite"; it is enlisted in some instances to externalize difference and in others to maintain a family identity's social coherence. Blood origin is variously excluded from or enfolded within social desire, but in all cases it lingers as racialized difference, a complex thing for many reasons.

Straight couples expressed varying levels of discomfort with regard to Chinese-culture as a potential threat to the family's coherence, that is, to broader social claims of kinship with the child.[9] This worry was most pronounced among some of the straight adoptive fathers.

You don't want to do too many Chinese things. As we grow with our daughter, I find myself questioning at what point it's more important growing within our family, you know, *or* us taking her for Chinese food or taking her to a Chinese parade. [Billy Peterson, straight white father]

I don't want her to have anything to do with that culture that threw her away.... I think you ought to spend your time trying to raise your kids to be happy well-adjusted little citizens, not happy well-adjusted little Asian-American people perhaps with a focus on their Fukinese abstraction [*sic*]. [Chet Cook, straight white father]

We read this either–or proposition—she is "Chinese" or she is "ours"—as a form of narrative labor on the gap between biology and desire, in which social intelligibility depends on containing the continuities of difference represented by Chinese-culture.

For some straight white couples, the "almost but not quite" of their kinship—a normative family structure with the obvious absence of the correspondence of blood and social origins—surfaced most palpably with regard to racialized difference. Sandra and John Padding both said they initially had wanted a baby that looked like them. John said that he experienced dissonance in "having a Chinese baby without a Chinese past in my life. If she wasn't Chinese, she'd be a Jewish baby to be raised—and my heritage would be her heritage, and there wouldn't need to be this other culture added." Sandra narrated the anxiety this way: "It's like, how do you honor the Chinese cultural stuff without it turning into a different religion? ... There's a connection in doing something that has some parallels to Chinese tradition, but it's [also] Jewish tradition." To deal with this tension, the Paddings had created a hybrid ritual for Jewish and Chinese festivals that fall at the same time of year—Sukkot and the Mid-Autumn Festival, respectively—in which, as a family, they erected a sukkah, looked at the moon, and thought of their child's birth family. Chinese-culture was integrated into a more general family narrative, creating a seeming detente between blood and social origins.

The salience of race in negotiating kinship is underscored in those few families for whom it actually helped to relieve anxiety around origins. George and Patty Lou, an interracial couple (he is Asian, she is white), conjured cultural intelligibility through the interplay of race, family, and nation:

Patty: There was no issue of culture, different country, different language than she was used
          to. We just brought her home and she was ours! We want her to know, of course, that
          she's adopted, and that she's Chinese but also American.
Dorow: How do those things fit together for you, that she's both Chinese and American?
Patty: It's not an issue. Because if we had a natural, a biological child, it would be half Chinese,
          half Caucasian.

For George and Patty, an interracial popular imaginary allowed their family to "pass" (especially if George was present),[10] something not available to the majority of couples adopting from China.

Queer couples seemed to most embrace Chinese-culture. Their narratives of Chinese-culture usually worked with the discontinuity of blood and desire rather than laboring to contain or manage difference. Jennifer Bartz compared her experience to that of straight couples she had observed.

Traditional married couples usually come from this place where they've tried to have kids themselves, they went through the whole infertility thing generally, struggled with that, they want their kind of traditional family. So adoption is a way for them to get what they always wanted. Whereas the rest of us are kind of more open to the alternatives.... [Some straight] people will say (lowers her voice with a swagger), "I didn't bring her here to be Chinese, I brought her here to be my daughter." And it's like of course she's our daughter. But I think it's partly that—I find it fascinating, too, the whole idea of her learning Chinese. [Jennifer Bartz, lesbian white mother]

For queer families, the entire adoption process is a reminder that they are on the margins of socially intelligibility; this reality is not carried only by racial difference. All queer families with whom Dorow spoke had to temporarily conceal their queerness in the course of the adoption process. Joyce and Marion, a white lesbian couple, put it this way:

Joyce: Since we're lesbians only one of us could be the adoptive parent.... Marion traveled to
          China. I did not go. Our agency actually prohibited it because they had had an experi-
          ence with two lesbians going, where one of the other families outed them, and then
          there was a real problem.
Marion: Because of the whole lesbian thing, they kept saying, "Don't tell anyone, don't tell
          anyone."

Such distance from—and yet felt presence of—the heteronormative ideal is evident in the way queer parents cautiously reveled in those moments when adoption, in its bureaucratic protocols, afforded a recognition or legitimation of their kinship. Debra recounted having to write biographies and a home study for the adoption agency, adding that it was "actually kind of fun—but it was fun because we were recognized as a family, and we were recognized as good future parents." It was their "pure" desire for a child apart from the question of social intelligibility that provided the relief of being recognized as family. Relief at such recognition and frustration with the continual undermining of such recognition are two sides of the same coin but not primarily matters of racial difference.

Rather than narratives that used Chinese-culture to contain and manage the question of social intelligibility, many queer parents seemed to desire (sometimes anxiously) a full account of their child's Chinese-culture. Consequently, it is not surprising that parents engaging in this type of narrative labor told stories that were the least about racial difference and the future and the most about making the child's past in China present in the cultural identity of the family: "Somebody said to us, I don't remember who, that what happens is that we all, just because we have a child from China, we are all as a family Chinese American. Not only our children, but we have assumed that identity.... We talk about China—almost daily it's brought up in conversation at some point" (Terry Schlitz, gay white father cofather).

The real limits to what these parents could know about the conditions surrounding their child's birth, and of what they could understand and experience of Chinese-culture, were a source of anxiety and, sometimes, anger.

> If we can't give her her birth parents, at least we can give her her birth culture, sort of?—but not all happy-slappy, to say that birth parents had to have loved her!
>
> I think that's the only thing that bothers me about adopting from China—that it's so hard to know ... I have occasionally fantasized about traveling to China and somehow going door to door if I needed to and saying ..., "Who left that little ... who abandoned a baby on ...?" [Joyce Cousins, lesbian white mother]

This narration of Chinese-culture was linked to a reworking of the relationship of blood and social origins—a process that Hayden (1995) has called the "dispersal" of kinship. Whereas Hayden uses the term to refer to the multiple conceptions of biology employed in lesbian kinship narratives,[11] we deploy the term to think about the social and historical interplay of biological and fictive (or chosen) kin in adoption narratives:

> She has two moms that dote on her. Usually you just have one mom, but she's got two that dote on her. Plus another [Chinese] friend who's like a grandmother, plus her real grandmas. [Marion Frank, lesbian white mother]
>
> I imagine that the way this whole thing evolved, that there were many people involved in getting Pan Pan from her birth mother, whom she spent a night with, to her foster mother. So she's been on a kind of an underground railroad, with people who've all along the way cared tremendously about her, have made sure that she hasn't had any lapses in any care or any love. I mean, she's been loved and challenged and taught and everything, every step of the way. [Lisa Walker, lesbian white mother]

Like Terry Schlitz, other queer parents suggested that dispersed kinship included the conscious embrace of racial difference as one of a continuity of differences. Joyce Cousins chuckled at this laundry list: "She was abandoned, she was adopted, she's got two mothers, she's got two mothers of a different race, she's left-handed."

Racial difference played a part alongside Chinese-culture in the enacting of kinship, but class was also a crucial corollary. It figured in the desire to provide for a child—including "providing" her with a cultural identity—in many ways that were economic. As one lesbian mother put it, "We're in a position now where we're not struggling too much financially at the moment, so we can do things that we need to do to try and take care of her. And we can let her go to a [Chinese–English] bilingual Montessori private preschool that costs a lot of money." Eng (2003) has argued that transnational–transracial adoptive kinship is legitimized in part by middle-class consumerism, perhaps especially for queer parents. Terry and Matt suggested, for example, that people "forgave" their being gay because they had brought a child into a better life. Across the board, adoptive parents variously saw their financial provision as making up for the lack of support given to their children by the Chinese birth family and the Chinese state, as a way to provide Chinese cultural opportunities, or even as giving girls, in particular, the kinds of opportunities they might not have had in China.

Conclusion: Kinship Anxiety and the Ambiguities of New Kinship

Adoption narratives reveal anxiety over a demand and a desire for intelligibility that applies to all forms of kinship. In the particular forms we consider here, from the anxiety emerges a kind of narrative laboring on racial and cultural differences, which are taken up as raw material through (and against) which to negotiate intelligibility. Narrative labor performed on "Chinese-culture" is of particular importance because of the ways it manages the discontinuous origins of transracial–transnational adoption, working to defer, contain, supplement, or disperse the conflation of blood and social origins demanded by ideologies of intelligible kinship. Parents' negotiations of Chinese-culture thus offer a unique entrée to the operation and circulation of desire in kinship—desire for particular kinds of kinships, even and especially when they do not and cannot involve blood relations. Insights into the particularities of this "instrumental case" (Stake 2005) of China–U.S. adoption might help scholars more generally understand, and perhaps raise new questions about, the relationship between blood and desire in the reproduction of intelligible kinship in a heteronormative context.

These insights might be especially productive given scholarly splits and uncertainties regarding adoptive kinship. On the one hand, transnational–transracial adoption is quintessentially a form of "new kinship," a dispersal of bloodlines and heterosex as the foundation of domestic belonging. On the other hand, the classed, gendered, and raced aspects that attend the desire for intelligibility in such adoptions belie the connotations of consent that accompany the concept of "chosen family." Our exploration of narrative labor on Chinese-culture is an attempt to think about these questions otherwise: to suspend the assumed newness of "chosen" kinship and the persistence of the social command of blood long enough to ask what secrets adoptive parents' stories might reveal about the social intelligibility of kinship.

Narrative labor in relation to cultural identity, especially when class and race are considered, can invent unexpected variations on the theme of heteronormativity. In some cases, as we found especially with single mothers, the blood–social relation was reworked as a deferral of heteronormative demands, because the discontinuity of origins left open the question of intelligibility. In other cases, labor on the gap between blood and social origins unexpectedly contributed to active remembering of birth families in China, thus stretching the normative bounds of the nuclear family unit. Although mobilized with different vocabularies, the dispersal of kinship appeared in the narratives at least as the acknowledgment of the uncertainty of the future or as a provision of "tools" for multiply positioned differences.[12] Debra and Christy commented on this uncertainty:

Debra: Well, we have this sort of funny vision of the conferences for Chinese adoptees in 20 years.

Christy: (lightly laughing with Debra) Yeah, breakout sessions for the daughters of lesbian parents, parents who divorced after they came home from China—

Debra: —single parents …

At the same time, our reading of China–U.S. adoptive parents' narratives also suggests some caution about the marriage of new kinship studies and adoption scholarship that such variation might invite. Certainly the early decades of transnational–transracial adoption (i.e., the 1960s and 1970s) were dominated by the assertion that assimilationist approaches were "best" for the child, and new kinship studies indicate how these discourses are not sustainable in the era of globalization and hegemonic multiculturalism. In this way, the "choice" of kinship is equivalent to one of a continuity of differences, which seems to upset the applecart of biological foundationalism. However, "difference" is tolerated only to a certain point: It is good to embrace another culture, but only so far as it remains within the limits of social intelligibility. As our discussion highlights, that intelligibility is not born of a straightforward conflation of blood and social origins; but it persists as a desire for particular kinds of kinship and as a narrative laboring on difference.

This makes us pause at the optimism expressed in new kinship studies over the multiplicity and hybridity of kinship forms. Are we to read the Paddings' hybridization of the Chinese Mid-Autumn Festival and the Jewish holiday of Sukkot as a dispersion or a conflation of the blood and social origins of kinship? What about a single mother's deflection of questions about her child's father or a white gay father's claim that he is now Chinese? If queer parents' recrafting of their children's histories into transnational and transracial stories of kinship does not clearly constitute an escape from the demand for social intelligibility, we might then ask anew what exactly constitutes that demand.

Wade (2005) has pointed out that essentialism is a "moveable feast," thus complicating the task of categorizing various forms of kinship as "traditional" or "innovative." Parents' multiple forms of labor on Chinese-culture suggest that the social intelligibility of kinship might itself be a moveable feast, or perhaps a moving target. We simply assert that one secret of socially intelligible kinship is related to the operation of heteronormativity on the level of desire, evidenced in the multiple and inventive forms of interplay between blood and social origins in these adoption narratives.

Notes

Acknowledgments. The authors would like to thank Charles Barbour and Karyn Ball for comments on a draft of the article. Sara Dorow gratefully acknowledges funding in support of field research from the Social Science Research Council and the University of Minnesota.

1. It is crucial to note that the percentage of healthy infant girls leaving China for adoption far exceeds the actual percentage of such children in orphanages; that is, healthy baby girls are the ones demanded by and sent for international adoption (Dorow 2006).

2. Anxieties over origins and the labor toward heteronormative reproduction are thus inextricable from institutional and state regulatory practices.

3. In other words, Judith Stacey's work also operates in the tension we have delineated between a kind of "hybridity" thinking and the power of intelligible kinship.

4. This analysis of double origins is akin to David Eng's argument that the transnationally adopted child serves as both subject and object of kinship formation.

5. The formalization of open adoption has effected great change in practices of and desires for "clean break" adoption, but in the case of transnational adoption, open adoption is the exception. Indeed, one reason many parents choose intercountry adoption is that "there will be no birth mother knocking on our door" (as one parent put it to Dorow in an interview).

6. It is also possible to understand this exchange not as one occurring between two mothers but, rather, as an exchange of mothers, reminiscent of the "exchange of women" theorized by Claude Lévi-Strauss (1969) as a fundamental structure of all (heteronormative) kinship. In this sense, the spectacle of exchange in adoption recapitulates relations of exchange configuring all kinship, in which "the woman from elsewhere makes sure that the men from here will reproduce their own kin" (Butler 2002:32).

7. This ease with the absence of the blood father might be explained by the dominant imaginary of fatherhood, whether adoptive or biological, as being, in contrast to the innateness of motherhood, not instinctive but learned (Miall and March 2003).

8. This is a phrase used by postcolonial theorist Homi K. Bhabha (1994) to theorize mimicry, although we do not mean to use it in exactly the way he does.

9. Anxiety about social intelligibility may be exacerbated by infertility; many couples who adopt from China are unable to have children by birth and have gone through some kind of process of grieving and of working through the associated feelings.

10. We do not want to neglect the role the national imaginary plays in underwriting heteronormative kinship, as suggested in Patty Lou's and also Chet Cook's narratives of family and national belonging for their children. We do not have space here to deal with this issue, but see Dorow 2006.

11. This dispersal of kinship sometimes coexists with the claim to a "doubling" of maternal love in lesbian narratives, which is itself a reworking of biology in its new intersections with chosen kinship (Hayden 1995).

12. As our method of reading Chinese-culture in adoption narratives demonstrates, relative "proximity" to heteronormative kinship makes a difference in the forms of labor available to adoptive families as they enact kinship. At the same time, this range of approaches is not fixed to some continuum of straight–single–queer; for example, Dorow interviewed some straight couples whose negotiations of Chinese-culture more closely resembled what we have identified as a queering of double biological and social origins and so forth. This point only underscores the larger point we wish to make: The reproduction of socially intelligible kinship may depend on the (heteronormative) collapse of blood and the social into each other but might, in fact, be reproduced through the flexibility of their shifting interdependence.

References Cited

A Åkerström, Malin, Katarina Jacobsson, and David Wästerfors
2004 Reanalysis of Previously Collected Material. Qualitative Research Practice. Clive Seale, Giampietro Gobo, Jaber F. Gubrium, and David Silverman, eds. Pp. 344–357. London: SAGE.

Anagnost, Ann
2000 Scenes of Misrecognition: Maternal Citizenship in the Age of Transnational Adoption. Positions: East Asia Cultures Critique 8(2):390–421.

Berebitsky, Julie
2000 Like Our Very Own: Adoption and the Changing Culture of Motherhood, 1851–1950. Lawrence: University Press of Kansas.

Bhabha, Homi K.
1994 The Location of Culture. London: Routledge.

Blackwood, Evelyn
2005 Wedding Bell Blues: Marriage, Missing Men, and Matrifocal Follies. American Ethnologist 32(1):3–19.

Borneman, John
1996 Until Death Do Us Part: Marriage/Death in Anthropological Discourse. American Ethnologist 23(2):21–35.

Butler, Judith
2000 Antigone's Claim: Kinship between Life and Death. New York: Columbia University Press. 2002 Is Kinship Always Already Heterosexual? Differences: A Journal of Feminist Cultural Studies 13(1):14–44.

Campbell, Kirsten
2002 The Politics of Kinship. Economy and Society 31(4):642–650. Carsten, Janet 2007 Tracing Trajectories of Information in New Contexts of Relatedness. Anthropological Quarterly 80(2):403–426.

Clark, Dannae
1998 Mediadoption: Children, Commodification, and the Spectacle of Disruption. American Studies 39(2):65–86.

Dempsey, Deborah
2004 Donor, Father, or Parent? Conceiving Paternity in the Australian Family Court. International Journal of Law, Policy and the Family 18(1):76–102.

Dorow, Sara K.
2006 Transnational Adoption: A Cultural Economy of Race, Gender, and Kinship. New York: NYU Press.

Eng, David L.
2003 Transnational Adoption and Queer Diasporas. Social Text 21(3):1–37.

Franklin, Sarah, and Susan McKinnon
2001 Relative Values: Reconfiguring Kinship Studies. Durham, NC: Duke University Press.

Hayden, Corinne P.
1995 Gender, Genetics, and Generation: Reformulating Biology in Lesbian Kinship. Cultural Anthropology 10(1):41–63.

Hertz, Rosanna
2002 The Father as an Idea: A Challenge to Kinship Boundaries by Single Mothers. Symbolic Interaction 25(1):1–31.

Lamphere, Louise
   2005   Replacing Heteronormative Views of Kinship and Marriage. American Ethnologist 32(1):34–36.
Lévi-Strauss, Claude
   1969   The Elementary Structures of Kinship. Rev. edition. J. H. Bell, J. R. von Sturmer, and R. Needham, eds. R. Needham, trans. Boston: Beacon.
Lewin, Ellen
   1993   Lesbian Mothers. Ithaca, NY: Cornell University Press. Miall, Charlene, and Karen March 2003 A Comparison of Biological and Adoptive Mothers and Fathers: The Relevance of Biological Kinship and Gendered Constructs of Parenthood. Adoption Quarterly 6:7–39.
Modell, Judith S.
   2002   A Sealed and Secret Kinship: The Culture of Policies and Practices in American Adoption. New York: Berghahn Books.
Ouellette, Françoise-Romaine, and Héléne Belleau, with Caroline Patenaude
   2001   Family and Social Integration of Children Adopted Internationally: A Review of the Literature. Montreal: INRSUrbanisation, Culture et Société.
Rapp, Rayna
   1999   Foreword. *In* Transformative Motherhood: On Giving and Getting in a Consumer Culture. Linda Layne, ed. Pp. xi–xix. New York: NYU Press.
Schneider, David M., and Kathleen Gough
   1984   A Critique of the Study of Kinship. Ann Arbor: University of Michigan Press.
Shanley, Mary L.
   2001   Making Babies, Making Families: What Matters Most in an Age of Reproductive Technologies, Surrogacy, Adoption, and Same-Sex and Unwed Parents. Boston: Beacon Press.
Stacey, Judith
   2006   Gay Parenthood and the Decline of Paternity as We Knew It. Sexualities 9(1):27–55.
Stake, Robert E.
   1995   The Art of Case Study Research. Thousand Oaks, CA: Sage. Sullivan, Maureen 2004 The Family of Woman: Lesbian Mothers, Their Children, and the Undoing of Gender. Berkeley: University of California Press.
Sullivan, Maureen
   2004   The Family of Woman: Lesbian Mothers, Their Children, and the Undoing of Gender. Berkeley: University of California Press.
Tessler, Richard C., Gail Gamache, and Liming Liu
   1999   West Meets East: Americans Adopt Chinese Children. Westport, CT: Bergin and Garvey.
Volkman, Toby Alice
   2003   Embodying Chinese Culture: Transnational Adoption in North America. Social Text 21(1):29–55. 2005 Cultures of Transnational Adoption. Durham, NC: Duke University Press.
Wade, Peter
   2005   Hybridity Thinking and Kinship Thinking. Cultural Studies 19(5):602–621.
Watkins, Mary
   2004   Adoption and Identity: Nomadic Possibilities for ReConceiving the Self. Electronic document, http:// uploads. pacifica.edu/gems/watkins/AdoptionIdentity.pdf, accessed September 2005.
Weston, Kath
   1991   Families We Choose: Lesbians, Gays, Kinship. New York: Columbia University Press 2001 Kinship, Controversy, and the Sharing of Substance: The Race/Class Politics of Blood Transfusion. *In* Relative Values: Reconfiguring Kinship Studies. Sarah Franklin and Susan McKinnon, eds. Pp. 147–174. Durham, NC: Duke University Press.
Yngvesson, Barbara
   2007   Refiguring Kinship in the Space of Adoption. Anthropological Quarterly 80(2):561–579.

Discussion Questions

1. The authors discuss *heteronormativity* in this article – what is this? Why is it important for us to recognize that this exists in our own culture?
2. What are some of the main ideas about identity and how it is created that are discussed in this article?
3. The authors discuss both *social* and *blood* origins – what is the difference here? Why is this an important distinction?
4. In the conclusion, the authors introduce the term *kinship anxiety* – what do they mean by this? Why is this important for us to study in terms of our understanding of modern kinship?
5. How have you constructed your own kinship? Do you place strong importance on blood kinship, or has your kinship identity been constructed in different ways? Why do you feel the way you do?

Chapter 10

Links Between Religion and Morality in Early Culture

Elsie Clews Parsons

W hat is the connection between religion and morality? This question has been examined – and will be examined – many times. In this article, Elsie Clews Parsons reasons that because the practices of some early cultures may not be judged as "moral" by Western standards, many assumptions about these cultures are ethnocentric and flawed. While this article was published in 1915, the reader should keep in mind that these problems anthropologists encountered 100 years ago can still be present in research today.

It is becoming a commonplace of ethnology that the connection between religion and morality is a late cultural fact. And yet this particular reaction against the ecclesiastical view of society is true only on the narrowest definitions of religion and of morals. It is not true if by morals we mean collective or social conduct as against conduct antisocial or individualistic, and by religion we mean supernaturalism.[1] To these meanings we shall undoubtedly hold unless our reaction against theology has not been thorough, leaving us still at heart theologues or their unwitting bastards, metaphysicians.

What then are the relations between religion and morality in early culture? They begin for the savage, as for us, in the nursery. In savagery, as in civilization, the supernatural sanction has a nursery rôle. Santa Claus, who writes down the names of the good children only in his book, the "bogey man" who carries off naughty children, the old witch who catches runaways, the god who promises longevity to filial offspring, all have their counterparts in the discipline of the savage child. In Australia, hard-pressed Illawarra mothers have been overheard to say, "Mirirul [the tribal high god] will not allow it."[2] Irritated West Victorian parents threaten to send for a moon spirit that does the bidding of Muurup, an epicure of child-flesh.[3] Samoans have a juvenile scarecrow in *Sina 'ai Mata,* or Sin a the Eye-eater, a bird-god. "Do not make such a noise; Sina the Eye-eater will come and pick out your eyes," an harassed parent would say.[4] Thompson River and Kootenay Indian parents also threaten noisy children with a bird. "The Owl will come and take you," or "I'll give you to the Owl," they say.[5] Eastman, the Sioux, remembers how, in his less sophisticated days, his grandmother would say to him at night, "Do not cry! Hmakaga (the Owl) is watching you from the tree-top."[6]

A "good" child does not cry. Nor, for the peace of his elders, must he be adventurous. It is troublesome to look for children who run away. And so would-be explorers are threatened with supernatural mishap. A Koita child who strayed in the bush at night would encounter a *vadavada,* a man who travels by night and

---

From "Links Between Religion and Morality in Early Culture" by Elsie Clews Parsons, as published in *American Anthropologist,* 17(1), 41–57, January 1915, American Anthropological Association.

---

[1] In our sense. The supernatural to us is in other cultures unquestionably natural. Cf. Lévy-Bruhl, L., *Les Fonctions Mentales dans les Sociétés Inférieures,* passim.
[2] Ridley, Wm., *The Aborigines of Australia* (Sidney, 1864), p. 137.
[3] Featherman, A., *Social History of the Races of Mankind* (London, 1881–91), Sec. Div., p. 172.
[4] Turner, G., *Samoa* (London, 1884), p. 74.
[5] Teit. J., "The Thompson River Indians." *Mem. Amer. Mus. Nat. Hist.* (New York. 1900). 11, 108.
[6] *Indian Boyhood* (New York. 1902). p. 9.

who brings sickness and death to those he meets.[7] The Euahlayi tribe of New South Wales have a bogey called from his cry Gineet Gineet. He goes about with a net across his shoulders into which he pops any children he can see.[8] Chemosit is a Nandi devil, half man, half bird, with one leg, nine buttocks, and a red mouth which shines at night like a lamp. He catches children who are foolish enough to be lured away from home by his night song.[9] 'Nenaunir of the Masai is a kindred monster; he is an invulnerable, stony-bodied creature with the head of a beast of prey and feet with claws; "Don't go too far," a mother says to her children, "or 'Nenaunir will get you!"[10] An obedient child among the Masai or elsewhere ordinarily stays at home or within call, but sometimes if he hangs around he may be in the way. When their elders begin to eat it is etiquette for Caffre children to leave the hut. The older comply, but the younger hang around for "just one taste." Then their father bids them go out into the veld to call Nomgogwana, a dangerous and peremptory monster. If the children demur, the father will say off-hand, "Very well, sit where you are; the food will not cook, as you know, till Nomgogwana comes, and then when he does come he will be so angry at seeing the food uncooked that he will eat all the children he can find." As the frightened children slip off, the father calls out to them: "Be sure you go far, far away into the veld, for otherwise Nomgogwana will not hear you; the reason why he did not hear you call before was that you did not go nearly far enough away; so be sure to go far away this time, lest you get eaten yourselves."[11]

Moral stories for the young are not lacking among savages. Once on a time in Pulu, an islet of the Torres straits, the boys and girls used to disobey their parents and play a game of twirling around with outspread arms. They played every night on the beach, until finally a great rock fell from the sky and killed all the islanders except one indispensable couple. Parents still tell their children never to play this game at night, and the old men remind bad children that by and by, if they are not good, the stone from Pulu will come and eat them Up.[12] In another of the folktales of the Torres straits, a mother and grandmother threaten a fractious girl with the Dògai if she will not stop crying. She fails to heed them, and the bogey does carry her off to torture.[13] The Bunya-Bunya of Queensland have a story about two boys who were once left alone in camp with strict orders not to leave it until the elders returned. Nevertheless, tiring of the camp, the boys went down to the beach. Then the Thugine, or Great Serpent of the Rainbow, came out of the sea, and, always on the watch for unprotected children, caught the boys and turned them into the two rocks that now stand between Double Island point and Inskip point. "Here you see," the old Blackfellow used to say to the boys, "the result of not paying attention to what you are told by your elders."[14] On Rogea off southeastern New Guinea once lived a little girl, say the islanders, a little girl over-fond of wandering about. "At all times her mother and father they said, 'Don't wander, or else the sorceress in the bush will eat you.' The girl didn't listen, she walked about. The old woman saw the girl and called her and said, 'You come.'" She took the girl to a cave and tattooed her.[15] "She boiled the blood and ate it." Had not the girl run home, she would have eaten her too.[16] In a story told by the Bètsilèo of Madagascar a naughty little boy is eaten up—by a *songòmby*, a creature big as an ox, but fleet-footed. The parents had put the boy outside of the house, calling out, "Here's your share, Mr Songòmby." The beast came and the child cried out, "Oh, here he

[7] Seligmann. C. G., *The Melanesians of British New Guinea* (Cambridge. 1910), p. 187

[8] Parker. K. L. *The Euahlayi Tribe* (London. 1905). p. 137.

[9] Hollis. A. C. *The Nandi* (Oxford. 1909). p. 41.

[10] Merker, M., *Die Masai* (Berlin. 1904). p. 202.

[11] Kidd, D., *Savage Childhood* (London, 1906), pp. 96–7.

[12] *Reports of the Cambridge Anthropological Expedition to Torres Straits* (Cambridge, 1904), v, 22.

[13] Ibid., v, 14.

[14] Howitt, A. W., *The Natives of South-East Australia* (London and New York, 1904), p. 431.

[15] The legend was told the investigator to account for tattooing.

[16] Seligmann. op. cit., p. 493. n. 2.

really is!" "Well, let him eat you," cried the parents, thinking the boy was fooling. And he did.[17] The Bilqula of the Northwest coast tell the story of a chief's daughter who one night would not stop crying. Finally her mother said to her, "Lie down and be still or the Snēnē'ik will come and get you." At midnight, when all were asleep, the Snēnē'ik did come in the shape of an old woman, and, catching the child through a hole in the wall, put her in a basket and carried her off.[18]

Terrifying ceremonial masks as well as "Sunday-school" stories are helps to primitive parents. In western Victoria the white kangaroo pouch masks worn over head and face by clowns at corroborees are often used to frighten misbehaving children.[19] In one of the Zuñi summer dances there is a mask of an old woman, a ceremonial scold, and part of her "business" is to threaten to eat up the children.[20] A kachina in a Hopi dance makes the same threat. The Hopi mask goes up to the child and says: "You are naughty and bad; we have come to get you. You fight the other children, kill chickens, etc., and we shall now take you away."[21] Among the Pueblo Indians of the Rio Grande I have collected several stories of refractory children frightened by masked figures, "like Santa Claus," one woman said to me. It is said that a "progressive" Santa Clara man once on a visit to San Juan tore the mask off a figure who was alarming the children and that because of the outrage he was kept imprisoned in the estufa for some time in danger of his life, and that he finally had to be ransomed with a horse and saddle.

Infantile bugaboos are replaced in many societies by spirits especially attentive to young people, "goody-goody" stories supposed to appeal to them succeed to the simpler nursery yarns, and renewed is the emphasis on the supernatural rewards or penalties for the filial or unfilial. Among the Tshis the family god is expected to appoint a *sassŭr*, a subordinate spirit, to walk behind the growing girls of the family.[22] Once on a time, goes a Kayan story, a woman and her daughter were reaping paddy. The girl left alone by her mother was told on no account to eat any of the rice, as it was against the tribal custom to eat while reaping. But the girl disobeyed. Thereupon hair began to grow all over her body and she had to take to the jungle like a coconut monkey.[23] Among the Fors, girls meddling with the milk-pots or stealing milk behind their mothers' backs are punished with epilepsy by a *zittan*, a spirit servant of the great mountain god of Gebel Marah.[24] At Ponape, in the Caroline islands, the ancestral spirits put an unending curse upon the unfilial.[25] Ainu women teach their daughters that were they to marry without being properly tattooed, after death the demons will do all the tattooing with very large knives and at one sitting.[26] Aztec youths were said to be warned by their fathers against unfilial conduct in order not to be devoured by wild beasts or come to an otherwise bad end.[27] The Ainu and the Aztecs do not represent, of course, as early a culture as some of the other groups from which we have been drawing illustrations, groups where dependence on parents or subjection to them ends with or even before adolescence. In these more primitive groups it is the tribal elders who go on with the education of a girl or a boy.

---

[17] Sibree. J., *Madagascar before the Conquest* (London. 1896). pp. 230–1.

[18] Boas. Franz, *Indianische Sagen won der Nord-Pacifischen Küste Amerikas* (Berlin. 1895), pp. 248–9. At Masset. Graham island, a Haida half-breed girl told me this summer mothers threaten naughty children with an old woman. She comes from under the earth to carry them off.

[19] Dawson. J., *Australian Aborigines* (Melbourne. etc., 1881). p. 83.

[20] Fewkes. J. W., "A Few Summer Ceremonials at Zuñi Pueblo." *Jour. Amer. Ethnol. and Archaol.*, 1 (1891). p. 42.

[21] Voth. H. R., "The Oraibi Powamu." p. 118. *Pub. Field Columbian Mus.*, Anthrop. Ser., III. Chicago. 1901–3.

[22] Ellis, A. B., *The Tshi-Speaking Peoples of the Gold Coast of West Africa* (London, 1887), p. 94.

[23] Hose, C. and McDougall, W., "The Relations between Men and Animals in Sarawak," *Journal of the Anthropological Institute*, XXXI (1901), p. 191.

[24] Felkin, R. W., "Notes on the For Tribes of Central Africa," *Proc. Roy, Soc. Edinburgh*, XIII (1884–6), p. 223.

[25] Christian, F. W., *The Caroline Islands* (New York, 1899), p. 72.

[26] Batchelor, J., *The Ainu and Their Folk-lore* (London. 1901), pp. 23-4.

[27] Clavigero, *The History of Mexico*, ed. 1807. 1, p. 332.

It is at the tribal initiation, of course, that the elders step in. During it the young get considerable moral teaching of both a direct and an indirect nature from the elders, and taboos are laid upon the initiates which serve to strengthen the social hold upon them of the state, i.e., the elders. Besides, these taboos may increase materially the privileges and prerogatives of the old people—the more so as the taboos may extend over considerable periods both before and after initiation. Breaking the taboos is apt to be supernaturally punished, particularly breaking taboos relating to food, to sex conduct, and to preserving secrecy. In Australia the boys and girls of the Lower Murray tribes thought that if before initiation they ate emu, wild duck, swans, geese, or black duck, or the eggs of any of these birds, their hair would become prematurely gray and their muscles would shrink.[28] Wotjobaluk boys are forbidden to eat of the kangaroo or the padi-melon on penalty of falling sick, breaking out all over with eruptions, and perhaps dying. If young Wakelbura men or women eat forbidden game, they will probably pine away and die, uttering sounds peculiar to the creature they have eaten. Its spirit enters into them and kills them. Howitt heard of a Kurnai boy who had stolen and eaten opossum before he was permitted, in accordance with the food taboos, to eat of it. The old men made him believe he would never grow up to be a man. He did lie down, in fact, under the belief, and within three weeks he died.[29] Death by meteorite or lightning punishes boys and girls who break the food taboos in other Australian tribes.[30][31][32] As for sex taboos[33] and their supernatural sanctions, among the Lower Murray tribes the sight of a woman for three months after the novice's teeth have been knocked out would bring numberless misfortunes upon him–withering up of limbs, blindness, general decrepitude.[34] Were a Kurnai youth to touch a woman at a certain stage in the initiation he would, he is told, fall seriously ill. Were a woman's shadow to fall upon him he would surely become thin or lazy or stupid.[35] At Bartle Bay, New Guinea, boys believe that if they do not keep from intercourse during and before initiation their hair will not grow.[36]

Initiates are told not only to keep away from women, they are explicitly warned to keep their secrets hidden from women lest supernatural evils befall. The Urabunna initiate is made to believe that should any woman see one of the secret sticks, he and his mother and sisters would drop dead.[37] In New Guinea, Kiwai Island initiates are warned to maintain secrecy at the risk, among other consequences, of being seized with a fearful incurable disease.[38] In the Elema district an impersonation of Kovave tells the initiates that if they

---

[28] Beveridge, P., in *Jour. and Proc. Roy. Soc. N. South Wales*, XVII (1883), p. 27.

[29] Howitt, pp. 769–70.

[30] Palmer, E., "Notes on Some Australian Tribes," J. A. I., XIII (1883–4). p. 294; Helms in *Proc. Linnean Soc. New South Wales*, Sec. S., x (189S), p. 393.

[31] Supernatural penalties for breaking food taboos are common, of course, outside of Australia; nor are they confined either in Australia or elsewhere to adolescence.

[32] The effects of food taboos, if not the alleged purposes, are more or less social or moral. They may protect the food supply of a favored class, the old against the young, men against women, chiefs against commoners. Pregnancy or lactation food taboos may convey a sense of parental "responsibility." The totemic taboos are anti-cannibalistic, it not being sociable to eat your kinsman. The mourning taboos show "consideration" for the dead.

[33] Australian elders are greedy about women as well as about food; but the sex restrictions they put upon initiates are not so much for purposes of immediate monopoly as they are to insure a good start, so to speak, on that separation of the sexes in public so characteristic of primitive society.

[34] Beveridge. p. 27.

[35] Howitt. "The Jeraeil, or Initiation Ceremonies of the Kurnai Tribe." *J. A. I.. XIV (1884–5). pp. 306, 316, and Native Tribes.* p. 402.

[36] Seligmann. p. 496.

[37] Spencer. B., and Gillen. F. J., *The Northern Tribes of Central Australia* (London and New York. 1904). p. 498.

[38] Chalmers. J., "Note on the Natives of Kiwai Island. Fly River. British Kew Guinea." *J. A. I.*, XXXIII (1903).

divulge the secrets to the uninitiated,[39] he will punish them with disease and death. If they let it be known that the whining of Tiparu, the bull-roarer, is not the cry of a god but the work of a man, the curse of Tiparu, equivalent to death, is upon them.[40]

Elema women flee their villages to escape the curse of hearing the voice of Tiparu.[41] In many other communities women are kept from prying by supernatural sanctions. Elsewhere[42] I have pointed out how thoroughly in other particulars they are kept in their place by supernatural sanctions or by their mere fear of the supernatural, how they are discouraged from trespassing or straying from home, from eloping or committing adultery or marrying again, how they are rendered docile and obedient. To their husbands are given magical means of detecting their infidelity; for the undetected, a difficult labor or death in childbirth is in store;[43] men disguised as ghosts or gods break their spirit for adventure or revolt. Sometimes the gods themselves condescend to discipline the wayward or the inquisitive.

Supernatural sanctions attach to violations of sex habits other than monogamy.[44] For illustrations of what dire things happen to men who break through the taboos upon a woman during menstruation let me refer again to another discussion.[45] But at Mowat, New Guinea, I have since noted a variation from the usual type of menstruation taboo. If a Mowat man have connection with a woman after he has had it with a menstrous woman, it is supposed that he will die.[46] Incest, a peculiarly abhorrent offense to primitive man however he defines it, is very apt to be punished, he believes, either automatically or by an outraged spirit. In the Kêi islands the incestuous are supposed to fall ill;[47] among the Khasis they are struck by lightning or killed by a tiger or they die in childbirth; in the Omeo tribe of Victoria they are beaten by "jidjigongs" or snakes, and the punishment is the more fearful because it may hang over them for years.[48] The Kenai ascribe their increase in mortality to breaking their exogamous rules.[49] Matthews once asked a Navaho what would happen if he married a woman of his gens. "I would have bad fortune," he said; "I would fall into the fire and get burned, the lightning would strike me, the cold would freeze me, or the gun would shoot me—something fearful would happen to me."[50] On the Herbert river, Queensland, anyone marrying into prohibited sub-classes will sooner or later die in consequence, his behavior being offensive to Kohin, an earth-roaming

[39] Aside from initiation, secrecy in esoteric affairs is often safe-guarded in primitive circles by a supernatural sanction. Among the Ewes the lightning-struck or poisoned are thought to be killed by Jehve for tattling about him (Spieth. J., "Der Jehve-Dienst der Evhe-Neger." in *Mitt. der Geog. Gesell. zu Jena.* XIII (1894). p. 19). When Fewkes insisted upon witnessing the Hopi ceremony of snake washing. he was cautioned to leave the kiva; if he stayed, he would "swell up and burst." Bursting·or other direful troubles came to one beholding rites none but a priest might see ("The Snake Ceremonials at Walpi," *J. Amer. Ethn. and Arch.,* IV (1894), p. 83).

[40] Holmes in *J. A. I.,* XXXII (1902), pp. 421, 425.

[41] Chalmers, J., "Toaripi," *J. A. I.,* XXVII (1898–9). p. 329.

[42] The *Old-Fashioned Woman* (New York. 1913), ch. xx. "Policing Her Super-naturally." See also Frazer. J. G., *Psyche's Task* (London, 1909). ch. iv.

[43] There are other supernatural punishments too—misfortune for the whole kampong among the Bataks (Steinmetz, S. R., *Ethnologische Studien zur ersten Entwicklung der Strafe* (Leiden and Leipzig, 1894, II. p. 357); "accidental death" in the Sawn islands, at the will of their deified lawgiver (ibid., p. 358); a plague of rain (for unchastity among the unmarried) among the Sea Dyaks (Perham, J., in *Jour. Straits Branch Roy. Asiatic Soc.,* No.8, pp. 149 sq., Singapore, 1882).

[44] Frazer has given illustrations (*Psyche's Task.* ch. iv) of the suffering falling super-naturally upon the group as well as upon the offender, and he suggests that this vicarious suffering leads to further collective pressure upon the individual to conform to custom—truly a very striking linking together of supernaturalism and morals.

[45] The *Old-Fashioned Woman.* ch. xi. "In Quarantine."

[46] Beardmore. E., in *Jour. Anthr. Inst.,* XIX (1889–90).

[47] Bartels, M., *Die Medicin der Naturvölker* (Leipzig. 1893). p. 29.

[48] Helms, p. 392.

[49] Steinmetz, II. p. 352.

[50] "The Study of Ethics Among the Lower Races." *J. Amer. Folk-Lore.* XII (1899). p. 6.

spirit of the Milky Way.[51] Among the Caffres, offspring of an incestuous union will be a monster, a punishment inflicted by an ancestral spirit.[52] Aleuts too believe that incest is always followed by the birth of a monster with walrus tusks or beard.[53]

Whether or not the practice of avoidance is a safeguard against incest,[54] it is apt to have, like indubitable exogamous rules, a supernatural sanction attaching to it. It is believed in Victoria that if a man see his mother-in-law, or is seen by her, evil spirits will afflict him or disaster of some other kind will befall him.[55] That a woman's hair will turn white if she speaks to her son-in-law or even looks at him is the belief of other Australian tribes.[56] If a Uganda woman hands anything to her father-in-law she will be afflicted, she thinks, with tremor.[57]

In Nias intercourse during pregnancy is punished by sickness.[58] In fact in very many places intercourse during pregnancy or during lactation is held to bring disaster to a woman or her offspring. In East Central Africa "it is believed" that a girl who does not mate at nubility will die.[59]

"It is believed," writes Macdonald of this African point of view. Who believes it? Presumably the girl herself, and assuredly because she got the idea from her elders. To make the young settle down in, marriage is a favorite undertaking of the elders, and an important factor in the subjection in which they keep not only the adolescents of the tribe, but all their juniors. This ascendency they establish at initiation, but most of the life of their juniors they regulate or at least meddle with. And this control is based for the greater part on their control of the tribal system of supernaturalism. Moreover, they may be heeded by their juniors, thanks merely to their very reputation as supernaturalists. In no end of places old women are feared because of the power of witchcraft imputed to them; besides, the curses of the aged,[60] like the curses of the dying, are held to be especially potent and dreadful.[61] The aged and the moribund alike are imminent ghosts, and ghosts are believed to be unusually well qualified to carry out threats. They are good at bestowing favors too, so that kindness to those with one foot in the grave is at least a prudent policy.

But respect for age is sometimes specifically imparted by the elders by means of the supernatural sanction. Once during a general quarrel Spencer and Gillen saw one of the younger men, i. e., a man between thirty-five and forty, and a medicine-man at that, try to strike one of the older men. At once at this grave offense his precious medicine powers left him.[62] An Aleut who is disagreeable and disrespectful to the elders has no luck in hunting; on the other hand attentiveness to the old insures longevity and good fortune in the

---

[51] Howitt. *Native Tribes*, p. 498.

[52] Shooter. J., *The Kafirs of Natal and the Zulu Country* (London. 18S7). p. 45.

[53] Petroff. I., "Report on the Population. Industries and Resources of Alaska." *Tenth Census of the United States* (Washington. 1884). VIII. p. 155.

[54] For another interpretation of it see *American Jour. of Sociology*. Jan. 1914.

[55] Smyth. R. Brough. The *Aborigines of Victoria* (Melbourne and London. 1878). I. p. 95. AM. ANTH., N. S., 17—4

[56] Howitt, *Native Tribes*, pp. 256–7.

[57] Roscoe, J., "Further Notes on the Manners and Customs of the Baganda," *J. A. I.*, XXXII (1902), p. 39.

[58] Bartels, p. 29.

[59] Macdonald, J., "East Central African Customs," *J. A. I.*, XXII (1892–3), p. 101.

[60] Westermarck, E., *The Origin and Development of the Moral Ideas* (London and New York, 1906), I. pp. 619 sq.

[61] Very entertaining is a recent illustration of this kind of gerontocratic control. "Not long ago," writes an observer of Turkish customs, "the wife of a former Grand Vizier, Haihiddin Pasha, died. On her death-bed she expressed as her last wish that her twelve-year-old daughter might take special courses in medicine, similar to those given to men. There was nothing for the government to do but to hastily open certain of these courses to women in order that they might not be cursed by ignoring the dying wish of a respected old woman." (Buell, Katherine, "Behind the Veil," *Harper's Weekly*, Aug. 15, I914.)

[62] Spencer and Gillen, p. 22.

chase or in war.[63] The ancient Hindus are well outside the circle of peoples we have been accounting in quite a general way primitive, but one of their expressions of respect for seniority is inculcated so primitively that I cannot forbear mentioning it. "The vital airs of a young man mount upwards to leave his body when an elder approaches," declares Manu, "but by rising to meet him and saluting he recovers them."[64]

A deferential treatment of the elders may be prompted, we noted, by the fear of what as malevolent ghosts they might do to the living.[65] Once they are ghosts the need of keeping them in a good humor is even more imperative. Hence the living and in particular the surviving kindred are bound to pay proper respect to the dead. Inattentiveness to a ghost is apt to be sorely punished by him. A slighted ghost in the islands of Torres straits would cause strong winds to destroy the gardens of his neglectful relatives and break down their houses! The Thompson River Indians believe that death or sickness would come upon one taking possession of the bow and arrows, leggings and moccasins of a departed kinsman.[66] Among the Koita of New Guinea relatives who infringed upon the dead man's funeral rights or who neglected them were punished by his *sua*[67]—in what way we are not told. Ghost haunting, a severe enough punishment in itself, is very commonly a consequence of funeral improprieties. Such considerations about the dead are quite pertinent, let me say, to a study of morality in early culture, for in it, we should not forget, the dead are an integral part of society. We have to realize, too, that in their treatment by the living morality and supernaturalism are indistinguishable.

Funerary destruction of property is partly prompted by the desire to preclude ghost walking, to keep the ghost from coming after his own, after what has been and still is a part of himself. It is one of the earliest and most marked ways of recognizing the right to property. But there are other primitive ways in which a supernatural sanction is invoked against the misappropriation of property, ways I particularly wish to indicate. Ignoring the fact that our own morality being a property morality compared with the morality of early cultures, primitive gods seem to us far more indifferent to theft than Jahveh or the god of the framers of our criminal codes. But like men, like gods—or ghosts. And theft, so far as it goes, is punished by primitive spirits. A ghost of the islands of Torres straits may be aggrieved not only by remissness as to his funeral rites, but by dishonesty toward his heirs, and he may be revengeful on their account also.[68] It was the special business of one of the gods of the Tracy islands to watch and kill thieves.[69] In East Central Africa magic stakes are driven into the ground on the edge of the corn fields. Thereafter anyone touching the crops will die on the spot.[70] The Wanika protect their plantations and fruit trees in like way.[71] Throughout the islands of the Malay archipelago sickness followed from eating food stolen from tabooed fields.[72] On the Bloomfield, in North Queensland, the older men to whom the country originally belonged will give out that certain tracts of it are "yirru" (*yirru* is an underground spirit), so that if any but themselves eat or camp there or disturb

---

[63] Petroff, pp. 153, 155.

[64] The Laws of Manu, II, 120, *Sacred Books of the East*, xxv.

[65] Other injuries in life besides neglect in old age may be punished by resentful ghosts. In the Elema district of New Guinea dead warriors visit their old enemies at night and keep them from sleeping by tickling their feet. The murdered invariably plague their murderers (Holmes, pp. 428. 429). Hudson Bay Eskimo have deserted the island of Akpatok since the murder on it of some shipwrecked sailors (Turner, L. M., "Ethnology of the Ungava District," *11th Rep. Bur. Amer. Ethn.*, 1894, p. 186). Greenlanders hold that an aborted child or an illegitimate deceased is transformed into an evil avenging spirit (Rink, H. J., *Tales and Traditions of the Eskimo.* (Edinburgh and London. 1875. pp. 45. 439 sq.).

[66] Teit, p. 331.

[67] Seligmann, p. 191.

[68] *Reports of the Cambridge Anthr. Exped. to Torres Straits. VI*, p. 127.

[69] Roth, W. E., *North Queensland Ethnography* (Brisbane, 1903), Bull. V, p. 29.

[70] Macdonald, p. 120.

[71] New, C., Life, *Wanderings, etc., in Eastern Africa* (London, 1874), p. 106.

[72] Bartels. pp. 28–29.

the soil in any way whatever, Yirru will punish them with grievous sores.[73] Indeed boundary fetishes of one kind or another are not at all uncommon among primitive peoples. The automatic supernatural sanction also attaches again and again to the preservation of property.

In the Bowditch islands a man dead is asked to confess through the voice of a priest what he had done to cause his death. Among other offenses he might confess to theft.[74] The god's proxy or priest is often called upon in cases of theft. Batak thieves were cursed through the magic staff of the great priest of Balige.[75] Pilfered, an Ossete goes with the *kurismezok*, "the wise man" or sorcerer, and his cat to the house of anyone under suspicion. "If thou hast stolen the article," exclaims the *kurismezok*, "and dost not restore it to its owner, may this cat torment the souls of thy ancestors!"[76] A Tshi bereft of his property will make an offering to his local god and ask his priest to beg the god to proceed against the thief.[77] Quakery, the Ju-Ju king of New Calabar, who ranked above the king in all purely native palavers, religious or civil, told de Cardi that if the king tried to detect robbers it would have little effect, because the king was a man like themselves from whom they would steal if they got the chance. "But if I sent round a notice that if the thieves did not immediately bring me the stolen articles, my Ju-Ju would cause them (the thieves) to swell up and burst, you would see how quickly they would come to me and deliver up the stolen goods."[78] To recover stolen or lost property, especially ponies, is one of the principal tasks of the Apache medicine-man. He does it through crystal gazing.[79] Through some unspecified magical means the Koita sorcerer also recovers stolen things.[80] In fact the medicine-man is for theft as for other offenses the first professional detective.

The medicine-man, or priest, is apt, too, to preside over ordeals, on the theory perhaps that his god will be on the side of the innocent.[81] At any rate the emphatic presence of the priest at the ordeal makes for an association in thought between the moral and the supernatural. So does his presence at initiation ceremonies. Quite often he is in charge of them, and it is he instead of the elders who teaches the youth the tribal morals. His tendency to take a hand in all the daily affairs of life, a tendency quite as marked in primitive as in modern times, has a like effect. Being a representative of deity his slightest interference with any social relation gives it a supernatural coloring.

A priest's authority is naturally supported by his god. From their priestly derivation, if for no other reason, early forms of chieftaincy might be expected to have a supernatural backing. But a mystical, representative quality too seems to attach to chiefs or leaders. They express or embody the welfare of the community and of each of its members. Subservience to them means communal and individual prosperity; contradiction or disobedience means disaster. The Massim of Bartle Bay work in the garden of their chief, believing" if they did this their own gardens would be good." In Nias a certain severe throat ailment is supposed to be due to [82]quarreling with a village headman.[83] The Tonga gods were under stood to punish disrespect to chiefs

---

[73] Roth. p. 29.

[74] Turner. G., p. 272.

[75] Brenner. J. von. *Besuch bei den Kannibalen Sumatras* (Würzburg. 1894). p. 226. Turner. G., p. 283.

[76] Haxthausen. *Transcaucasia* (London. 1854). pp. 398–9. Needless to say the imprecation is often effectual.

[77] Ellis. p. 75.

[78] de Cardi. C. N., in *Jour, Anthr. Inst.* XXIX (1899). pp. 51–2.

[79] Bourke, J. G., "Medicine Men of the Apache," *9th Ann. Rep. Bur. Ethn.* (1887–8). p. 461.

[80] Seligmann, p. 133.

[81] That the ordeal (or the oath) may be merely magical (see Westermarck, 11, pp. 118 sq., 687 sq.) does not concern us, for we are not weighing the character, moral or non-moral, of the gods. It is enough for us that to the ordeal (and to the oath) a supernatural sanction attaches. But into a fuller dissension along this line I will not go, as its viewpoint would be somewhat different from that to which I am limiting our discussion.

[82] Seligmann, p. 458.

[83] Bartels, p. 28.

almost as severely as disrespect to themselves.[84] In the Mortlock islands the spirits of dead chiefs punished offenses against their colleagues in the world with sickness, curable only by the gods through the mediation of the living chiefs.[85]

It is not only political rebels who have been punished by ghosts. Among the Dakota and in the Malay archipelago they are believed to torment iconoclasts of all kinds.[86] For any infringement of tribal customs the Koita *sua* might smite offenders with sickness or call down upon them bad luck in hunting or fishing.[87] Elsewhere the gods, too, posing as backers of custom as custom, are against iconoclasts. If the Narrinyeri are asked why they keep to any custom, they answer that Narundere, their "All Father," commanded it.[88] Daramulun, the high god of the coast Murring was believed to have laid down the food rules and to punish those who broke them.[89] The Tchiglit Innuit believe that they are injuring deity and calling down divine punishment upon themselves because they are adopting foreign customs.[90] Ainu iconoclasts know they are sure to suffer from the wrath of the gods.[91] With these instances from primitive society of what is perhaps in modern life the most conspicuous part of its rôle, its support of custom as custom, I may fitly conclude, my sketch of the supernatural sanction on morals.

At the outset of this paper we contented ourselves with identifying moral with social conduct and then passed on at once to give illustrations of the supernatural sanctions attaching to such conduct. It is plain, I trust, that from this far from novel point of view morality has been little if anything but the prevailing system of keeping people in their place, out of other people's way, juniors out of the way of seniors, one sex out of the way of the other, kindred out of the way of kindred, the desitute or the subject out of the way of the man of property or the chief, lay or ecclesiastic, the dead out of the way of the living, the adventurer out of the way of everybody. For accomplishing this social distribution there seem to be three main methods: public opinion (including, of course, ridicule, its most potent weapon), the sanction of the group working naturalistically (ostracism, i. e., execution, exile, imprisonment, and mutilation or fine), and the sanction working supernaturally, i. e., automatically or magically, or through spirits. The availability of these several methods varies in different cultures. In particular the availability of the supernatural sanction varies, as one might expect, with the scope of supernaturalism characteristic of the given culture. Just as supernaturalism is far more a part of life in early culture than in modern, so concomitantly is the supernatural sanction. Our obliviousness to this fact has been due mostly to our unwillingness to recognize how insignificant religion has become to us, to what extent we get on without it,[92] how remote it is from our daily

---

[84] Mariner. W., *An Account of the Natives of the Tonga Islands* (London. 1817). 11. pp. 155. 237.

[85] Kubary. J., in *Milth. d. Geogr. Gesell. in Hamburg.* 1878–9. p. 256.

[86] Eastman. M., *Dacotah* (New York. 1849). pp. xx. 87. Schoolcraft. H. R., *Indian Tribes* (Phila., 1851–57). 11. pp. 195–6. Bartels. p. 28.

[87] Seligmann. p. 192.

[88] Woods. J. D., *The Native Tribes of South Australia* (Adelaide. 1879). p. 55.

[89] Howitt. in J. A. I., XIII (1883). p. 192.

[90] Petitot. E., *Les Grands Esquimaltx* (Paris. 1887). p. 35.

[91] Batchelor. pp. 58. 177–8.

[92] How seldom, for example, do we hold that an untoward event is a punishment for our sins, a point of view common enough in primitive circles. When several deaths occur about the same time in the same For family, it is thought to be due to lying by one of its members (Felkin, pp. 230–2). In Samoa, if the offspring of a consanguineous marriage died prematurely, it was taken as a sign .of the disapproval of the marriage by the household god (Turner, G., p. 92). Several centuries ago, the Chinese of the province of Camul, urged on by a reform governor, gave up their practice of sexual hospitality. Poor harvests and general misfortune ensued, because, said the people, they had foregone a custom cherished by the gods (*Marco Polo*, ed. by Yule, London, 1871, I, pp. 189–90). When the Merkedes, an Arab tribe, became Wahábys, they had to give up the same custom; a drought followed and, considering it a punishment, they got permission from the Waha.by chief to return to the good old practice of their forefathers (Burckhardt, J. L., *Notes on the Bedouins and Wahábys*, London, 1831, p. I02).

life.[93] Furthermore, denial of a relation between morality and religion in early culture may be due to our habit of studying the content of one moral code in terms of another, the Blackfellow's, for example, in terms of our own. An offense great enough in our eyes to keep its perpetrator out of heaven may be too petty in the eyes of the Blackfellow for such an automatic penalty to attach to it as attaches to the breaking of Australian food taboos or the rules of class exogamy, offenses quite without meaning to us.[94] The very claim that only the historical religions are related to morality is part and parcel of the antique conception that only our own morality or the morality of kindred cultures is morality at all. It is the final attempt of self-righteousness to pull the wool, so to speak, over the eyes of ethnology.

STONOVER FARM

LENOX, MASSACHUSETTS

Discussion Questions

1. How does Parsons define religion? How does she define morals? Do you think these definitions are accurate? Why or why not?
2. What does Parsons mean when she says that religion and morals begin in the nursery? Do you agree with this?
3. How does Parsons make a case for historical particularism, using religion and morals as an example?
4. How does Parsons view religion and its relationship to morality?
5. After reading this article, do you think religion is a necessary precursor to morality? Can morality exist without religion? Explain your answer.

---

[93] Of its remoteness the mere existence of spirits is evidence according to Professor Lévy-Bruhl. The primitive mystic has no need of spirits; everything has for him an immediate mystical quality. The gods originate, so to speak, in secularization. From this point of view, the magical automatic sanction is earlier than the sanction imposed by deity. Such sanctions on morality as those of the historical religions may mean therefore that our morality is less religious than the morality of the savage.

[94] To the savage the supernatural or mystical attaches to much that to us is natural and merely objective. Defilement through death or through sex, for example, is still assumed in certain ways by us, but it does not begin to 100m upon us as upon the savage. Impressed by such mysticism in savage life, one of its close observers writes me that to him there appears to be little or no relation between religion and morality in primitive life, supernaturalism attaching primarily to matters of a non-moral character. Even so, docs it not attach as well to the social organization?

Chapter 11

Excerpts from Sexual Risk-Taking and Health-Seeking Behavior in Orange County Adults: A Survey of Potential Influences

Keri Canada

Germany: Vering Dr. Muller Press

What is the role of the anthropologist in clinically applied research? This has been asked in many forms; it's become a somewhat more common question since the resurgence of applied anthropology in the 1970s. In this excerpt, Keri Canada describes clinically applied research and examines the niche medical anthropologists can fill in this particular field. Like many studies, this one asked more questions than it answered – but the data here provide an opening to ask something important: why do people make the decisions they do about their health?

Introduction

What do sexual risk-taking and health-seeking have in common? Do these behaviors, in fact, have anything in common? I suggest that these two behaviors are inherently related—if one dislikes his or her doctor or medical professional (and it therefore is difficult to schedule regular medical visits), he or she is more likely to engage in risky sexual behavior (sex without a condom or other birth control, irregular testing for sexually transmitted diseases, etc.).

However, there is more at stake than just not liking one's doctor. To what extent do cultural and/or religious practices affect risk-taking and health-seeking behavior? For example, Catholics generally eschew all birth control—members of this religion may be practicing risky sexual behavior, but not because of problems with doctors. It is important to take into account as many behavioral influences as possible when attempting to analyze such behavior. In my study, I hope to find to what extent these cultural factors are related, it at all.

Statement of the Problem

Populations of lower socioeconomic status often do not utilize available health care as often as they should (Asch et al. 2006). However, data available from the Orange County Health Needs Assessment (OCHN A) indicate that this is not a problem unique to those of lower socioeconomic status; individuals from higher income and insurance levels also report irregular medical visits. If infrequent medical visits cannot be fully explained by ability to pay, it is important to identify additional causal factors. OCHNA's 2005 data indicate that the majority of respondents did not utilize medical services due to lack of insurance, but a variety of other factors are cited as well, including Jack of transportation, limited medical office hours, language barriers, and overall satisfaction with the last medical visit. Only 43 percent reported being "very satisfied" with previous medical visits (OCHNA 2005:200); this is interesting, as more than 50 percent of respondents report not using birth control frequently (OCHNA 2005:328)—it is possible that satisfaction with medical care is related to the tendency to use birth control? In addition, more than 80 percent of respondents reported that they do not use condoms to prevent sexually transmitted diseases (OCHNA 2005:332). It is important to note, however, that OCHNA's data are not uniform—the data available on health-seeking behavior are more likely to be accurate than the data on sexual behavior, as the questions about sexual behavior were asked of much smaller numbers of people, and therefore the numbers may not be completely comparable. This is why, rather than simply analyzing the available data and attempting to draw conclusions, I felt it was important to collect original data on risk-taking and health-seeking behavior.

No link has been previously identified between sexual risk-taking and health-seeking behavior in Orange County adults, and no effort has been made to compare risky sexual behavior, ethnicity, and socioeconomic status; this creates a serious problem if medical services (particularly reproductive health services) are under-utilized due to substandard care. Further, if it becomes apparent that utilization of medical services is more ethnicity-specific, this may indicate that additional cultural competence training of area medical providers is needed.

Significance

This study is significant in that it has the potential to provide clinics and other medical establishments providing reproductive health services with valuable information that may improve their quality of care, leading to greater patient utilization and retention, and perhaps more in-depth cultural competency. While the study was not able to prove that certain ethnic groups are under-utilizing available healthcare (which would be an indicator that there is a communication breakdown between medical personnel and the population they are attempting to serve), the results did indicate that at least one ethnic group docs not seek sexual health care services due to religious beliefs.

Methods

Beginning in June 2006, I contacted approximately 20 community health clinics in Orange County, California Because I sought to study sexual risk-taking and health-seeking behavior, I felt this would be the most convenient way to reach my intended population (individuals over 18 years of age living in Orange County).

My goal was to enroll five community clinics in the study, with each clinic completing 100 surveys (50 in English and 50 in Spanish). I wrote a cover letter to each clinic explaining the study, and asking that they assist me in distributing the surveys. I explained that I would provide the surveys and a box in which to collect them; the clinics needed only to distribute the surveys to their clients (please see Appendix I, page 82).

I initially mailed 15 information packets, containing a cover letter, copies of the surveys in both English and Spanish, a copy of my thesis proposal, and a copy of the approval letter from the California State University, Fullerton Institutional Review Board (Application No. HSR-06-0096). I felt I was providing the clinics with ample information about what I was asking for and what the study was about, although I did invite them to contact me if they had any further questions or concerns about participation.

I was not able to enroll any clinics from the first mailing (despite repeated follow-up contact attempts), so in consultation with my thesis advisor, I decided to ask community college and university campus clinics to participate. While I had hoped to reach a wider age range of participants, it was my belief that perhaps clinics in an academic setting would be more willing to participate in a study being done by a student. I also mailed information packets to several more community clinics in an attempt to supplement college-age participants with a broader age range.

Within a week of the second mailing (mid-July 2006), I enrolled three community college campus clinics and one community clinic in the study. One month later, I enrolled one more community college clinic, meeting my goal of having five participating clinics.

I would like to have had more clinics from the Orange County Coalition of Community Clinics (which arc important providers of free and low-cost healthcare in Orange County), but these clinics either did not respond after repeated attempts or refused to participate. The exception here is the Laguna Beach Community Clinic, which did enroll in the study, and the five Planned Parenthood clinics in Orange County, which I did not ask. As a previous employee of Planned Parenthood, I knew that the patients at these clinics would be overwhelmingly female, and I was hoping for a fairly even· female-to male ratio. I also did not get any response from public health clinics not belonging to the Orange County Coalition of Community Clinics.

Problems

The first problem I encountered after enrolling the clinics in my study was language. I was offering the surveys in English and Spanish, and these were not necessarily the languages that the community college clinics felt they needed. The English surveys were welcomed by all the clinics, but the health clinic on the Golden West College campus requested surveys in Vietnamese, and Irvine Valley College told me their second-highest spoken language after English was Farsi. I did not have the resources to have additional surveys translated, so these clinics distributed a large number of English surveys, compared with a much smaller number of Spanish surveys. This may have been something I could have compensated for had I planned initially to include college campus clinics in the study; due to the demographic information I hold obtained beforehand from the Orange Country Health Needs Assessment data (and again, from my experience working at a Planned Parenthood clinic), I assumed I would be working with largely English- and Spanish-speaking populations.

Because of this, I was not able to give 100 surveys to each clinic. Each clinic did take 50 English surveys, but only the Laguna Beach Community Clinic took 50 Spanish surveys; the community college campus clinics each took approximately 20 Spanish surveys, and advised me they would likely have trouble completing even that many. In all, between 350 and 400 surveys were distributed, rather than the initial target of 500. I asked each participating clinic to complete the survey distribution and collection within a time frame of approximately one to one and a half months.

Suggestions for Future Research

This study could have been done using only community clinics if more time had been allotted. The study (from the time of initial proposal until completion) had a time frame of less than six months. In addition, while four out of the five participating clinics received the surveys in July 2006, the community college campus clinics had a very limited amount of time in which to distribute them because of the academic year schedule. All the participating college campuses typically have far fewer students enrolled during the summer session, and therefore did not have the opportunity to distribute many surveys until the regular fall semester began in late August. It was necessary for me to collect the surveys from the clinics in late September 2006, giving the community college campus clinics only one month to collect data. If more time was available, more surveys could have been distributed in order to reach my goal of 500 respondents. It was really my own personal time frame that may have rushed the process.

The time constraints may have been a factor in the refusal of other clinics to participate. I was very clear in that I hoped to have all the surveys distributed "as soon as possible," and this may not have been a convenient time for these clinics. If a larger period of time was available (or even if the study was being conducted during a different time of the year), the clinics' responses may have been different.

Time also comes into play when considering the content of the survey. After a more extensive review of available literature, I discovered it would have been helpful to have included questions on communication between sexual partners, as this seems to have direct bearing on sexual risk-taking, as well as questions about substance use/abuse and its relationship with risky sexual behavior. When I composed the survey, I based it on one already distributed by OCHNA, which was less than adequate. I did supplement it with questions I thought were important, but given more time, I would have done more initial research into available literature for assistance in developing additional questions. I incorporated, nonetheless, literature on communication and substance abuse into the finished thesis, as I felt it too important to leave out.

It may also have been beneficial to have mailed a less-detailed cover letter. I was very specific in what I wanted (see Appendix I, page 82), and because it contained so much information and may have looked to be rather long, this may have not made it a priority for busy clinic manages. In fact, because of one response I got (which ended with a clinic manager hanging up on me), it was clear to me that the managers may not have even read all the information and were therefore confused about what I was asking.

While my cover letter was not subject to review by the California State University, Fullerton Institutional Review Board, I used most of the information on the application I submitted to write the cover letter—that the detail in the letter provided to be overwhelming is ironic, given that I would not have gotten approval if the same detail had not been present on the application.

Overview of OCHNA Data

The OCHNA was originally developed in 1997, in partnership with the Country of Orange Health Care Agency and the Hospital Association of Southern California to meet the legal requirements of SB 697. This bill requires nonprofit hospitals in the state to engage in a needs assessment of their service areas every three years.

The data I use from OCHNA comes from a four-month (May 2004 to August 2004) household survey conducted by that organization; the data were collected using telephone interviews (the numbers dialed were generated randomly). The total number of interviews conducted was 3,378.

The information in the 2005 Data Report I was not interested in, obviously, was that of sexual risk-taking and health-seeking behavior. I was also interested in the demographic information (ethnicity, insurance status, etc.), as I hypothesized that this information may have bearing on risk-taking and health-seeking behavior. While the OCHNA report contains this information, it does not analyze or explain the relationship between the data presented. The surveys I distributed were based largely on the questions asked on the OCNHA survey; however, I felt the questions asked about sexual behavior were inadequate and my survey was thus supplemented with additional questions.

Data of Specific Interest: Health-Seeking

The following tables are results from the 2005 OCHNA Spring Data Report. I have included OCHNA's own questions about health-seeking in this section; although they do not exactly parallel the questions I asked, I felt they were representative of the data. The table captions represent the questions asked in the OCHNA survey.

In the OCHNA report, all of the information in Tables 1–4 is also broken down into the following categories: race/ethnicity, income level, education level, and age group. In addition to the questions represented

TABLE 1 Q: Do You Have Any Type of Health Care Coverage?

Any health care coverage		
YES	Population Estimate	2,000,698
	Percent	**89.6%**
	Unweighted Count	3,099
NO	Population Estimate	232,859
	Percent	**10.4%**
	Unweighted Count	266
Total	Population Estimate	2,233,556
	Percent	**100.0%**
	Unweighted Count	3,365

Source: 2005 OCHN Spring Data Report, page 87

TABLE 2 Q: How Long Has it Been Since You Last Saw a Doctor?

Time Since Last Saw Doctor		
Less than 6 months	Population Estimate	1,652,886
	Percent	**74.4%**
	Unweighted Count	1,260
Six months to less than one year	Population Estimate	280,590
	Percent	**11.6%**
	Unweighted Count	199
One year to less than two years	Population Estimate	167,923
	Percent	**7.6%**
	Unweighted Count	112
Two years to less than five years	Population Estimate	87,517
	Percent	**3.9%**
	Unweighted Count	54
Five or more years ago	Population Estimate	26,232
	Percent	**1.2%**
	Unweighted Count	24
Never been for treatment	Population Estimate	7,875
	Percent	**0.4%**
	Unweighted Count	12
Total	Population Estimate	2,223,023
	Percent	**100.0%**
	Unweighted Count	1,661

Source: 2005 OCHNA Spring Data Report, page 153

TABLE 3 Q: Have Language Problems Been a Barrier in Receiving Health Care?

Language Barrier to Care		
YES	Population Estimate	121,743
	Percent	**5.4%**
	Unweighted Count	87
NO	Population Estimate	2,112,202
	Percent	**94.6%**
	Unweighted Count	1,585
Total	Population Estimate	2,233,945
	Percent	**100.0%**
	Unweighted Count	1,672

Source: 2005 OCHN Spring Data Report, page 181

above, questions were also asked regarding satisfaction with medical care, including wait time before obtaining an appointment, demeanor of doctor and medical staff, and hours of the medical clinic.

TABLE 4 Q: Have You Felt You were Discriminated Against in Regards to Receiving Health Care in the Past Year?

Any Discrimination in Health Care		
YES	Population Estimate	137,083
	Percent	6.2%
	Unweighted Count	76
NO	Population Estimate	2,089,816
	Percent	93.8%
	Unweighted Count	1,586
Total	Population Estimate	2,226,899
	Percent	100.0%
	Unweighted Count	1,662

Source: 2005 OCHN Spring Data Report, page 223

Data of Specific Interest: Sexual health

The following tables (Tables 5–7, page 7) are samples from the 2005 OCHNA Spring Data Report's questions on sexual health. I chose to include these tables as they closely parallel the questions I asked for my study.

The information on sexual health is broken down into the same categories as general health-seeking behavior. In addition to the information presented above, the OCHNA survey asked for information on specific birth control methods being used. However, that is the extent of the questions on sexual health.

Shortcomings and Inaccuracies

As I mentioned earlier in this chapter, the OCHNA data set has what I feel are numerous shortcomings and inaccuracies, which is why I felt it was important to collect my own data, rather than simply attempt to analyze what was available.

To begin, the major shortcoming of the OCHNA data set is that an extremely large amount of data are presented, but no relationships are analyzed. Reportedly, of the 3,000 respondents, 1,676 were adults, but not every adult interviewed responded to every question, and this is largely not accounted for when the data are presented.

The following table (Table 8, below) is an example given in the OCHNA 2005 Spring Data Report on how to interpret the data.

Because every table contains very different numbers, the data as a whole are difficult to analyze. The weighted response (that which refers to the estimated number of people in the population that are represented by the response) is given much more prominence in the data tables than the unweighted response (that which refers to the actual number of respondents). I do understand that this report is generated for County and medical professionals, however, the data are presented in a misleading way and may not be understood by those not intimately familiar with statistical analysis. With the exception of the introductory section on how to analyze the data, the discrepancies in the data presented are not mentioned.

In addition, there are occasional tables where higher or lower unweighted counts than are warranted by the percentage of the population estimate are shown. The OCHNA explains this by stating that these mismatches tend to occur when a survey question had only a small number of respondents. In this case, however, the data are not necessarily identified and no additional attempt is made to explain the information.

TABLE 5 Q: Are You or Your Partner using Birth Control Now?

Using any birth control		
YES	Population Estimate	528,318
	Percent	**46.5%**
	Unweighted Count	398
NO	Population Estimate	608,265
	Percent	**53.5%**
	Unweighted Count	428
Total	Population Estimate	1,136,583
	Percent	**100.0%**
	Unweighted Count	826

Source: 2005 OCHN Spring Data Report, page 328

TABLE 6 Q: Do You or Your Partner use a Condom to Prevent Sexually Transmitted Diseases?

Use condoms		
YES	Population Estimate	147,838
	Percent	**16.1%**
	Unweighted Count	104
NO	Population Estimate	771,938
	Percent	**83.9%**
	Unweighted Count	58
Total	Population Estimate	919,776
	Percent	**100.0%**
	Unweighted Count	690

Source: 2005 OCHN Spring Data Report, page 333

TABLE 7 Q: Have You Ever Been Tested For Hiv?

Ever tested for HIV		
YES	Population Estimate	843,392
	Percent	**38.4%**
	Unweighted Count	620
NO	Population Estimate	1,350,250
	Percent	**61.6%**
	Unweighted Count	1,008
Total	Population Estimate	2,193,642
	Percent	**100.0%**
	Unweighted Count	1,628

Source: 2005 OCHN Spring Data Report, page 339

TABLE 8 Q: SAMPLE

Sample Response Table			
YES	Population Estimate	39,801	Estimated number in the Orange County populations.
	Percent	**89.6%**	
	Unweighted Count	3,099	
NO	Population Estimate	232,859	Percentage reflect the estimated number in the Orange County populations.
	Percent	**10.4%**	
	Unweighted Count	266	
Total	Population Estimate	2,233,556	Actual number of responses to a question.
	Percent	**100.0%**	
	Unweighted Count	3,365	

Source: 2005 OCHNA Spring Data Report, page 8

Future Chapters

While the OCHNA data was the basis for the idea behind this study, it is useful for comparative purpose only. The majority of the thesis is composed of literature review and original data.

This thesis is an example of clinically applied medical anthropology. The lines between anthropology and sociology are often blurred in the field of medical/social research; the chapter includes discussion of clinically oriented research and applied medical anthropology, and concludes with a discourse on the future of clinically applied research. Chapter Two is an important chapter, as I discuss the role of the anthropologist in clinically applied research.

Chapter Three incorporates an extensive literature review on risk-taking and health-seeking trends, focusing especially on sexual risk behavior, cultural context, risk perception, and factors influencing health-seeking behavior. In addition, cultural decision-making and culturally appropriate care are discussed and analyzed.

I discuss the results of ray study in Chapter Four; I present and analyze the data on risk-taking and health-seeking behavior I collected during my research. The data in this chapter are the cumulative results of five medical clinics; individual clinic results can be found in the Appendix II. I compare and contrast these data to the data published by OCHNA.

Finally, I give concluding thoughts and remarks on this study in Chapter Five, including further suggestions for future research. I discuss what I have learned during the course of the study and what I may have done differently.

THE ROLE OF THE ANTHROPOLOGIST

The lines between anthropology and sociology are often blurred in the field of medical/social research. The purpose of this chapter is not only to highlight the differences between anthropology and sociology, but to give an overview of medical anthropology, especially reproductive health and clinically applied medical anthropology.

More than 40 years ago, William Caudill noted in the first review paper encompassing medical anthropology that "social anthropologists and the other social scientists have recently been doing some unusual things" (Chrisman and Johnson 1996:88). He went on to examine a number of these behaviors: working closely with physicians, teaching in medical schools, collaborating with public health services, and studying hospitals and patients.

There have been difficulties deciding how to define what anthropologists do in clinical settings—in Caudill's time and up until the mid-1970s, it made sense to include anthropological activities in clinical settings simply as part of medical anthropology (Chrisman and Johnson 1996:89). A "clinical setting" can be described as taking place in a hospital, medical clinic, or other establishment providing medical services. Now, however, there are more specially trained applied anthropologists, and those who work in clinical settings are able to document unique contributions to both Western medicine and anthropology; in short, we see medical anthropology as the study of health-related phenomena (Chrisman and Johnson 1996:89).

It has been noted that applied medical anthropology is properly distinguished and distinguishable from medical anthropology and other social sciences by virtue of this focus on using the concepts of anthropology to explain and suggest changes for the health care system and patients within the systems (Chrisman and Johnson 1996:90). In addition, it is important to note that *clinically oriented* and *clinically applied* anthropology are often used as separate terms in medical anthropology; they are not, however, necessarily competing terms.

The difficulty, as noted by Joan Ablon, with the appellation of "clinical anthropology" is that it may not accurately describe the activities of the anthropologist and may imply a more extensive therapeutic role than is desirable or can be accomplished following traditional anthropological training (Chrisman and Johnson 1996:91). While the literature has yet to agree on a single term, I prefer the term "clinically applied medical anthropology"—the implication of research in medical anthropology taking place in a clinical setting. In this chapter, I differentiate between *clinically applied research* and *applied medical anthropology* only because they appear under these terms in current literature.

Clinically Applied Research

Clinical anthropology, as a topic, has provoked considerably lively and occasionally hot debate among medical anthropologists in recent years; much of the controversy has focused on the specific issue of the anthropologist as a therapist and the recommended or requisite training for such a role (Bennett et al. 1982:18). In 1994, Linda Bennett published/reviewed the career experiences of four anthropologists who worked as teachers, administrators, consultants, and researchers in clinical situations, and these personal documents addressed some of the gray areas in which their professional activities have had an impact upon patients or clients using clinical services.

These first-hand accounts were first presented at the 1982 meetings of the Society for Applied Anthropology. Bennett's initial interest in organizing this particular session evolved out of her own experience over several years conducting research with alcoholic families; she found herself recommending to some families that they follow up on their own research participation with another sort of therapy. She realized that while she continued to identify herself as a researcher, she also became aware that she entered the realm of providing information and advice to participants that could have clinical implications for their own lives and the lives of their children (Bennett 1994:18).

I have included on the following pages the experiences of four anthropologists (Bennett 1994:19-26). I felt that including these four different experiences (which all fall under what I call clinically applied medical anthropology) would help to further define the field, as well as illustrate the holistic nature of the field.

I would like to begin with Margaret Lock, as her experience is a wonderful example of what the field of clinically applied medical anthropology has to offer. Shortly after joining the faculty at McGill University, she was asked to take over the coordination of the Interdisciplinary Behavioral Sciences course, a core 80-hour course required of all first-year medical students. In teaching the formal content of this course, the anthropologist is required to present both empirical and experimental framework with as rigorous scientific background as possible. She felt there is a danger inherent in this method, which is pointed out by Chrisman and Maretzki (1982:12): 'There is . . . the tendency for health professionals to learn only what they believe is relevant about culture, health beliefs, and practices, lifestyle, ethnic identity, and the like. The transitions to clinical practice [under these conditions] are likely to be made in the context of biomedical framework, reducing the potential for the humanizing and holistic influences of anthropology."

This is where a role for which anthropologists are particularly well-trained is vital — the role of making hidden meanings explicit and hence promoting reflexivity (Bennett 1994:20). One can maintain one's integrity and walk the liminal line as an anthropologist "in" medicine but only if one steps outside regularly to refresh oneself with the anthropology "of" medicine (Bennett 1994:20).

Next, I would like to discuss the experiences of Thomas Maretzki. The University of Hawaii (where Maretzki was a faculty member) has a postdoctoral training program to prepare anthropologists for research on ethnomedical approaches to broad mental health concerns in the biomedical health care system. The program began to shift, in 1982, from its original psychiatric focus to a more general base in the School of Medicine; when the program began, the staff members were not sure how their role as social scientist researchers should be articulated in relation to biomedical problem solving–they tried to identify the cultural components of clinical problems in psychiatry. In the end, they developed the role of the clinical anthropologist as suggested by Kleinman (1982). They saw this role within the clinical framework of ethnomedical analysis and as such related to an interest in health and illness which transcends our own clinical institutions.

As anthropologists, it is important to retain a broad cross-cultural perspective, and this should remain foremost in our orientation (Bennett 1994:22-23); Robert Straus is a good example of this. As a consultant in many different medical settings over the years, Straus makes several suggestions for thoughts that anthropolgtsts (as nonclinicians) should keep in mind: First, anthropologists should become enculturated to the attitudes the values, the customs, and the ways of thinking of their colleagues. Second, it is important to become comfortable with ourselves and whatever the conflicts, indignations or biases we face, maintain our own equanimity, our equilibrium, our self-worth, and our sense of humor. Straus felt that every budding anthropologist or sociologist (his Ph.D. was in sociology) should learn to appreciate the importance of beginning research endeavors by asking potential subjects "what are the questions?" Far too often, he felt, we spend our time in isolation designing "beautiful" instruments with "skillfully" worded questions and only after we have amassed large amounts of data do we learn that the really relevant questions were never addressed.

Straus' experiences and suggestions can be applied to not only clinically oriented research, but to all fields of anthropology, which underscores the ease with which anthropological experience and research methods fit into this area of research. Anthropologists will tailor their research methods to fit their specific area, but broad anthropological principles will be applicable to many fields.

Hazel Weidman's experience is another good example of how clinically applied medical anthropology can be utilized. Weidman joined the faculty at the University of Miami School of Medicine in 1968, with the goal of transforming a uniculturally oriented environment into one that could incorporate a transcultural perspective into its research, training, and service functions. As director of the Office of Transcultural Education and Research, Weidman's role is multifaceted: providing cultural consultations on hospital wards and in clinics; conducting general education continuing education workshops on clinical issues from a transcultural perspective; developing presentations on transcultural aspects of specific healthcare problems encountered in separate clinical divisions of the hospital; and delivery of lectures, seminars, and scientific presentations on topics of particular relevance to the provision of healthcare from a transcultural perspective.

In the eyes of health professionals in these types of medical settings, there is a specialty called "clinical anthropology," and there is a person who functions as a "clinical anthropologist." It is likely that *this* precedent will encourage repetition and the field will be increasingly visible as the number of clinical anthropologists grows (Bennett el al. 1994:26). I feel, however, that while it might be wise to *call* oneself a "clinical anthropologist" when touting anthropological services to the medical profession—if this is indeed the term the medical profession is comfortable with—there should not necessarily be a distinction made between clinical anthropology and applied medical anthropology, I would like to again stress that I am discussing these two terms separately as they have appeared in recent literature, but I do not believe they are truly separate subfields of anthropology.

Applied Medical Anthropology

Pertti Pelto and Gretel Pelto argue in a 1997 article that the concept of knowledge, as utilized by public health professionals, is best regarded as cultural belief, as defined in anthropology. The purposes of this article are threefold: to critically examine the twin concepts of cultural knowledge and cultural beliefs with respect to people's behaviors; to place these concepts in a theoretical model of health-seeking behaviors; and to outline an approach to empirical data gathering that can produce systematic data concerning cultural beliefs and knowledge that can be directly useful in health care programs (Pelto and Pelto 1997:147).

There has been a persistent, long-term communications gap between anthropologists and health care policymakers and practitioners; anthropologists working in various primary-health contexts have frequently felt frustration that health-system policymakers and practitioners pay little heed to the importance of understanding cultural beliefs and knowledge systems of the peoples they are meant to serve (Pelto and Pelto 1997:148). In addition, policymakers and practitioners have found it difficult to see how anthropological descriptions and interpretations of cultural belief systems can be directly and systematically related to specific health care applications (Pelto and Pelto 1997:148).

The type of anthropology found in health science centers is part of a growing applied arm of the discipline: anthropology devoted to helping health practitioners do their work better. One medical educator has noted that applied medical anthropology is "properly distinguished and distinguishable from medical anthropology and other social sciences by virtue of this focus on using the concepts of anthropology to explain and suggest changes for the health care system and patients within the systems" (Chrisman and Johnson 1996:90).

Anthropologists generally have quite a different approach to conceptualizing "knowledge/beliefs" than do health educators and other health professionals, and these differences often lead to miscommunication; public health professionals often *appear to* view *knowledge* and *beliefs* as contrasting terms (Pelto and Pelto 1997:148). *Knowledge* refers to people's "knowing" about modern biomedical information, such as the risk of acquiring HIV from unprotected sex. The term *knowledge* contains the implicit assumption that the information is "scientific fact," based on universal, cross-culturally valid "facts"; the term *beliefs*, in contrast usually refers to traditional ideas or "folk models" (Pelto and Pelto 1997:148). Often, *beliefs* is used to connote ideas that are erroneous from the perspective of biomedicine and that constitute obstacles to appropriate behavior (Pelto and Pelto 1997:148). For example, health professionals would apply the term *belief* to that feature of a folk model that explains fever-related convulsions in infants as a sign of spiritual possession and that lead families to seek help from a spiritual leader rather than a trained medical professional. In contrast, the term *knowledge* would be the more likely label for a mother's use of a thermometer to assess elevated body temperature.

In the anthropological lexicon, *beliefs* and *knowledge* are not contrastive terms. Perhaps the only difference between these words is that "beliefs" are generally thought of as conscious and available for verbalization, while "knowledge" includes elements that are not readily available for discussion. For example, a mother may "know" when her child is seriously ill, but she may not be able to provide an explanation at how she arrived at that conclusion.

Beliefs constitute another core concept useful to practitioners. Ward Goodenough's definition—beliefs are propositions accepted as true—is succinct. However, like culture, beliefs are invisible and thus difficult for clinicians to deal with; the anthropologist must emphasize that patient beliefs need constant attention by clinicians (Chrisman and Johnson 1996:104). Most practitioners recognize the possibility that patients may have beliefs that differ from theirs, whether health related or not. It is useful to discuss a variety of beliefs—not just health beliefs—with clinicians so they can begin to recognize the general utility of the term.

The growing recognition of a pervasive "health care pluralism" has directed anthropologists, as well as other researchers in international health care fields, to develop ways to examine how people choose, or make decisions among a range of therapeutic options, in given cases of illness (Pelto and Pelto 1997:152). This brings the focus of ethnographic research closer to the concerns of health care administrators and practitioners.

At the heart of the focused ethnographic research strategy is the fundamental assumption that building more effective theoretical models about beliefs/knowledge and behaviors in health and illness requires adequate measurements of the key constructs. The pathway to better measurement of health beliefs/knowledge has two main components: attention to emic constructions, gleaned by eliciting peoples' cultural vocabularies and terminology, and by understanding the attributes or qualities they assign to illnesses or symptoms, and a focus on specific diseases so that emic constructs can be examined in relation to peoples' actual behavior and in relation to approximately equivalent etic concepts (Pelto and Pelto 1997:161).

In terms of reproduction, it is important to remember that all societies shape their members' reproductive behavior. This cultural patterning of reproduction includes the beliefs and practices surrounding menstruation; proscriptions on the circumstances under which pregnancy may occur and who may legitimately reproduce; the prenatal and postpartum practices that mothers-to-be and their significant others observe; the management of labor, the circumstances under which interventions occur, and the form such interventions may take; and comparative study of the significance of menopause (Browner and Sargent 1996:219).

Reproduction also refers to the activities and relationships involved in the perpetuation of social systems. Recent controversies concerning the use of the reproduction concept underscore the need for continued exploration as to how its distinct dimensions are interrelated and determined culturally and socially (Browner and Sargent 1996:221).

At the same time, it is important to stress that the initial focus on cultural knowledge does not in the least imply a completely cognitive explanation of illness behaviors; the cognitive components, beliefs and knowledge, are essential elements to which the economic, material, and political factors must be joined for a full-scale understanding of behavior patterns (Pelto and Pelto 1997:161). It is possible and practical to gain to obtain operationally important information and insights on specific health problems that are required by communities and program planners through the use of focused ethnography.

The Future of Clinically Applied Research

The unique approach of clinically applied anthropology has valuable contributions to make to both clinical medicine and general anthropological theory. There is, however, a basic conflict between the pragmatic needs of clinical medicine and the theoretical needs of medical anthropology. The clinical imperative of medicine forces clinically applied anthropologists to analyze medical care from the perspective of the patient-clinician interaction with the goal of improving therapeutic efficacy; moreover, to effectively communicate with physicians (in Western cultures), the anthropologist must use the language of the biomedical model (Phillips 1985:33).

Perhaps the key question for clinically applied anthropology is: What can anthropologists do with and for health practitioners? Many anthropologists find it difficult to assume the limited and specialized role of providing information narrowly—to package their information to fit the time demands of clinical settings and to be congruent with the dominant information-processing style of their clinician colleagues-(Chrisman and Johnson 1996:96). An important dynamic in the relationship between clinicians and anthropologists has to do with the paradigm into which information concerning the care of patients will be put (Chrisman and Johnson 1996:97).

Nevertheless, anthropologists are invited to many health care institutions to provide the information necessary to help physicians and others deal with cultural issues as clinicians see them emerging (Chrisman and Johnson 1996:97). Thus, a key issue in clinically applied anthropology is how to formulate anthropological theory and data in ways that will be responsive to the imperatives of clinical settings—time consciousness and direct relevance to patient care (Chrisman and Johnson 1996:97)

In addition, the continuing debate over the definitions of illness and disease is a paradigmatic example of the tension between the needs of theoretical and applied anthropology (Phillips 1985:33). On the theoretical side, there is value in extending the debate because it is a convenient vehicle to address basic epistemological issues in mainstream anthropology, while on the applied side, there is a need to stop the debate, or at least limit it to the theoretical constructs of clinically applied anthropology that can be consolidated and applied to the practical problems of clinical medicine (Phillips 1985:33).

While Phillips' paper was published in 1985, many of his statements are still true today. In sum, clinically applied anthropology has not yet (although it is on its way) realized the goal of becoming a catalyst of a new and better kind of medical practice. The greatest weakness of clinically applied anthropology, at this point, is that it does not have a service mandate that legitimizes it as part of the "health care team." The continued viability of anthropologists in clinically applied roles will depend on their ability to establish areas of expertise and prerogatives that are accepted by other medical care professionals. On the other hand, though, to develop epistemologically sound theories that address general anthropological principles and challenge the existing assumptions of medical institutions, clinically applied anthropologists must be able to transcend the limitations of medicine (Phillips 1985:35).

Discussion Questions

1. What are the research questions being presented here? How could this research be beneficial?
2. How does the author define *clinically applied medical anthropology*?
3. How is this study an example of applied and/or medical anthropology?
4. What is the role of the medical anthropologist in research like this? What different, unique perspectives can an anthropologist provide?
5. What problems are present in the research methodology discussed here? How could these problems be corrected?

Judith Holland Sarnecki

411 Main Hall, Lawrence University,
115 S. Drew Street Appleton,
WI 54912

Judith.H.Sarnecki@Lawrence.edu

What does it mean to memorialize an event – and why would someone want to remember something painful? A dominant theme in this article is that images may speak louder than words – and tattoos, ostensibly, speak permanently. Everyone experiences pain – but everyone deals with pain differently. In this article, Judith Sarnecki explores the role tattoos play in memorializing pain and trauma; through this narrative, the reader examines events worthy of being committed to memory. Ultimately, the ideas presented here are part of a larger conversation on identity and self-expression.

Abstract

This article examines how tattoos may function as a way to deal with personal trauma. First, I examine a recent theory of how personal trauma cannot be fully experienced; thus, it calls for a return to the event in order to incorporate it into the psyche. Second, I look at how that return, often achieved symbolically, might include the process of acquiring a tattoo. Finally, I turn to various examples, taken from memoirs, film, and an interview, of trauma that has been expressed through tattooed images that turn bodies into memory-laden texts. *Keywords: tattoo, trauma, healing*

The first time I began to connect trauma and tattoo, I was reading Peter Trachtenberg's (1998) *Tattoos: A Memoir in the Flesh.* I originally became captivated by tattoos, however, during the summer of 1997 as I stood in line at my local Dairy Queen. The young man ahead of me was wearing a Stanley Kowalski-style undershirt that allowed my gaze to fall upon the delicate fine-line tattoo that graced his upper back and shoulders. Up until that moment my conception of tattoos was limited to bikers' skulls and sailors' South Sea Island beauties. Wow, I thought to myself, that's lovely, as I resisted an overwhelming urge to reach out and touch this stranger's shoulder and question him about his body art. When did tattoos become so artful, I wondered. As it happened, I was going through a trauma of my own when this seemingly insignificant event took place: I had just moved my nearly ninety-year-old mother into my home for hospice care; she died only days later. At the time, however, I made no link between trauma and tattoo. Why would I?

A month later, I accompanied a friend to a nearby tattoo parlor (my first visit to one) where she received a dainty flower tattoo on her ankle by an artist known as "Little John," a Vietnam veteran who, several months later, drowned in the river behind his studio. As I observed while my friend acquired her small tattoo, Little John tolerated my abundant (and abundantly naive) questions, which he answered good-naturedly. While he told me the process would sting a little, my friend confided in me afterward that "it hurt like hell." Little John, an unusually slight, short man sporting long hair and a long gray beard, came late for an appointment looking world-weary and smelling of stale beer; yet, he took his work very seriously. As blood slowly seeped from the minuscule wounds inflicted by the electric tattoo machine on my friend's ankle, I was not yet tuned in to the link between trauma and tattoo.

When I gave a paper on tattoo and narrative at Dartmouth College in April, 1999, I also had the privilege of hearing a wonderful talk by Cathy Caruth (1996), author of *Unclaimed Experience: Trauma, Narrative, and History.* As Caruth spoke, I began to think more seriously about a possible relationship between trauma and tattoo. Caruth, a professor of English and Comparative Literature at Emory University, talked of her own first encounter with death when her mother, a well respected child psychoanalyst, died following a serious illness. Caruth posed the question: "What does it mean for life to bear witness to death?" She reminded us of Freud's little Ernst and the fort-da game that reenacts the departure and (fictionalized) return of the mother. Little Ernst was Freud's grandson, child of his daughter Sophie, lost to them both when she dies prematurely. In the fort-da game, the child substituted the pleasure of creation for the pain of loss, "playing" symbolically with the mother's body. In other words, the child repeats the painful memory of losing his mother, linking repetition of the loss or separation to the creative act of invention; in so doing, the child forges a new relationship between consciousness and life.

Extraordinarily knowledgeable about and interested in Freudian theory, Caruth has developed her own theories about how we experience (or do not experience) trauma. For Caruth, true trauma is characterized by what we are unable to take in due to its suddenness and enormity. When we are victims of a traumatic event, according to Caruth, we are unable to synthesize it, to incorporate it into our psyche. Because we both experience and do not experience trauma, we are doomed to repeat the traumatic event in some way as we come to terms with it. In other words, we must find some way to incorporate the trauma that has occurred but remains unsynthesized. We have to re-experience an event that, because of its traumatic nature, passed through us without our being truly able to take it in. It is as if the event did and did not happen to us. That is the contradiction that causes mental unrest, an unrest that forces us to return to the initial traumatic event in order to understand it, or at the very least, to understand why we cannot understand it. Whether this return happens while we are dreaming or waking, we will be driven to resolve the conundrum caused by the unresolved event and our survival beyond it. Caruth theorizes, therefore, that trauma is essentially a break in the mind's consciousness (or perception) of time. The danger that leads to the traumatic experience is not perceived in time; it is realized a moment too late. That lapse results in a state of anxiety that causes us to repeat the experience (if only in memory) in order to master what was not grasped fully the first time. According to Caruth, life (or survival) attempts to serve as witness to what consciousness could not. For Caruth, the incomprehensible act of survival is also a not wholly understood imperative to live. Caruth goes back to Freud's recounting of little Ernst's fort-da game and how in repeating a death or departure it creates something entirely new. In other words, little Ernst repeats the performance to which he owes his existence. The child bears witness to the death of his mother by enacting it in a different way, a way that in its very creativity points to a future life. Language plays an important role in this creative process; it stages departure in a way that creates a new story of life. Freud, for example, translates his grandchild's stammer into the new language of psychoanalysis in *Moses and Monotheism* and *The Pleasure Principle* (The Standard Edition, 1953,74). While the lack or inability of language to represent the traumatic event leaves a gap in our psyche, this gap eventually leads to creating the stories that help us to heal. Creative mourning, in other words, leads away from melancholia toward survival by marking the absence and filling the void. According to Caruth what is called for is a different kind of signification that separates life from death yet contains both while bearing witness to the trauma.

Since I was attending the same conference as Caruth but giving a paper on tattoos, I began to consider how the trauma of receiving a tattoo, might, in certain instances, function as the "different kind of signification" that Caruth (1996) mentions as a way to survive and heal. The process itself is traumatic and certainly painful, but the pain and trauma are, to a considerable extent, controlled and mediated by another human being (recalling how some tattooers see their role as a kind of "shaman"). Some people who have incurred bodily trauma mark their bodies on the very site of the trauma, reinforcing Caruth's notion that we are compelled to repeat the trauma in some new, creative setting that will allow for a different, life-affirming signification of the event while still bearing witness to it.

The most poignant example I can give is the women who use tattoos to cover their mastectomy scars as a way to facilitate recovery from the loss of a breast to cancer. The repetition of pain and trauma is evident, but the painful return is also different in that it marks the place where the trauma occurred with a life-affirming design of the woman's choosing. Receiving a tattoo becomes a way to understand and incorporate a physical and psychological loss while regaining some sense of control and a new sense of empowerment. In her book irreverently titled *Stewed, Screwed and Tattooed,* Madame Chinchilla (1997), a self-named tattoo artist from Fort Bragg, California, relates how she feels about the act of tattooing the body of another human being:

> Tattooing is an intimate art form. There is a synergetic connection between the artist and his or her canvas. The tattoo artist is a facilitator. . . . The relationship is many-faceted, psychological, spiritual, medical, philosophical as well as a technical, creative process. (p. 61)

Madame Chinchilla has tattooed many persons who have sought a living memorial that also stands as a *memento mori.* She tells us that "[c]hoosing an image associated with the loss of a loved one is a transcendental act....We do many tattoos in our Main Street upstairs studio that are a ritual part of grieving and healing" (p. 67). One of the cancer survivors that Chinchilla pictures in her book with arms outstretched and head uplifted, Deena Metzger, writes movingly about the tattoo she acquired over her mastectomy scar:

> I am no longer afraid of mirrors where I see the sign of the amazon, the one who shoots arrows. There is a fine red line across my chest where a knife entered, but now a branch winds above the scar and travels from arm to heart. . . . I have designed my chest with the care given to an illuminated manuscript. . . . On the book of my body, I have permanently inscribed a tree. (Chinchilla, p.31)

Peter Trachtenberg (1998),a writer, commentator, and performance artist rarely at a loss for words, uses his seven tattoos (acquired at strategic moments during his life) as a way to grapple with unwieldy memory. The back cover of his book alerts us to the fact that this memoir is Trachtenberg's way of responding "ingeniously and emotionally to the harrowing events of his life: funerary rites in Borneo, heroin addiction on Manhattan's Lower East Side, and the deathwatches of both his parents." Trachtenberg's tattoos become the narrative tool he uses to penetrate the surface of his life, plumb its depths, and transform it into meaningful text. Each tattoo, illustrated on the title page of every chapter, leads into chaotic twists and turns of mind and body that represent the author's life experiences, preserved in pictorial recollections. The tattoos are keys that unlock the mysterious processes of memory, helping to unravel the tangled narrative strands that weave together a life story both unconventional and altogether human. The provocative chapter headings with their accompanying illustrations, "I Acquire a Wound" and "I Go Primitive," capture our imagination and invite us to probe the author's motivations for acquiring his body art.

Like the many tiny punctures of the tattooer's needle, Trachtenberg's pen probes the recesses of memory in order to explain what led him to acquire his idiosyncratic tattoos in the first place. In one chapter, for example, Trachtenberg recounts how he had to go to New York and find a tattooist named Slam before he could acquire the unusual second tattoo he sought: a replica of the wound in Christ's side. Never losing his sense of humor, Trachtenberg quips, "You'll admit this is an outré thing for a Jew to want," then goes on to explain his reasoning:

> A tattoo, I've always believed, is a visual reminder of pain, which has the tendency to be forgotten quickly and so sometimes requires documentation. This tattoo was my document of a particular kind of suffering, suffering I wanted to keep in mind and was afraid I wouldn't: I knew what a fickle slut my memory can be. (p. 38)

Trachtenberg poignantly recalls his struggles with what one might name the spiritual self, discussing along the way experiences from his Jewish childhood, his teenage encounter with drugs and Zen Buddhism, his flirtation with Catholicism, and his eventual slide into drug addition.

Many years later and newly sober, Trachtenberg happened to be reading Philip K. Dick's autobiographical science fiction novel *VALIS* (1978) in the middle of the night to combat insomnia. During the course of the reading, Dick's admitted schizophrenia proves contagious: Trachtenberg comes to the conclusion that he is Jesus' secret twin and begins to behave accordingly (the story is vastly more complicated; you'll just have to read the book). But by the time Trachtenberg's delusion ends, he has gained the habit of prayer, although he has no idea to whom he is praying. But he does know what tattoo he wants to commemorate this portion of his life when he finally finds Slam in New York City. She copies a Dürer woodcut onto his rib cage and tells him to hold still: "This may hurt," he writes, quoting Slam, but by that time, we the readers know that hurting is the whole point (p. 67).

The author clearly does not want to forget the self-inflicted suffering of heroin addition. On the other hand, he has been "clean" for several years and needs to mark that painful recovery period as well. He repeats the act of a self-inflicted wound by picking a particularly painful tattoo to apply. He knows enough about tattoos to realize what it will feel like to be tattooed directly over his rib cage, where there is little fat to serve as a cushion. The wound he chooses, Christ's bleeding side, depicts bleeding from the inside out: an internal, gut-wrenching wound that Trachtenberg wants to bring to the surface of his body so that it remains permanently visible. Why does he want to punish himself, we may ask, especially after he has kicked his habit? Each time he sees the wound in his side, he will be reminded of his fall from grace. On the other hand, by choosing to replicate Christ's wound on his own side, Trachtenberg is also sign fying an all-too-vulnerable humanness that seeks and anticipates an ascensior

Trachtenberg's me noir (1998) prods me to ask: Do tattoos usually mark painful stories rather than happy ones? Does pain, loss, and suffering require more drastic ways of telling, ways that involve our entire being? Does writing in the flesh in some permanent way help us both to let go and to memorialize a particularly painful or traumatic event in our life? In his final chapter, Trachtenberg gives us a clue:

> But pain, of course, is another way in which the body becomes remarkable. It is often the route chosen by those who feel unloved, or unworthy of love. Pain is what we settle for when we believe that pleasure is beyond us. (p. 234)

Shortly before reading Trachtenberg's memoir, I met a young ranch hand while vacationing on a ranch outside of Tucson, Arizona. He sported several highly visible tattoos and was very frank about having been recently released from prison. He was somewhat suspicious of my motives when I asked if he would allow me to interview him about his tattoos, but with some reluctance he finally agreed. When he did not show up for our initial interview, I hesitated whether or not to pursue the matter. Ultimately my curiosity (or voyeurism) got the best of me, and we arranged another meeting. This time he showed up, and the result was an enlightening as well as emotionally draining conversation.

Sky, all of twenty-two as of November 2000, had spent three years in prison for his part in a gang-style killing that he admitted to committing. Having begun to drink at age ten, he told me, he was whacked out on drugs and alcohol and running with a much older group of skin-heads by the time he was a teen-ager. His birth mother disappeared so early from his life that he never knew her. His father and stepmother seem not to have paid much attention to him while he was growing up. Most of his tattoos were acquired in prison, where they are illegal but omnipresent. His tattoos, he claimed, were part of his defenses, a clear statement to others to leave him alone (an enormously sad declaration from such a seemingly lonely young man). In a program on the Discovery Channel titled "Beauty, Art and Pain" (October 17, 1999), prisoners spoke of how they view their prison-crafted tattoos as a way to inspire fear and respect on the inside. Tattoos are also their sole means of demonstrating individuality in a penal setting. In her book, Madame Chinchilla (1997) writes of prison tattoos as "the ones you earn," and goes on to quote an anonymous inmate:

> In this life, someone can take everything we have, our clothes, home and family. They can make us lose our pride, our minds and our will power. They can lock us up. But these tattoos are mine. They will have to skin me to get them. (p. 69)

Speaking of the tattoo culture in Arizona's prisons, Sky, a fifth generation cowboy, said that all tattoos applied there have significant meaning. Prisoners may not always talk to one another, but they can read another inmate's body to discover both his "political" affiliations and his "life story." Each spider web, Sky explained, represents one year in prison. It captures the feeling of entrapment that every inmate feels. Each tear drop on the left side of the body indicates someone killed; each tear drop on the right stands for someone in the gang "family" who died. Sky emphasized the intimidation factor of tattoos: "I don't have to explain myself," he said, suggesting that in his case, images speak more eloquently and succinctly than words.

During our interview, Sky removed his shirt and showed me his own tattoo collection. It was his way of telling me his life story. His back is covered with a cowboy on a bucking bronco; before he dropped out of high school, Sky explained, he was a champion bareback rider on the teen rodeo circuit. The statement on his chest, "fear no man," speaks for itself. I looked at the tall, gangly kid who stood before me and I imagined the fear that he, as a seventeen-year-old active alcoholic, must have felt when he was incarcerated alongside hardened criminals. His survival in such an environment strikes me as something of a miracle in itself. Have the tattoos he so proudly displays helped him to begin to heal from a life of substance abuse, violence and neglect? The two sparrows that adorn his pectoral muscles are in memory of his best friend, killed in a gang war. Sky interrupts his story to tell me that his body is his sole possession, his tattoos the one thing that cannot be taken from him. He explains to me how his father overdosed on drugs and alcohol when Sky was a boy and how his stepmother was later diagnosed with schizophrenia. His tale is frighteningly convincing. By the age of twenty he was proud to be a recovering alcoholic. He was not proud that he has been shot and stabbed, had taken a life, and had spent three years in prison.

Now out on parole, Sky claims that his tattoos are constant reminders "of where I never want to go again." The dragon on his left arm, "that was the demon I beat," he says as he tells me that he attends an AA meeting every day. Becoming an AA representative in prison, in fact, earned him his early parole. The flames surrounding the dragon are "for the hell I went through." Sky's tattoos are his visual aids, helping him to articulate his life story; they allow him to remember those moments he chooses never to forget. In their own way, they memorialize his pain and loss. Yet they also, in some life-affirming way, facilitate the healing process and mark his continuing survival. I am left with the impression of a young man who has already had a lifetime of grim experience that surpasses language's ability to express it. Etched on the skin, his tattoos capture some of the trauma, the pain, and the loss he has endured and inflicted during his brief lifetime. Shaken and teary, I come away from our interview with a glimpse of a world I can barely imagine.

Sky's real-life story brings to mind the shocking 1998 film *American History X*, an X-rated history of a gen-X ex-con, in which Edward Norton creates a frighteningly realistic portrayal of a neo-nazi gang member. The enormous tattooed swastika he brazenly sports on his chest foreshadows the hate crime he will commit against a rival African American gang member. Edward Norton's character, the intelligent but oh-so-angry Derek, is drawn into the rowdy neo-nazi gang following the sudden and traumatic death of his father, a firefighter gunned down by members of a black street gang. We watch the television news interview with Derek, a teen overcome with grief and shock, spouting a racist rhetoric that only deepens as he comes under the spell of Cameron, a white supremacist father-figure who encourages racial hatred and violence. Stacy Keach gives a marvelously smarmy performance as an adult who revels in leading his youthful protégées down the path of hate. Under Cam's constant encouragement, Derek develops into the group's leading hate-monger.

After brutally murdering two young blacks that tried to highjack his car in retaliation for his forcing them off the community basketball court, Derek is sent to prison for three and a half years.

Once inside, Derek displays his swastika, a symbol of identity that serves to link him to other neo-nazis. But when he veers away from this group and befriends his co-worker, a black inmate, his so-called buddies turn on him, raping and beating him in the communal shower room. Traumatized by the violence committed against him by the very group with whom he had identified, Derek undergoes a slow, yet radical transformation. When he is finally released from prison, he returns home to find his mother seriously ill and his younger brother, Danny, well on his way to becoming Derek's clone. Derek knows he must confront Cam and persuade his brother to renounce his former neo-nazi gang. He attends a rally organized by Cam and announces that he is through with the group's philosophy of hate once and for all. After a physical scuffle with Cam, Derek returns home and takes a long shower, as if to wash away his "dirty" past. Yet when he steps out of the tub he is confronted by his own naked image in the bathroom mirror. What stands out is, of course, the swastika, black and menacing on his slender, white, and newly vulnerable body. As he gazes into the mirror, there is the shock of recognition on his face. His past is there, emblazoned on his chest for all to see, but more importantly, it is there for him to face for the rest of his life. In this all-important scene, the tattoo returns Derek to the scene of his traumatic and terrifyingly violent past, a past that, like the tattoo, can never be eradicated. In addition, the tattooed swastika prefigures the film's tragic conclusion.

Although Derek can remove all traces of his neo-nazi gang membership by dismantling his room, he can never remove the large tattoo over his heart nor can he undo the massive harm he has done—the two black teens he killed cannot be brought back to life. The film's moral lesson is clear: hatred and violence can only beget more hatred and violence. In the horrifying climax Danny, Derek's younger brother, is senselessly shot at point-blank range in the high school's boys' restroom by an equally young and impressionable angry black teenager. As Derek careens into the high school to find his brother lying in a pool of blood on the bathroom floor, he drops to his knees, grabs Danny in his arms and laments: "Oh my God, what have I done." With this final repetition of brutality and violence, we are reminded of how the tattooed X marks not only Derek's own violent act, personal trauma and survival, it also memorializes Danny's death. Tattoos are a form of self-inflicted wound, a bodily sensation of pain that some of us freely choose. Whether part of a personal ritual of recovery or a memorial to pain, tattoos "turn inside out" by bearing witness to feelings too inchoate to express in words. Yet the very fact of their existence as a part of our body's landscape serves as a testimonial to survival. By choosing tattoos, many find a creative, life affirming means to memorialize life's traumatic events.

References

Caruth, C.
   1996 Unclaimed Experience: Trauma, Narrative, and History. Baltimore: The Johns Hopkins University Press.

Chinchilla, M.
   1997 Stewed, Screwed & Tattooed. Fort Bragg: Isadore Press.

Dick, P.K.
   1978 VALIS. New York: Vintage Books.

Discovery Channel. (Producer)
   1999 Beauty, Art and Pain.

Morrissey, J. (Producer).
   1999 American History X. New Line Cinema Home Video.

Strachey, J., ed.
   1953–1974 The Standard Edition of the Complete Psychological Works of Sigmund Freud. London: Hogarth Press.

Trachtenberg, P.
   1998 7 Tattoos: A Memoir in the Flesh. New York: Penguin Books.

Discussion Questions

1. What do you think Sarnecki means when she says "personal trauma cannot be fully experienced; thus, it calls for a return to the event in order to incorporate it into the psyche"? What role might a tattoo have in this process?
2. The article states that "tattoos are a form of self-inflicted wound" – do you feel this is true in all cases? Why or why not?
3. Does pain (physical or emotional) have to be memorialized to be truly experienced? Why or why not?
4. Have you ever memorialized an important event in your life? How? This can be any event, not just something painful or traumatic.
5. If many tattoos have a function – to tell a story, to memorialize an event – can they be considered a form of art? Be very specific in your answer.

CPSIA information can be obtained
at www.ICGtesting.com
Printed in the USA
LVOW09s0608140717

541156LV00002B/4/P

9 781524 933203